D1261625

CONTEMPORARY Black Biography

ISSN-1058-1316

CONTEMPORARY

Black

Biography

Profiles from the International Black Community

Volume 65

GALE
CENGAGE Learning

Detroit • New York • San Francisco • New Haven, Conn • Waterville, Maine • London

Contemporary Black Biography, Volume 65

Kepos Media, Inc.: Paula Kepos and Derek Jacques, editors

Project Editors: Margaret Mazurkiewicz, Pamela M. Kalte

Image Research and Acquisitions: Leitha Etheridge-Sims

Editorial Support Services: Nataliya Mikheyeva

Rights and Permissions: Vernon English, Barb McNeil, Edna Shy

Manufacturing: Dorothy Maki, Cynde Bishop

Composition and Prepress: Mary Beth Trimper, Gary Leach

Imaging: Lezlie Light

For product information and technology assistance, contact us at
Gale Customer Support, 1-800-877-4253.
For permission to use material from this text or product,
submit all requests online at **www.cengage.com/permissions.**
Further permissions questions can be emailed to
permissionrequest@cengage.com

Gale
27500 Drake Rd.
Farmington Hills, MI, 48331-3535

ISBN-13: 978-0-7876-9542-2
ISBN-10: 0-7876-9542-4

ISSN 1058-1316

This title is also available as an e-book.
ISBN 13: 978-1-4144-3786-6
ISBN-10: 1-4144-3786-2
Contact your Gale sales representative for ordering information.

Printed in the United States of America
1 2 3 4 5 6 7 12 11 10 09 08

Advisory Board

Contents

Introduction

Contemporary Black Biography provides informative biographical profiles of the important and influential persons of African heritage who form the international black community: men and women who have changed today's world and are shaping tomorrow's. *Contemporary Black Biography* covers persons of various nationalities in a wide variety of fields, including architecture, art, business, dance, education, fashion, film, industry, journalism, law, literature, medicine, music, politics and government, publishing, religion, science and technology, social issues, sports, television, theater, and others. In addition to in-depth coverage of names found in today's headlines, *Contemporary Black Biography* provides coverage of selected individuals from earlier in this century whose influence continues to impact on contemporary life. *Contemporary Black Biography* also provides coverage of important and influential persons who are not yet household names and are therefore likely to be ignored by other biographical reference series. Each volume also includes listee updates on names previously appearing in *CBB*.

Designed for Quick Research and Interesting Reading

- **Attractive page design** incorporates textual subheads, making it easy to find the information you're looking for.

- **Easy-to-locate data sections** provide quick access to vital personal statistics, career information, major awards, and mailing addresses, when available.

- **Informative biographical essays** trace the subject's personal and professional life with the kind of in-depth analysis you need.

- **To further enhance your appreciation** of the subject, most entries include photographic portraits.

- **Sources for additional information** direct the user to selected books, magazines, and newspapers where more information on the individuals can be obtained.

Helpful Indexes Make It Easy to Find the Information You Need

Contemporary Black Biography includes cumulative Nationality, Occupation, Subject, and Name indexes that make it easy to locate entries in a variety of useful ways.

Available in Electronic Formats

Diskette/Magnetic Tape. Contemporary Black Biography is available for licensing on magnetic tape or diskette in a fielded format. Either the complete database or a custom selection of entries may be ordered. The database is available for internal data processing and nonpublishing purposes only. For more information, call (800) 877-GALE.

On-line. Contemporary Black Biography is available on-line through Mead Data Central's NEXIS Service in the NEXIS, PEOPLE and SPORTS Libraries in the GALBIO file and Gale's Biography Resource Center.

Disclaimer

Contemporary Black Biography uses and lists websites as sources and these websites may become obsolete.

We Welcome Your Suggestions

The editors welcome your comments and suggestions for enhancing and improving *Contemporary Black Biography*. If you would like to suggest persons for inclusion in the series, please submit these names to the editors. Mail comments or suggestions to:

The Editor

Contemporary Black Biography

Gale, Cengage Learning

27500 Drake Rd.

Farmington Hills, MI 48331-3535

Phone: (800) 347-4253

Peter Jasper Akinola

1944—

Archbishop

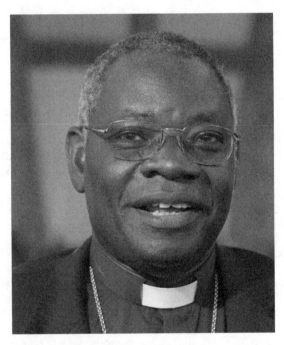

Akinola, Peter Jasper, photograph. AP Images.

Peter Jasper Akinola, the Archbishop of Nigeria, emerged as a key figure in a looming split inside the worldwide Anglican Church. Outspoken in his conservative views, Akinola has strongly opposed the ordination of openly gay clergy and the blessing of same-sex unions. He has called on Anglican prelates in the more liberal West to reconsider their liberal policies, and he has become a leader of what is sometimes described as the coming "southward shift" of Christianity in the twenty-first century—meaning that for the first time there will be more adherents to the faith in Asia and Africa than in the Christian world's longtime centers of power in Europe and North America. Some of Akinola's public remarks have been perceived as homophobic and have brought the archbishop a degree of infamy outside of Africa. "I have been so demonised by the Western media," Akinola told *Times* of London journalist Ruth Gledhill. "If this is the price I have to pay for leading the Church at this time, so be it. They can punch me here, punch me there, but in the midst of all that are people who say Akinola is the right thing."

Feared Sacrificial Death

Akinola was born in 1944 in Abeokuta, a city in the state of Ogun in southwestern Nigeria. He is a member of the Yoruba ethnic group, one of the three main groups in the country, and was raised by an uncle following the death of his father. He entered school at the age of ten and finished at sixteen. He wanted to continue his education, but instead his family urged him to move to Lagos, the capital city at the time, to learn a trade. There he stayed with family members and began to learn carpentry and cabinetmaking. "Very ugly things happened to me while I was there," he recounted in the interview with Gledhill. "Another uncle of mine was not thinking well of me. He was going to sacrifice me for a ritual to make money…. I had premonitions. I saw a very clear vision of what was going to happen," he continued, and said that events then began to mimic his premonitions. Finally, he said, "I came out of the house to go to where I was supposed to be sacrificed and I saw this figure far away at the other end of the road, beckoning me to

---

At a Glance . . .

Born on January 27, 1944, in Abeokuta, Ogun, Nigeria; married; six children. *Religion:* Anglican. *Education:* Theological College of Northern Nigeria, DipTh, 1978; Virginia Theological Seminary, MTS, 1981.

Career: Worked as a carpenter until 1973; ordained deacon, 1978; ordained priest, 1979; St. James Church, Abuja, Nigeria, vicar, 1978–82; canon missioner in Abuja, 1984–89; consecrated bishop, 1989, and served as diocesan bishop for Abuja, 1989–97; Archbishop of Province III, Nigeria, 1997–2000; Metropolitan and Primate of All Nigeria, 2000–09; head of the African Anglican Bishops' Conference, 2004—, and the Global South group of Anglican provinces, 2005—.

Addresses: *Office*—Archbishop's Palace, PO Box 212 ADCP, Abuja, Nigeria.

come. In white. I ran and ran and ran. The faster I ran, the further distance between me and the figure. I never found it. I believe very strongly that the Lord was taking me away from that dungeon."

Akinola spent much of the 1960s working as a carpenter—a particularly symbolic line of work, given the fact that it was also Jesus' profession before he began preaching—and became increasingly active in the Anglican Church in Nigeria. The religion was established there by English missionaries in the 1840s and continued to grow even after Nigeria achieved its independence as a sovereign state in 1960, after years as a British colony. The promise of the new era soon faded with the outbreak of a devastating civil war, and in the 1970s the country struggled to recover. A brutal military regime came to power in 1983 and persisted well into the 1990s. The corrupt, despotic rule seemed to prompt an increasing number of Nigerians to turn to the Anglican faith—aided in part by an evangelical push to gain new converts—and the membership rolls swelled.

Akinola began training as a catechist, or someone who instructs others in the tenets of the faith in preparation for baptism or confirmation, in 1968. In 1973 he entered the Theological College of Northern Nigeria and earned his diploma of theology in 1978. He was ordained a deacon in the Anglican Church that same year, then ordained as a priest in 1979 and went on to earn a master of theological studies from Virginia Theological Seminary in Alexandria, Virginia. He was

made a vicar at a church in Abuja, the city that would become Nigeria's new federal capital, and he was consecrated a bishop in 1989. As the Anglican community in Nigeria continued to grow, a number of new dioceses were created, and in 1997 Akinola was elevated from diocesan bishop in Abuja to the office of archbishop. He headed Province III in Nigeria for three years before being made Metropolitan and Primate of All Nigeria in 2000. By then, the Anglican Church in Nigeria—which is formally known as the Church of Nigeria (Anglican Communion)—had nearly tripled its membership, which was just five million when Akinola was ordained in the late 1970s.

Strife Erupted over Gay Rights

The Anglican Church in Nigeria belonged to what is known as the worldwide Anglican Communion. No national church has a position of authority within the Communion. The Church of England, however, is considered the mother church, and its primate, the Archbishop of Canterbury, is considered a symbolic leader for the world's Anglicans. The Episcopal Church of the United States is the American branch of the Anglican Communion. Since its ordination of the first women priests in the mid-1970s, the U.S. Episcopal church has become increasingly liberal, though conservative elements within it have periodically raised concerns over this new direction. In 2003 Episcopalian leaders elected the first openly gay bishop in the U.S. church, V. Gene Robinson of New Hampshire, which prompted protests both at home, from more tradition-minded U.S. parishes, and in Africa, from church leaders who adhere to a much more conservative interpretation of the Bible.

Akinola had already emerged as a crusading force on this issue in the summer of 2002, when a Canadian diocese within the Anglican Communion agreed to bless same-sex unions. He warned that such actions could be construed as a break with the Anglican Communion, a sentiment echoed by Anglican leaders in the West Indies and South America. In 2004 he summoned the first conference of African Anglican bishops, which issued a formal statement in October supporting the call for a moratorium on the election and consecration of bishops living openly as gays or lesbians and the halt of Anglican rites for blessing same-sex unions. The statement mentioned by name the Episcopal Church of the United States and the Anglican Church of Canada.

In 2005 the primates of several African, Asian, and Latin American Anglican churches organized themselves as the Global South. Among the twenty Anglican Communion provinces that joined were Kenya, Rwanda, the Philippines, South India, Bangladesh, the West Indies, and the Southern Cone of the Americas, which includes South American Anglicans. The primates elected Akinola to head the group, and in November of 2005 they issued an open letter to

Rowan Williams, the Archbishop of Canterbury, in which they criticized the Church of England for its lack of leadership on the issue of gay bishops and same-sex unions.

At the same time, Akinola sensed an opportunity to strengthen ties with U.S. Episcopal parishes that also disapproved of the liberal shift. In December of 2006 a few conservative Episcopalian dioceses made a formal break with the U.S. Episcopal church and allied with Akinola's Nigerian diocese instead. This news was followed by a controversial interview that Akinola gave to the *New York Times,* published on Christmas Day. Its opening paragraphs featured quotes from Akinola recounting the time he "jumped back" after realizing he had just shaken the hand of an openly gay person. In responding to questions by the paper's religion writer, Lydia Polgreen, Akinola attempted to justify his objections to homosexuality. "Why didn't God make a lion to be a man's companion?" he countered, in remarks that were widely publicized. "Why didn't he make a tree to be a man's companion? Or better still, why didn't he make another man to be man's companion? So even from the creation story, you can see that the mind of God, God's intention, is for man and woman to be together."

Anglicans Resisted Islam

Akinola's stance on homosexuality has deeper roots, however, involving Christianity in Africa and the spread of Islam. Parts of Nigeria are the few remaining places in the world where actual religious violence threatens the neighborly coexistence of Christians and Muslims together. In northern Nigeria, where Muslims are in the majority, several provinces have adopted the strict Islamic religious law known as sharia as their legal code. In some of these areas, Christians have been persecuted and their homes looted. Akinola's Nigerian church—which is expected to reach the twenty-million mark by 2010—is poised to play a significant role in the country's future direction. Its numbers have swelled because of an active recruitment effort, but Islam has also engaged in zealous recruiting activities. Indeed, throughout Africa "Muslims have tried to make converts by arguing that the Christian West is decadent and sexually irresponsible," explained Philip Jenkins in the *Atlantic Monthly,* "a belief that finds daily confirmation in Western films and television. If the Anglican Communion accepted gay bishops or approved gay unions, Muslims would gain an enormous propaganda victory in Nigeria—and in a dozen or so other African countries in which Christians and Muslims compete for converts, sometimes violently."

In 2006 Akinola consecrated Martyn Minns, a longtime friend, to serve as bishop for the Convocation of Anglicans in North America (CANA), the churches that had broken with their U.S. Episcopal diocese. Minns was the rector of Truro Church in Virginia, a wealthy parish that objected to the ordination of gay priests and bishops. In May of 2007 Akinola traveled to Wood-bridge, Virginia, to install Minns as the CANA leader. Truro is one of about thirty U.S. parishes that have aligned with African dioceses. The event only fueled opposition to Akinola, with critics claiming that he is attempting to use the disagreement to wrest control of the Anglican Church from its seat at Canterbury, England, via the Global South group. He has dismissed such charges, stating that he intends to retire as archbishop in 2009 and return to serve as a simple village priest. Some religious scholars have even wondered if the Archbishop of Canterbury and other Anglican Communion leaders are attempting to stall a formal debate or decision on the matter of gay priests and same-sex unions until that date. But Akinola is firm in his belief that the controversy will not end simply because he has exited the fray. "The Church is already receiving hundreds of people who are better, stronger," he asserted to Gledhill. "God raised Peter Akinola to what he has done. The same God will raise hundreds of people more gifted than me to get the job done. It is God's Church not mine."

Sources

Periodicals

Atlantic Monthly, November 2003.
New York Times, December 25, 2006; May 6, 2007.
Time, February 19, 2007; May 14, 2007.
Times (London, England), July 5, 2007.

—Carol Brennan

Alphonse Ardoin

1915–2007

Musician

The French-speaking, African-American Creoles of southwest Louisiana have maintained a unique musical tradition. The contemporary expression of that heritage is called zydeco, and was made popular by Clifton Chenier during the 1970s and 1980s. For the older folks of the region, the blues-inflected two-steps and waltzes played on accordion and fiddle are simply "la musique creole." One of the last surviving musicians to play in the old style was Alphonse "Bois Sec" Ardoin, an accordionist who died on May 16, 2007, at the age of ninety-one. Ardoin and fiddler Canray Fontenot, musical partners for half a century, influenced countless musicians and embodied the link between the rural music of the nineteenth century and the urbanized, electrified sound of zydeco.

Alphonse Ardoin was born on November 16, 1915, in l'Anse de Prien Noir (Black Cyprian's Cove) near Duralde, Louisiana, in Evangeline parish. His family had lived and worked as sharecroppers in the region since the 1830s. When Ardoin was four years old, his father died, and Ardoin grew up helping his mother and other relatives in the fields. According to Ardoin, a white neighbor named Alfred Veillon also helped him get a start in life by offering him odd jobs to make money. It was Veillon who first called him by the nickname "Bois Sec" ("dry wood") because Ardoin was always the first farm worker to run for the barn or hide inside a hollow tree when rain began to fall.

Ardoin's older cousin Amédé Ardoin was the first African-American Creole musician to make commercial recordings, starting in 1929, and was the first to expand the possibilities of Creole music by incorporating the syncopations of blues and jazz. Bois Sec Ardoin often heard his cousin play at dance parties, and began to accompany him on the triangle.

The music stayed with the young man, and he resolved to master the single-row, or button accordion, himself. When he was about seven, he began to borrow his older brother Houston's instrument surreptitiously, while Houston was away from the house. In Michael Tisserand's book *The Kingdom of Zydeco,* Ardoin recounted how he would practice in the hayloft of the family's barn, saying "it was not a good hiding place, because you could hear me for miles." Houston soon caught him in the act, but hearing that his brother's musical prowess surpassed his own, allowed Ardoin to keep borrowing the instrument. Soon, Ardoin had saved enough to buy one of his own.

Unlike his cousin Amédé, Ardoin never attempted to earn a living solely from his music. He continued to work as a farmhand on the local cotton fields and tend the eight-acre plot next to the house in which he was born. He grew rice and soybeans and raised pigs and chickens. With his wife, Marceline, he raised fourteen children. He did a little carpentry on the side, and he played music, at home and at the roving dance parties held by neighbors, a lively tradition in the Creole community.

In 1948 Ardoin began playing with Canray Fontenot, another farmhand from nearby Welsh, Louisiana. They called their duet the Duralde Ramblers. Gradually, the pair branched out from house parties to the saloons and clubs of southwestern Louisiana, where they often shared the bill with Clifton Chenier and his brother Cleveland. During the 1950s, they had a radio broadcast every Sunday on KEUM in Eunice, Louisiana. Over many years of playing together, Ardoin and Fontenot developed an uncanny rapport. They traded leads and vocals, switched tempos and improvised together seamlessly. "We can read each other's mind," Ardoin told Tisserand. "It's not like that with anyone else."

By the 1960s, folklore enthusiasts had begun to take an interest in the indigenous music of the Louisiana bayou. Musicologist Ralph Rinzler invited Ardoin and Fontenot to perform at the prestigious Newport Folk Festival in 1966; the assembled crowd was the largest either player had ever seen. Their performance at Newport represented the first time traditional Creole music had received such wide exposure. On their way home from Rhode Island, the duo made a studio recording in Virginia with producer Richard Spottswood. The result was the first full-length album by an African-American Creole band, *Les Blues du Bayou* (later reissued as *La Musique Creole*).

After their success at Newport, Ardoin and Fontenot received offers to play concerts and music festivals across the United States and in Europe. The pair performed at Carnegie Hall and became a mainstay of the annual New Orleans Jazz and Heritage Festival. Ardoin's sons Morris, Gustav, and Lawrence also teamed up with their father to form the Ardoin Brothers Band. The band, usually featuring Fontenot's fiddle as well, recorded a single and began to get steady club work.

The family suffered a severe blow when Ardoin's son Gustav was killed in an auto accident in 1974, and Ardoin briefly reined in his musical endeavors after his son's death. His traditional Creole style was waning in popularity, as it was being overtaken by its new incarnation as zydeco and by rock and roll. However, he remained a visible and respected leader in his local community. He performed at Mardi Gras, at the annual Fourth of July festival in the hamlet of Elton, and always at home. Twice a year, the Ardoin clan butchered a pig and hosted a "boucherie."

As Ardoin aged, he was increasingly appreciated as a link to the passing cultural traditions of his people. His music and agrarian lifestyle were captured in the 1973 documentary *Dry Wood* by independent filmmaker Les Blank. Blank featured Ardoin again sixteen years later in *J'ai Ete au Bal* (*I Went to the Dance*), a broader film history of Cajun, Creole, and zydeco music. In 1986 Ardoin and Fontenot were awarded the National Heritage Fellowship by the National Endowment for the Arts.

Ardoin carried on after Fontenot died in 1995; he began playing and recording with a new generation of musicians. He had made the album *A Couple of Cajuns* with the white fiddler Dewey Balfa in the early 1980s and returned to the studio in 1998 to record *Allons Danser* with Balfa Toujours, a band led by Balfa's daughter.

During Ardoin's final years, his children and grandchildren carried on the family's accordion tradition, including son Lawrence "Black" Ardoin, and grandsons Dexter Ardoin, Chris "Candyman" Ardoin, and Sean Ardoin, who leads the band ZydeKool. Bois Sec Ardoin told Tisserand, "All my grandchildren play zydeco now, but I can't change them. Oh no, I got to let them go."

Selected discography

Albums

Les Blues du Bayou, 1971 (reissued as *La Musique Creole*).
The Cajuns, Vol. 1, 1972.
Zodico: Louisiana Creole Music (various artists), 1979.
Bois Sec Ardoin and Dewey Balfa: A Couple of Cajuns, 1981.
Allons Danser: Bois Sec with Balfa Toujours, 1998.

Sources

Books

Savoy, Ann Allen, *Cajun Music: A Reflection of a People,* Bluebird Press, 1984.
Tisserand, Michael, *The Kingdom of Zydeco,* Arcade, 1998.

Periodicals

London Independent, May 21, 2007.
New York Times, November 22, 1998; May 20, 2007.

Online

"Dry Wood: Bois Sec and Canray," *Folkstreams,* http://www.folkstreams.net/context,42 (accessed December 27, 2007).

"Lifetime Honors: 1986 National Heritage Fellowships," *National Endowment for the Arts,* http://www.nea.gov/honors/heritage/fellows/fellow.php?id=1986_01 (accessed December 27, 2007).

Other

Bois Sec Ardoin is featured in two documentaries by filmmaker Les Blank: *Dry Wood* (1973) and *J'ai Ete au Bal* (*I Went to the Dance*), 1989.

—Roger K. Smith

Vernon Joseph Baker

1919—

U.S. Army soldier

On January 13, 1997, the U.S. government delivered belated recognition to some unheralded heroes of World War II. In a small ceremony at the White House, seven World War II veterans received the Congressional Medal of Honor. They were the first African-American veterans of that war to receive the nation's highest military award. More than half a century had passed since the war, and six of the seven honorees were dead. The sole survivor to receive his medal in person was Vernon Joseph Baker. In decorating Baker and his fellow veterans, President Bill Clinton said, "They were denied their nation's highest honor, but their deeds could not be denied, and they cleared the way to a better world."

Vernon Baker was born on December 17, 1919, in Cheyenne, Wyoming. Both his parents were killed in an auto accident when he was four years old. He and his sisters were raised by their grandparents, and in his stern and husky grandfather, Joseph Baker, he found a figure to idolize.

Joseph Baker gave his grandson his first gun as a Christmas present, when the boy was twelve. For every shot he fired, his grandfather insisted, he must bring home meat for the family. Baker quickly mastered marksmanship. He graduated from high school, while working summers on the Union Pacific railroad. He was twenty when his grandfather died. With limited prospects for employment, he decided to enlist in the army because he had heard he could make a decent living as a quartermaster. When he went to enlist, however, a racist recruiting officer told him, "We have no quotas for you people."

Undeterred, Baker tried again. He requested a post with the Quartermaster Corps, then watched the recruiting officer write on his enlistment form, "Infantry." Baker held his tongue, happy just to have been accepted. He married his sweetheart, Leola, on June 25, 1941, and left the next day for basic training.

Arrived at the Italian Front

After Baker went through basic training in Texas, he was sent to Officer Candidate School in Georgia. In the Deep South, Baker experienced racial animosity surpassing anything he had encountered in Wyoming. During World War II the army was segregated, and Baker endured harsh discrimination from whites both above and beneath his rank. He was abused by enlisted whites after he was promoted to sergeant; some whites refused to respect his rank or obey orders from him. Commissioned in early 1943 as a second lieutenant, Baker was assigned to the Ninety-second Infantry Division, named the Buffalo Division, after the African-American "buffalo soldiers" of the Native American wars. Serving in a black unit under white officers rankled the young lieutenant. "The army decided we needed supervision from white Southerners," Baker told Allan Mikaelian, "as if war was plantation work and fighting Germans was picking cotton." He gradually earned the respect of the men under his command.

Half a million African Americans served overseas during World War II. Baker's unit stayed out of the war until July of 1944, when he landed in Naples, Italy. For several months, he went on night patrols as a platoon

At a Glance . . .

Born on December 17, 1919, in Cheyenne, WY; son of Manuel Caldera and Beulah Baker; raised by grandparents, Joseph Samuel Baker and Dora Baker; married Leola, 1941 (divorced); married Fern Brown, 1953–86 (deceased); married Heidy Pawlik, 1993; children: two.

Career: Enlisted in U.S. Army, 1941; commissioned January 11, 1943; fought in Italian campaign during World War II, 1945; reached rank of First Lieutenant; retired 1965; American Red Cross, counselor to military families, 1968–87.

Awards: Bronze Star, Purple Heart, Distinguished Service Cross, 1945; Congressional Medal of Honor, 1997.

Addresses: *Home*—St. Maries, ID.

leader. By October they had moved north into Tuscany. Under orders to capture a farmhouse near Seravezza, he sent three men ahead of him along the path to the house. All three were killed, and Baker was haunted by his responsibility. Baker himself was wounded in the same operation. At first, he did not feel the bullet that struck his wrist, and he carried on until his men had taken the house. He woke up in a hospital near Pisa, and was out of action for two months.

In early April of 1945, Baker and the Buffalo Division were in the foothills of the Apuan Alps. Joining them was the 442nd Regimental Combat Team, comprising Japanese Americans who had escaped the internment camps by volunteering for the armed services. The Germans were holding Castle Aghinolfi, a mountain fortress dating back to medieval times. Below the castle were three hills that the Americans called hills X, Y, and Z. The U.S. forces launched a major offensive to capture the garrison and suffered heavy casualties as the dug-in Germans repelled several assaults.

Penetrated Enemy Lines

On April 5, Baker and his men were ordered to attack the castle. Baker started uphill at the head of his platoon before dawn. He took his M-1, but declined to put on his helmet, which impaired his hearing. Soon he spotted two figures crouching in a machine-gun nest. He shot them, and his men advanced. He observed, and destroyed, another machine-gun position and an observation post, and walked on ahead of all his men.

As he went, he used wire cutters to destroy the enemy's communication lines.

The castle was now one deep canyon away; Baker had come closer than anyone on his side expected. His company's new commander, Captain Runyon, caught up with him on the hill. A German soldier appeared and tossed a grenade, which failed to explode. Runyon jostled Baker's rifle in his panic, but Baker recovered and shot the fleeing German. In the meantime, Runyon had disappeared.

Baker pressed on alone. He came dangerously near one camouflaged dugout, whose crew had paused for breakfast. He killed these enemy soldiers. Mortar shells began to fall and hit his men. Over the radio, his unit called in for support, but commanders refused to believe they had penetrated so far past enemy lines. Baker found Runyon hiding in a stone house. The captain said he was going back for reinforcements, but he never returned. Later, Baker learned that Runyon had told command that Baker's men would not survive.

While waiting for reinforcements, Baker decided to set up a perimeter and attempt to hold their position. This was a fatal error, he admitted in retrospect. After a fierce German counterattack, the unit was down to eight men. Baker collected the dog tags from his dead comrades, and watched for the reinforcements until he realized they were not coming. Then he led a retreat back down hill X, taking out two machine gunners and a tank along the way.

That was Baker's final day in combat. He had lost nineteen of his men, but the attack was a decisive victory. The Germans pulled out that night. One month later, Benito Mussolini and Adolf Hitler were both dead, and the war in Europe was over.

The experience left Baker bitter and angry. He had experienced the futility of warfare. He would never stop regretting the deaths he might have prevented, among the Germans as well as his own men. What rankled him most of all was that he had gotten no thanks, no recognition that his men had surpassed all expectations, and no apology for the failure to send reinforcements.

On July 4, 1945, Baker received the Distinguished Service Cross for his bravery, the nation's second-highest military award. He had been recommended for the Medal of Honor, it turned out, but the paperwork was never forwarded to Washington, and Baker was never told.

Facing uncertain job prospects back home and divorced from his wife, Baker elected to remain in the military after the war. He remained in Italy for two years, and reenlisted when his commission expired in 1947. He volunteered for combat duty at the start of the Korean War in 1950, but he was not assigned to a battle unit. The army was preparing for desegregation and needed decorated minority officers such as Baker to assume command positions. When desegregation became effective in 1951, Baker became a company commander in charge of white troops at Fort Campbell, Kentucky.

In 1953 Baker married Fern Brown, a divorcee with two daughters. They moved to California when Baker was transferred to Fort Ord, and there they had another daughter. The final addition to their family was an orphan, half-Korean and half-black, whom Baker adopted while serving in postwar Korea.

After his retirement from the military in 1968, Baker worked for the Red Cross for nearly twenty years counseling military families. Among the places this work took him was Vietnam, during the height of that country's long war. His wife died in 1986, and Baker retired to a small property in a part of rural Idaho that reminded him of his childhood years in Wyoming. He married Heidy Pawlik, a native of Germany, in 1993.

Recognized for War Service

In the winter of 1996 Baker received a phone call from historian Daniel Gibran, who had been awarded a grant to investigate why no African Americans had received the Medal of Honor for service during World War II. Gibran's study found clear evidence of a racial disparity in the selection of Medal of Honor winners. On Gibran's recommendation, a panel of generals reviewed the records of ten Distinguished Service Cross recipients; that review led to the White House ceremony belatedly honoring Baker and the six deceased veterans. That month Baker was swamped with attention from the news media. One journalist, Ken Olsen of the *Spokane Spokesman-Review,* wrote a series of pro-

files of Baker, and later collaborated with him on the memoir *Lasting Valor.*

As President Clinton spoke of Baker's heroic actions on the Italian front, Baker's mind returned to Hill X, and to the nineteen men he lost that day. While Baker continued to brood over how he could have prevented their deaths, he told the Public Broadcasting System that, to him, receiving the belated Medal of Honor meant "that every black solider that fought in the Second World War has been vindicated, every one."

Selected writings

(With Ken Olsen) *Lasting Valor,* Bantam, 1999.

Sources

Books

Mikaelian, Allen, *Medal of Honor,* Hyperion, 2002.
Smith, Larry, *Beyond Glory,* Norton, 2003.

Periodicals

New York Times, January 14, 1997.

Online

"Idaho: A Portrait—Vernon Baker,"*Public Broadcasting System,* http://idahoptv.org/productions/idahoportrait/about/baker.html (accessed December 27, 2007).
Kelly, S. H., "Seven WWII Vets to Receive Medals of Honor," *Army News Service,* http://www4.army.mil/ocpa/read.php?story_id_key=2187 (accessed December 27, 2007).

—Roger K. Smith

Harry Belafonte

1937—

Singer, actor, activist

Belafonte, Harry, photograph. AP Images.

It has been said that in the life and work of entertainer Harry Belafonte, the worlds of music and morality do not collide, but balance harmoniously. In the 1950s Belafonte introduced the colorful, bouncy melodies of calypso music to the United States, and American listeners began swaying to the jaunty Caribbean beat and singing "Day-O" along with the masterful crooner. Since that time, Belafonte has used his visibility as an entertainer to cast a political spotlight on humanitarian causes ranging from world hunger to civil rights to the plight of children in the third world. Belafonte's accomplishments, and the awards bestowed on him in the spheres of entertainment and activism, show a man equally committed to musical excellence and political virtuousness.

Known as the "consummate entertainer," Belafonte was born in New York City in 1927. His parents were West Indian, and he moved with his mother to her native Jamaica when he was a child. In the five years he spent on the island, he not only absorbed the music that was such a vital part of the culture but also observed the effects of colonialism, the political oppression that native Jamaicans had to endure under British

rule. "That environment gave me much of my sense of the world at large and what I wanted to do with it," Belafonte was quoted as saying in the *Paul Masson Summer Series*. "It helped me carve out a tremendous link to other nations that reflect a similar temperament or character."

Was Fascinated by Acting and Singing

Once back in Harlem, another culturally and artistically rich environment, Belafonte became street smart, learning the hard lessons of survival in the big city. When the United States entered World War II, he ended his high school education and enlisted in the U.S. Navy. After an honorable discharge, he returned to New York City, where he bounced between odd jobs. His first foray into the world of entertainment came in the late 1940s, when he was given two tickets to a production of the American Negro Theater. He was hooked after one performance. "I was absolutely mesmerized by that experience," he told the *Ottawa Citizen* in 1990. "It was really a spiritual, mystical feeling I had that night. I went backstage to see if there was anything I could do."

At a Glance . . .

Born Harold George Belafonte Jr. on March 1, 1927, in New York, NY; son of Harold George and Melvine Love; married Marguerite Byrd, 1948 (divorced); married Julie Robinson, 1957; children: (with Byrd) Adrienne, Shari; (with Robinson) David, Gina. *Education:* Attended Dramatic Workshop of the New School for Social Research, studying under Erwin Piscator.

Career: Acted in various theater, movie, and television productions, late 1940s—; helped organize *We Are the World* recording session, 1985; named cultural advisor to the Peace Corps by President John F. Kennedy; Southern Christian Leadership Conference, member of the board of directors; Martin Luther King Jr. Memorial Fund, chair; appointed UNICEF Goodwill Ambassador, 1987.

Awards: Tony Award, 1953; Emmy Award, 1960; Grammy Award, 1985; U.S. Committee for UNICEF, Danny Kaye Award, 1989; National Medal of the Arts, 1994; Grammy Lifetime Achievement Award, 2000; Black Entertainment Television's Humanitarian Award, 2006.

Addresses: *Office*—Belafonte Enterprises Inc., 830 Eighth Ave., New York, NY 10019.

His first leading role with the company was in Irish playwright Sean O'Casey's *Juno and the Paycock*. Impressed by the power and message of O'Casey's words, and by the promise of theater in general, Belafonte enrolled in the Dramatic Workshop of the New School for Social Research, studying under famous German director Erwin Piscator, whose other students included renowned actors Rod Steiger and Beatrice Arthur.

Belafonte was concerned about the scarcity of work for African-American actors but got a break when, as a class project, he sang an original composition called "Recognition." His audience was spellbound. Among the listeners was the owner of the Royal Roost Nightclub, a well-known Broadway jazz center. Belafonte was offered a two-week stint that, due to such positive reception, blossomed into a twenty-week engagement. At the Roost and later at other clubs, such as the Village Vanguard in New York City's Greenwich Village, Belafonte charmed audiences with his husky-yet-sweet-voiced adaptations of popular and West Indian folk songs.

Recognized Nationally for Acting and Singing

In 1949 Belafonte was approached by representatives of Jubilee Records. Armed with a recording contract and the praise of critics, this bright new talent started making his mark. He first appeared on Broadway in *John Murray Anderson's Almanac,* for which he won a Tony Award. In the 1954 film *Carmen Jones,* based on French composer Georges Bizet's opera *Carmen,* Belafonte played the lead role and endeared himself to a national audience. Throughout the next few decades, he continued to act in films such as *Island in the Sun* and *Uptown Saturday Night* and produced television programs such as *A Time for Laughter,* in which he introduced U.S. audiences to then nationally unknown humorists Richard Pryor and Redd Foxx.

It was in 1956, with the release of his album *Calypso,* that Belafonte sealed his status as a superstar and consummated America's love affair with Caribbean music. His most famous recordings, "Banana Boat Song" (popularly known as "Day-O") and "Matilda," recall the melodies, rhythm, and spirit of Jamaica and other West Indian cultures. Throughout the 1960s, 1970s, and 1980s, Belafonte reached into the lore and music of other cultures, most notably those of South America and Africa. He also continued with his celebrated interpretations of American folk ballads and spirituals, but he has always been most closely associated with the zest and spunk of calypso.

Belafonte's *Calypso* was the first album to sell more than one million copies, a benchmark that led to the establishment of the Grammy Awards. The album was only one of many illustrious firsts in Belafonte's life. He was the African-American man to win an Emmy Award as well as the first African American to work as a television producer. He was also the first entertainer—African American or white—to be named cultural advisor to the Peace Corps by U.S. president John F. Kennedy.

Belafonte's success on vinyl and tape has always translated well in his live concerts, where he uses sing-alongs, dialogue with audience members, and a contagious energy and excitement to get the crowds responding jubilantly. Dave Hoekstra wrote in the *Chicago Sun-Times* in 1990 that Belafonte "sings from discovery and fulfillment.... So when you listen to the Belafonte songbook on a perfect summer night, you know the dignity, poise and spiritual exploration will still be heard long after the voice has passed. That is Harry Belafonte's lasting contribution to American popular music."

Merged Political Activism with Performing Career

As a young boy keenly aware of British domination over the lives of Jamaicans, Belafonte learned a lasting lesson about the power of art in general, and song in particular, to express and shed personal meaning on the physical, psychological, and cultural constraints generated by colonialism. "People living in that sort of oppression are always very creative," he was quoted as saying in the *Summer Series* magazine. "The environment was terribly musical. People sang while working in the fields, while selling their wares in the streets, in church, during festivals. That background had a great impact on me."

Even though he would always believe that music should be a cherished vehicle for commentary on the human condition, Belafonte recognized in the 1960s that song alone, no matter how politically and moralistically charged, would not right the wrongs suffered by society's disenfranchised people. Taking advantage of the fame garnered from his music and theater successes, Belafonte donned the cape of activist and quickly earned the respect of those who might have worried that he was simply an entertainer dabbling self-servingly in politics.

After World War II, in which he was first exposed to what he viewed as an honorable fight waged on moral grounds, Belafonte found political mentors and ideological inspiration in former first lady Eleanor Roosevelt and actor and singer Paul Robeson. He saw in Roosevelt an irrepressible dedication to human rights and the courage to take stands with which mainstream America might have disagreed. Robeson, a trailblazing, African-American entertainer, was an early campaigner against racial segregation and had been blacklisted by the U.S. government for his pro-communist beliefs. Of Roosevelt and Robeson, Belafonte was quoted as saying in the *Ottawa Citizen,* "Both taught me by example to be resilient and fight for things I believed in even if it could get me into trouble."

Throughout the 1960s, Belafonte's primary ethical focus was on the Jim Crow laws of segregation. He unified cultural elements behind the civil rights marches in Selma and Montgomery, Alabama, and helped organize the celebrated 1963 Freedom March in Washington, DC, at which his close friend, Martin Luther King Jr., delivered the historic "I Have a Dream" speech. Years earlier, Belafonte had been forced to stop a South Carolina performance at intermission because of rumors that the Ku Klux Klan was intending a violent demonstration. But in viewing the development of American society and the evolution of the civil rights struggle, Belafonte has come to realize that the racism he and others have long decried is evident throughout society's cultural mosaic and not merely in the Klan's vicious epithets and signature white sheets. "There's a lot of racial tension coming out of our communities," he told *Summer Series* magazine. "There's a tremendous amount of crack and dope in black neighborhoods, which I think is an extension of racial inequalities. Racism has become more insidious, sometimes more clandestine, sometimes more blatant, as in the case of the Skin heads and others who represent the new wave of white, lower-middle-class people who have come together to preach racial violence. It's quite unnerving."

In 1966 Belafonte performed in Paris, France, and Stockholm, Sweden, in the first European-sponsored benefit concert on behalf of King. As a result of his efforts to fight segregation and racism, he was appointed to the board of directors of the Southern Christian Leadership Conference, a leading civil rights organization, served as chairman of the Martin Luther King Jr. Memorial Fund, and was named one of the three executors of the King estate after the celebrated leader was assassinated in 1968.

Focused Political Activism on International Issues

In recent years, Belafonte has used his celebrity to draw attention to civil rights issues and injustices on a global scale, particularly in respect to children suffering from malnutrition and sickness. In 1985 Belafonte, with friend Ken Kragen, organized the hugely successful and inspirational *We Are the World,* which won a Grammy Award, and more important for Belafonte, raised millions of dollars for and heightened an awareness of victims of famine and drought in Africa. An outgrowth of that record was the USA for Africa Foundation, on whose board of directors Belafonte has served with, among others, Lionel Richie, Quincy Jones, and Kenny Rogers. Belafonte was also deeply involved in Hands Across America, an outgrowth organization benefiting hungry and homeless Americans.

In 1987 Belafonte was appointed UNICEF Goodwill Ambassador, only the second American ever to hold the title. His first humanitarian odyssey in that position brought him to Dakar, Senegal, where he served as head of a four-day symposium in which African intellectuals and artists strove to publicize and consider solutions to the variegated problems besetting children on that continent. His commitment to the survival and health of third-world children led *Ebony* magazine to dub him "The Children's Patron Saint" and a "prime minister of hope," and earned him the 1989 Danny Kaye Award by the U.S. Committee for UNICEF. Vigorously pursuing a UNICEF drive to immunize children in developing counties, Belafonte has been called on frequently to testify before congressional committees. Through a fund bearing his name, Belafonte has opened new cultural exchanges with African nations, enabling African students to pursue an education in the United States.

As an outspoken critic of South Africa's apartheid government, Belafonte orchestrated a burst of artistic, if not political, liberation with the 1988 release of his critically acclaimed album *Paradise in Gazankulu*. Because of his arrest years earlier during an antiapartheid protest outside the South African embassy in Washington, DC, his advocacy of strict international economic sanctions, and his repeated calls for the release of then imprisoned African National Congress leader Nelson Mandela, Belafonte was considered a persona non grata—unaccepted or unwelcomed—in South Africa and could not go to that country to work on the album. Instead, musicians recorded the music there and the tapes were sent to the United States, where Belafonte added the vocals. Though banned on South African radio, *Paradise* was praised internationally for beautifully capturing in music the painful and haunting stories and poems describing life in a land infamous for its oppression.

In 1989 Belafonte was one of the recipients of the Kennedy Center Honors for lifetime achievement in the performing arts, arguably the most prestigious award given to artists by the U.S. government. "I couldn't help thinking how much of my life had been spent at odds with these people, with the establishment, and here they were honoring me," he was quoted as telling the *Ottawa Citizen*. "I've been critical of government actions and I will continue to be critical, and here I was being recognized for my accomplishments. It made me fall in love with America all over again."

Belafonte was a host for the World Summit for Children, which was held in September of 1990 at the United Nations (UN), where world leaders and social workers met to discuss and debate the current state of children's issues. Leaders of the summit produced the *World Declaration for the Survival, Protection, and Development of Children,* a document that codified the goals of UN members toward protecting children's rights across the globe. The effects of the World Summit translated into direct legislative efforts in many countries to enhance legal and social services for children.

In 1994 he received the National Medal of the Arts for his lifetime achievements in both film and music. He continued performing and acting throughout the 1990s, often winning critical acclaim for his performances. In 1995 he appeared in the racial drama *White Man's Burden*; he also appeared in the 1996 Robert Altman film *Kansas City,* in which he portrayed "Seldom Seen," the head of a criminal organization in Altman's stylized homage to Kansas City's underworld of the 1930s. In 2000 Belafonte was honored with a Grammy Award for lifetime achievement.

Became a Vocal Critic of Bush Administration

After the election of George W. Bush in 1999, Belafonte emerged as one of the most outspoken critics of the Bush administration. In a 2002 interview with San Diego radio station KFMB-AM, Belafonte likened Secretary of State Colin Powell to a "house slave," who had been allowed entrance to his "master's" house but was still beholden to his master's bidding. Belafonte's remarks brought sharp criticism from both the White House and supporters of the Bush administration, who dismissed Belafonte as a "celebrity liberal" whose accusations were uninformed. The incident elevated Belafonte's activism to the national stage as both Belafonte and Powell were asked to comment on a number of television and radio programs. Belafonte refused to apologize for his characterization of Powell and expanded his criticisms to other African Americans in the administration.

In 2006 Belafonte joined a group of activists and scholars that met with Venezuelan president Hugo Chavez to discuss Chavez's leadership, the state of democracy in Venezuela, and the Bush administration's opposition to Chavez's government. In interviews given during the meeting, Belafonte defended the "socialist revolution" in Venezuela and characterized Bush as a "tyrant" and "terrorist," who was attempting to portray Chavez as a dictator for political benefit.

Despite the controversy surrounding his political activities, Belafonte's activism continued to win him praise from within the African-American community. In 2006 Belafonte was honored by Black Entertainment Television with the Humanitarian Award for his passionate and multifaceted services to African Americans. When he accepted the award, *E! Online* quoted him as saying, "This award doesn't just touch vanity. It is a validation of what I stand for, what Paul Robeson stood for. It's a validation of what W.E.B. Dubois stood for, what Malcolm X and Dr. King stood for."

Selected discography

Albums

Mark Twain, RCA, 1954.
Calypso (includes "Banana Boat Song"), RCA, 1956.
Belafonte (includes "Matilda"), RCA, 1956.
Belafonte Returns to Carnegie Hall, RCA, 1960.
To Wish You a Merry Christmas, RCA, 1962.
Homeward Bound, RCA, 1970.
Paradise in Gazankulu, EMI, 1988.
Harry Belafonte: All Time Greatest Hits, RCA, 1988, volumes 2 and 3, 1989.
Belafonte '89, EMI, 1989.
Belafonte '89 (abridged version), EMI, 1990.

Sources

Books

Fogelson, Genia, *Harry Belafonte,* Holloway, 1980.

Periodicals

Chicago Sun-Times, July 27, 1990.
Chicago Tribune, July 26, 1990.
Ebony, September 1988.
Fun and Gaming, March 1, 1990.
New York Times, March 21, 2006.
Ottawa Citizen, January 13, 1990.
Paul Masson Summer Series, June 1989.

Online

"Belafonte: Bush 'Greatest Terrorist in the World.'" *MSNBC Online,* http://www.msnbc.msn.com/id/10767465/ (accessed December 18, 2007).
"Belafonte Won't Back down from Powell Slave Reference," *CNN Online,* http://archives.cnn.com/2002/US/10/15/belafonte.powell/ (accessed December 18, 2007).
Finn, Natalie, "BETs for Blige, West, Foxx and Brown," *E! Online,* http://www.eonline.com/news/article/index.jsp?uuid=7f8be5bf-0d96-4a87-abb5-8361c90d9e8e&entry=index (accessed December 18, 2007).
"Powell, Rice Accused of Toeing the Line," *Fox News Online,* http://www.foxnews.com/story/0,2933,66288,00.html (accessed December 18, 2007).

Other

Additional information obtained from a 1991 Belafonte Enterprises Inc. biography.

—Isaac Rosen and Micah L. Issit

Cuesta Benberry

1923–2007

Quilt historian

Cuesta Benberry was a self-taught historian of quilt-making who was instrumental in tracing African-American influences on the art. She died in 2007, leaving behind a rich trove of research that became part of the library of the American Folk Art Museum in New York City. "I think we get so emotional about quilts because they're such an integral part of many people's lives," she once told a reporter, according to an obituary by Patricia Sullivan that appeared in the *Seattle Times*. "They're on the bed. They're there at birth. They're there at death. They're part of the marriage bed. They're part of our lives, and they give us so many memories."

Born in 1923 in Cincinnati, Ohio, Benberry grew up in St. Louis, Missouri. As a young woman, she earned a degree in education at St. Louis's only historically black college, Harris-Stowe State College, which later became Harris-Stowe State University. She later pursued a degree in library science at the University of Missouri's St. Louis campus. From about the mid-1940s until her retirement in 1985, she worked as a teacher and librarian with the St. Louis public school system.

In 1951 she wed a Kentucky man, George Benberry. The women in his family were longtime quilters, and the newlyweds received a quilt as a wedding gift. At first, she recalled, she kept it underneath the bedspread, but then she visited her new in-laws in Kentucky and saw that "they took such great pride in their quilts," she told Jerri Stroud of the *St. Louis Post-Dispatch*. "They entered the quilts in county fairs and state fairs and put their quilts in to vie for prizes."

Intrigued by this enduring form of textile art, Benberry began collecting the block patterns that quilters regularly traded with one another, and she embarked on a decades-long research mission by visiting county fairs during her summers off from teaching to photograph and document the wide variety of quilt patterns that had developed in the United States since the colonial era.

There were hundreds of quilt block patterns, but Benberry discovered many were duplicates, often called by different names in different regions of the country over various time periods. Her exhaustive attempt to trace the history of these names marked the first time this had been attempted. She began writing on the topic in the 1970s, just as quiltmaking was becoming a serious research area for historians specializing in American folk art. Some of the more established scholars maintained that a small series of quilts, with distinctive patterns and vivid colors, that had been made by African-American women in the Deep South represented the sole black contribution to the form. Benberry countered this assertion in her writings and lectures, noting that generations of African-American women from around the country—in the South, New England, northern cities, and on the expanding Western frontier—had been quiltmakers and contributed significantly to the form, not just copied the work of white quilters. "When I saw that African-American quilt history was becoming the property of a group of scholars that had a very limited outlook on what African-American quilters have done over the years, I believed it was my task to try to give a more accurate

At a Glance . . .

Born on September 8, 1923, in Cincinnati, OH; died of congestive heart failure on August 23, 2007, in St. Louis, MO; married George Benberry, 1951; children: George Jr. *Education:* Harris-Stowe State University, degree in education; University of Missouri at St. Louis, MLS.

Career: Teacher and librarian in St. Louis, MO, c. 1945–85; quilt historian, beginning in the 1950s; author of articles and books on the subject and curator of museum exhibits.

Awards: Quilters Hall of Fame, inductee, 1983.

and varied picture," she once said, according to her *New York Times* obituary by Dennis Hevesi.

Recognized as a unique element in American folk art, the quilt had a special significance for African-American history. Even slave women sewed quilts, which made it one of the oldest African-American artistic traditions; in families torn asunder by slavery and in households with scarce material comforts, quilts were often the prized heirlooms in African-American families, and sometimes even the oldest of all the family's material possessions. They served as both a practical item and a link between generations, and with the renewal of interest in quiltmaking in the late twentieth century came a revival of traditional African-American quilting circles in communities across the United States. Some scholars even asserted that messages were hidden in nineteenth-century quilts that served as code along the Underground Railroad that guided escaped slaves to freedom in the North. "It is important to listen to what African-American quiltmakers say about their work and to give them credence, whether or not their comments coincide with researchers' theories and interpretations," Benberry wrote in a 1993 article for *American Visions.* "It is certainly not useful to view African-American quilts merely as isolated folk art objects, divorced from the lives of blacks and the social, political and economic conditions under which they have lived."

That article appeared a year after her first book, *Always There: The African-American Presence in American Quilts,* which was also the title of a museum exhibit she curated in Louisville, Kentucky. She worked

with Carol Pinney Crabb to compile two other books on quiltmaking: *Patchwork of Pieces: An Anthology of Early Quilt Stories, 1845–1940* and *Love of Quilts: A Treasury of Classic Quilting Stories.* Other museum exhibits she curated included *20th Century Quilts, 1900–1970: Women Make Their Mark,* held at the Museum of the American Quilter's Society in Paducah, Kentucky, in 1997, and *Piece of My Soul: Quilts by Black Arkansans,* held at the Old Statehouse Museum in Little Rock, Arkansas, in 2000.

In 2004 Benberry donated her vast collection of archival materials to the American Folk Art Museum in New York City. She died three years later, on August 23, 2007, just a few weeks shy of her eighty-fourth birthday. Survivors include her husband and their son, George Jr., along with two grandchildren and two great-grandchildren, but Benberry also left behind a vital body of research on American quiltmaking and its history. Her interest was purely scholarly: though she owned several quilts, she never made one herself. "Although I am not a quiltmaker, I wear the badge of quilt scholar with honor and pride," she wrote in a 1998 article that appeared in the *St. Louis Post-Dispatch.* "This field in which I spent so many years embodies ideals in which I strongly believe. The history of American women's quilts parallels and at times surpasses the country's historical progress toward enlightened democratic ideals."

Selected writings

Nonfiction

Always There: The African-American Presence in American Quilts, Kentucky Quilt Project, 1992.
(With Carol Pinney Crabb, comp.) *Patchwork of Pieces: An Anthology of Early Quilt Stories, 1845–1940,* American Quilter's Society, 1993.
Piece of My Soul: Quilts by Black Arkansans, University of Arkansas Press, 2000.
(With Crabb, comp.) *Love of Quilts: A Treasury of Classic Quilting Stories,* Voyageur Press, 2004.

Sources

Periodicals

American Visions, December–January 1993.
New York Times, September 10, 2007.
Seattle Times, September 9, 2007.
St. Louis Post-Dispatch, March 6, 1998; February 24, 2000.

—Carol Brennan

Corbin Bleu

1989—

Actor, singer

By the age of eighteen, when most young adults are just starting to focus on career possibilities, Corbin Bleu already had a substantial body of work behind him as both an actor and a recording artist. Best known for his role in the phenomenally successful Disney Channel movies *High School Musical* (2006) and *High School Musical 2* (2007), he has been performing since age two in television and film. In addition, Bleu released his first music album and spent the summer of 2007 on a concert tour that showcased his singing and dancing abilities. A teen heartthrob with a memorable mop of curly hair, Bleu expresses a levelheaded response to fame, and stresses that for him "it's not all about the fame and fortune; it's really putting out good work."

Began Career as a Child Model

Born Corbin Bleu Reivers in Brooklyn, New York, on February 21, 1989, Bleu is the son of David (an actor) and Martha Reivers. He got a jump on the competition by beginning his professional life as a toddler. At the age of two, he began appearing in television commercials for such products such as Life cereal, Hasbro, and Nabisco. By age four, he was working as a model, with his image appearing in advertisements for such high-profile clients as Macy's, Gap, Target, and Toys R Us. During this period, Bleu also made his stage debut in the off-Broadway production *Tiny Tim Is Dead,* playing an abandoned, homeless mute.

Bleu moved with his family from New York to Los Angeles in 1996. He worked steadily in episodic television and feature film roles, including a recurring role on the short-lived ABC police drama *High Incident* and an appearance on *E.R.* His feature films from this period include the Tim Allen comedy *Galaxy Quest,* the sci-fi thriller *Soldier,* and the comedy *Mystery Men,* which starred Ben Stiller. Additionally, Bleu was developing his dance skills and in 2001 began intensive training at the Debbie Allen Dance Academy in the Los Angeles area. There he undertook a full gamut of dance instruction, including ballet, jazz, tap, modern, hip-hop, African, break dance, salsa, flamenco, and ballroom. Allen, the famous choreographer who starred in the TV series *Fame,* told *Dance Spirit* magazine, "I think [Bleu] really has a career. Success is one thing, but a career is a much longer, broader journey."

Bleu attended the Los Angeles County High School for the Arts, a magnet school like the New York High School for the Performing Arts, which was portrayed in the movie and television series *Fame,* and which Bleu's mother had attended. During his freshman year, he won his first sizable film role in the teen action caper *Catch That Kid.* During high school, he performed in such student productions as *Footloose* and *Grease,* winning the honor of Theatre Student of the Year.

Took Part in Disney Megahit

In 2004 Bleu landed a starring role in the television series *Flight 29 Down,* which aired for three seasons on the Discovery Kids network. The program, a juvenile version of the ABC series *Lost,* concerned a group of teenagers stranded on a tropical island after their

At a Glance . . .

Born Corbin Bleu Reivers on February 21, 1989, in Brooklyn, NY, son of David and Martha Reivers.

Career: Model and actor in television commercials, 1991–96; film and television actor, 1997—; recording artist, 2007—.

Awards: Los Angeles County High School for the Arts, Theatre Student of the Year, 2004–05.

Addresses: *Agent*—Bonnie Liedtke, Liedtke, Bradwell and Associates, 9229 Sunset Blvd, Suite 405, West Hollywood, CA 90069; TalentWorks, 3500 West Olive Ave., Suite 1400, Burbank, CA 91505; (music) William Morris Agency, 1 William Morris Pl., Beverly Hills, CA 90212.

plane crashes. Bleu played Nathan McHugh, a Boy Scout whose leadership skills do not quite measure up to his self-confidence.

Although popular with its young audience, the success of *Flight 29 Down* pales in comparison to Bleu's next television project: the Disney Channel original movie *High School Musical*. The youngest of the six lead actors who were catapulted to fame by the film, Bleu portrayed the basketball player Chad Danforth, who tries to persuade his teammate Troy Bolton (Zac Efron) to give up his interest in theater and focus on winning the basketball championship. *High School Musical* premiered on January 20, 2006; with an audience of 7.7 million television viewers, it was the Disney Channel's most successful TV movie up to that point.

The broadcast of the original *High School Musical* production was just the first phase of a marketing blitz across the full panoply of media platforms commanded by the Disney enterprise. The film's soundtrack album went to number one on *Billboard's* charts. Disney aired sing-along, dance-along, and pop-up editions of the program. The cast members performed musical numbers from the movie during a national concert tour in late 2006, with new solo songs for Bleu and other members of the ensemble. The sequel *High School Musical 2* became the most-watched basic cable event in history with an audience of 17.2 million viewers on its debut in August of 2007.

The phenomenon of *High School Musical* has changed Bleu's life, delivering him to the heights of media celebrity while still in his teens. He told *TV Guide*, "Well, I used to be able to go to a mall, and now I can't!" On the other hand, he has prepared well for this success: "I know for me, as a person, I've pretty much stayed the same. I still have a great background. My dad comes with me everywhere I go and I wouldn't be able to do it without him, and [I'm] just glad to have him there to keep me grounded."

Recorded the Album Another Side

Bleu played the lead role in another Disney Channel original movie, *Jump In!*, which aired on January 12, 2007. The film, concerning a young boxer with an enthusiasm for double-dutch jump rope, was another ratings smash, further proving Bleu's appeal to the youth market. Again, Disney scored a crossover hit with the bouncy *Jump In!* soundtrack album, on which Bleu sings the track, "Push It to the Limit."

A pianist and vocalist, Bleu's first studio effort was a song called "Circles," recorded for an episode of *Flight 29 Down*. Disney's Hollywood Records label signed him on the strength of that single track. Bleu recorded his first solo album, *Another Side,* in the fall of 2006. The album fuses rhythm and blues with hip-hop and other pop genres in an upbeat, wholesome commercial blend. Bleu, who admires Prince, Michael Jackson, and Justin Timberlake, cowrote five songs on the album. In 2007 he toured in support of *Another Side* with the teen sister duo Aly & AJ.

Bleu presents an appealing combination of star quality and adolescent normality. He graduated from high school in 2007 and was admitted to Stanford University, but declined to matriculate because of scheduling commitments. As of 2007 he continued to live at home with his parents and three younger sisters.

For Bleu, the future seems limitless. A third *High School Musical* production is scheduled for release in late 2008, this time slated for theatrical release. In addition, Bleu is taking a producing credit on his upcoming film *Metal Burning*. He told *TV Guide*, "I'm at a point in my career right now that I definitely want to make a little more impact on the projects that I'm working on. And I definitely want to have a little bit more creative control as well." He told an interviewer for *Scholastic*, "What would be ideal for me would be to continue doing features, go work Broadway, and then go on a worldwide tour for another album. I want to do it all."

Selected works

Films

Beach Movie (also known as *Board Heads*), 1998.
Soldier, 1998.
Family Tree, 1999.
Galaxy Quest, 1999.
Mystery Men, 1999.
Catch That Kid, 2004.

Television

High Incident, 1997.
Flight 29 Down (series), 2005–07.
Dancing with the Stars, 2006.
High School Musical, 2006.
The Disney Channel Games, 2006–07.
Flight 29 Down (movie), 2007.
High School Musical 2, 2007.
Jump In!, 2007.
Ned's Declassified School Survival Guide, 2007.

Albums

Another Side, Hollywood, 2007.

Sources

Books

Contemporary Theatre, Film, and Television, Vol. 78, Thomson Gale, 2008.

Periodicals

Dance Spirit, July–August 2007, p. 136.
Los Angeles Times, December 31, 2006.
The Plain Dealer (Cleveland, OH), August 24, 2007.
TV Guide, January 12, 2007; October 9, 2007.

Online

"Another Side of Corbin Bleu!," *Scholastic,* http://content.scholastic.com/browse/article.jsp?id=3745960 (accessed December 27, 2007).

Corbin Bleu, http://www.corbinbleu.com (accessed December 27, 2007).

"Corbin Bleu," *Star Scoop,* http://www.thestarscoop.com/archives/corbin-bleu.php (accessed December 27, 2007).

—Roger K. Smith

J. Robert Bradley

1919–2007

Gospel singer

J. Robert Bradley, sometimes called "Mister Baptist," was one of the most influential vocalists in the history of gospel music. The power of his deep, resonant baritone was enough to lift him from squalid boyhood poverty to worldwide renown. He performed throughout the world in concerts that combined a classical repertoire with African-American spirituals.

Bradley was born in Memphis, Tennessee, on October 5, 1919. His father left the household early. His mother struggled to support him and his younger brother by working in a laundry. Bradley told interviewer T'Ebony Torain, "I know what it is to be hungry. I know what it is to need shoes. I know what it is to not have a house to live in, because they had set our little furniture out on the street because my mother couldn't pay the rent." He also suffered the trauma of losing his right eye to a severe infection during his early years. He went to school only occasionally after the third grade, without learning to read and write properly. He spent many hours by himself on the banks of the Mississippi River.

Sang Like an "Angel"

On Christmas Eve of 1931, the twelve-year-old Bradley stood outside the Front Street auditorium in Memphis, listening to children inside singing "Silent Night" at a Baptist holiday event. Unable to afford a ticket, he began to sing along with the carol. A policeman took notice of the boy, then entered the hall. He returned with Lucie Campbell, the program's music director. As Bradley recalled, the policeman asked Campbell what

she heard, and she replied, "I hear an angel singing." This was his first encounter with the woman who would become his mentor and chief supporter.

Campbell was no ordinary church lady. A gifted songwriter and educator, she was the music director of the National Baptist Convention and was largely responsible for introducing artists such as Marian Anderson and Thomas A. Dorsey to nationwide exposure through the black church. Some refer to her as the "mother of gospel music."

Campbell and Bradley's second meeting, two years later, was as memorable as their first. Bradley had been fishing in the Mississippi when, once again, he was attracted by music emanating from the Front Street auditorium. This time he found his way on to the stage, holding his bucket of crawfish. Some audience members cried to remove the urchin, but Campbell remembered him. As Bradley recounts in his foreword to Charles Walker's biography *Miss Lucie,* she wiped his muddy face with a handkerchief and stood him on a chair to sing. After he wowed the audience, National Baptist Convention president L. K. Williams asked Campbell where the boy had come from, and Campbell said, "Out of the river."

From then on, Campbell made Bradley her protégé. She took him in to the Baptist convention and its Sunday School Congress, and chose him to introduce her songs, some of which became standards of the gospel repertoire. She helped launch him into a professional career as a singer. Later in the 1930s, Camp-

At a Glance . . .

Born on October 5, 1919, in Memphis, TN; died on May 3, 2007, in Nashville, TN. *Education:* Trinity College (London), 1955.

Career: Singer; National Baptist Convention Sunday School Publishing Board, director of music promotion, 1957–63; National Baptist Convention, music director, 1963–2000.

Memberships: National Baptist Convention; World Baptist Alliance.

Awards: Knighted by President William Tolbert of Liberia, 1975.

bell organized a male gospel quartet called the Good Will Singers. With Bradley as the lead singer, the group toured the country and became highly popular. He also toured with the Hall Johnson Singers, and as a soloist at Baptist revivals.

Trained for Concert Stage

In 1938 Charles Faulkner Bryan, a music professor at Tennessee Polytechnic Institute, took the young baritone under his wing. Bryan attended a revival and was thunderstruck by Bradley's voice, but feared that without training he would overtax his larynx and injure himself. He gave Bradley a few lessons, and later the singer went to Cookeville, Tennessee, to study for a year with Bryan. Bryan's wife, Edith, instructed him in reading and writing as well. Because the campus was segregated at that time, Bryan was putting his own career and reputation at risk to work with an African-American student by night. The campus president gave his approval, however, after hearing Bradley sing.

In the early 1940s Bradley left Tennessee to study music more intensively in New York under Madame Edyth Walker, the famous Wagnerian soprano. He then spent six years in London. He sang for BBC radio and studied at Trinity College of Music. With classical training to support his natural gifts, Bradley's career reached new heights. In 1955 he gave a debut recital at the Royal Albert Hall in London, with the British royal family in attendance. The program featured classical pieces by Wolfgang Mozart, Giuseppe Verdi, and other composers, as well as African-American spirituals and gospel songs. It was the first performance of gospel music on the concert stage in Great Britain.

That same year, the Baptist World Alliance met in London, with Lucie Campbell in attendance. She introduced Bradley to the large international congregation of Baptists, and he sang a program that included her version of "The Lord Is My Shepherd." This success led to classical and sacred performances in Europe and Scandinavia, and many repeat performances at meetings of the World Alliance, where he became known as "Mister Baptist," the most visible public face of his denomination.

Performed on Five Continents

Besides his performances, Bradley also took on administrative tasks for the National Baptist Convention, first as Campbell's assistant, then as director of music promotion for the Baptist Sunday School Publishing Board, based in Nashville. He was responsible for selling millions of copies of the Baptist Standard Hymnal. After Campbell's death in 1963, he succeeded her as the convention's music director.

Bradley's recording career spanned five decades, from his first single on the Apollo label in 1950 to tracks on several compilations released by Shanachie in the 1990s. His concert career took him to the great concert halls of the world, spanning five continents. He always made sure to include gospel material and spirituals, such as "Amazing Grace" and "Sometimes I Feel Like a Motherless Child," in his concert repertoire. He sang in Brazil, Mexico, Israel, and Africa. In 1975 he was knighted by William Tolbert, the president of Liberia.

Gospel great Mahalia Jackson declared that Bradley's was the greatest voice she ever heard. His performance at her funeral in 1972 was so stirring that newspapers carried photographs of people swooning in the aisles of Chicago's Aerie Crown Theater. With enunciation reminiscent of Paul Robeson, he combined the intensity of operatic singing with the emotional accessibility of blues artists such as Bessie Smith. Martin Luther King Jr. named Bradley as his favorite singer, according to Bradley's obituary in the *New York Times*.

Bradley published a memoir, *I Have Always Been in the Hands of God,* with Rev. Amos Jones Jr. in 1993. He performed until 2005, despite failing health brought on by the complications of diabetes. His last years were spent confined in his small apartment in Nashville, and he died there on May 3, 2007. In Memphis the street where Bradley grew up was renamed in his honor.

Selected works

Books

(With Rev. Amos Jones Jr.) *I Have Always Been in the Hands of God,* Townsend Press, 1993.
Foreword to *Miss Lucie* by Charles Walker, Townsend Press, 1993.

Albums

God's Amazing Grace, 1960.
(With Rev. C. L. Franklin) *I Heard the Voice,* 1962.
I'll Fly Away, 1973.
(Contributor) "Amazing Grace," live performance included on *When Gospel Was Gospel,* 2005.

Singles

"Didn't My Lord Deliver Daniel," 1950.
"Hear My Prayer," 1950.
"If Jesus Had to Pray," 1950.
"Poor Pilgrim of Sorrow," 1950.
"The Day Is Past and Gone," 1992.
"Something Within Me," 1992.

Sources

Books

Boyer, Horace Clarence, *How Sweet the Sound,* Elliott and Clark, 1995.

Cosby, Camille O., and Renee Poussaint, eds., *A Wealth of Wisdom: Legendary African American Elders Speak,* Atria Books, 2004.
McNeil, W. K., ed., *Encyclopedia of American Gospel Music,* Routledge, 2005.
Walker, Charles, *Miss Lucie,* Townsend Press, 1993.
Who's Who Among African Americans, 20th ed., Gale, 2007.

Periodicals

New York Times, May 4, 2007.
Tennessee Tech Visions, Fall 2003.

Online

Sir J. Robert Bradley, http://jrobertbradley.com/ (accessed December 27, 2007).

Other

Personal correspondence with Anthony Heilbut, November 5, 2007.

—Roger K. Smith

Robert Brown

1936–2007

Cartoonist

Robert "Buck" Brown was a cartoonist whose work helped define the unique sensibility of *Playboy* magazine over the course of five decades. With a bright palette of acrylics, a gently subversive wit, and a smattering of erudition, Brown became one of the first African-American visual artists to cross over into the mainstream and attain prominence as a cartoonist.

Buck Brown was born Bobby Brown on February 3, 1936, in Morrison, Tennessee. Brown's parents separated when he was five years old, and he moved with his mother to Chicago's South Side. By his teenage years at Englewood High School, he was already showing an abiding interest in art.

After graduating from high school in 1954, Brown entered the military, serving as a hydraulics specialist in the air force. It was then that he began to express himself in artwork, especially cartooning. His commanding officers were amused by his sly humor and encouraged him to spend his spare time sketching. When he was discharged in 1958, Brown returned to Chicago, taking art classes at Wilson Junior College and working days as a bus driver with the Chicago Transit Authority. After earning a two-year degree, he enrolled at the University of Illinois at Urbana-Champaign and completed a bachelor of fine arts degree in 1966.

Brown entered his studies believing that he would eventually find steady employment in the advertising business. However, he was still developing his talent for cartoon humor, and he began submitting work to

magazines. At this time, few African-American cartoonists were finding markets for their work. The first comic strips created by black artists to be published in daily newspapers, such as Morrie Turner's *Wee Pals* and Ted Shearer's *Quincy,* did not appear until later in the 1960s. Even long after the civil rights era, the majority of cartoons portraying African-American characters and themes were drawn by white artists.

Found Niche at Playboy

However, at the age of twenty-five Brown got his first break and found his most enduring supporter. On a whim, he went to the Chicago office of *Playboy* magazine and dropped off some sketches. Hugh Hefner, the magazine's flamboyant publisher, appreciated Brown's sophisticated style immediately and purchased several pieces. His first cartoon appeared in the March 1962 issue. His final work for *Playboy* appeared posthumously in August of 2007. In between, the men's magazine ran nearly six hundred Buck Brown cartoons, bringing the artist a steady income and considerable fame. His work was featured in several book compilations published by Playboy Press, including the solo compilation *Playboy's Buck Brown* (1981).

Over the years, Brown published cartoons in many other publications, including the *Chicago Sun-Times, Ebony, Esquire, Jet,* and the premier American magazine for single-panel cartoons, *The New Yorker.* It was

Playboy, however, with which he was primarily identified, and where his restrained, sardonic humor fit best. Brown was one of a small set of cartoonists, including Jules Feiffer, Gahan Wilson, and Shel Silverstein, whose work contributed greatly to *Playboy*'s hip and libertine mystique from the 1960s onward. Between the nude photographs and the ribald artwork, the magazine projected a singular mind-set and lifestyle, embodied by the freewheeling Hefner.

Like most *Playboy* cartoonists, Brown submitted plenty of material about sex, but he was not interested in titillation or leering humor. His most memorable character was a dirty old lady who came to be known as Granny. "She was just an older woman my father drew," Brown's daughter, Tracy Hill, told the *Chicago Sun-Times,* "but every time he would go into the *Playboy* offices, the receptionist would laugh and say, 'I love that little granny of yours.' And the name stuck."

Granny first appeared in the magazine in 1966; subsequently, she was often seen in states of undress in comical situations. "Could you put your clothes on, ma'am?," a stagecoach bandit says in one caption— "You're scaring the horses." Granny's wrinkled, uninhibited exhibitionism served as a foil to the airbrushed image of the Playboy Bunny. In one cartoon included in the book *Playboy: 50 Years: The Cartoons,* Brown employs Granny to gently taunt his patron. She disrobes before the bed where Hefner sits in his famous smoking jacket with an attractive young woman by his side, and the caption reads, "Awright, Hef, baby, let's see you put *this* in your pipe and smoke it!" Granny achieved the ultimate *Playboy* honor in the magazine's September 1980 issue: she was the centerfold.

Painted in the Soul Genre

Brown used acrylic paints in his color cartoons to achieve a distinctive painterly style. The bold use of color gave his work great visual appeal. Many of his cartoons made visual reference to historical periods or parodied well-known works of art or literature. In these pieces, the richness of his drawings was integral to their comic effect, as in his send-up of Michelangelo's famous *Creation of Adam* fresco from the Sistine Chapel. The caption: "Pull my finger!"

Active during a key period in the civil rights movement, Brown dealt directly with race relations in many of his cartoons. His achievement in these works was to incorporate incisive social commentary while avoiding overt or strident political expression. Using disarming humor, he was able to provoke both thought and laughter from blacks and whites alike. An example of his approach appeared in *Playboy*'s October 1967 issue. Black marchers holding signs that read, "Equal Opportunity," "Open Housing," and "We Shall Overcome, Baby!" show surprise at the enthusiastic reception from their white neighbors, whose banner says, "Welcome Neighbors! We Can Work It Out." One marcher warns another: "It must be a trap!"

Besides his cartoon work, Brown also produced works in the larger format of painted canvas. These paintings also reflected his sense of humor and his flair for playful social commentary; he painted, he said, in the soul genre. Some of his paintings were purchased by celebrities. In the *Chicago Sun-Times,* Hill described one that was purchased by comedian Bill Cosby: it was "a scene on a beach. Out in the ocean was a big ship. He had all of these Africans coming out to greet the ship, and they were all dressed as basketball players. There was a coach standing there with them."

Brown was known as an unpretentious, easygoing gentleman. He continued to draw cartoons, paint, and exhibit his artwork into his later years and died on July 2, 2007, after suffering a stroke.

Sources

Books

Hefner, Hugh, ed., *Playboy: 50 Years: The Cartoons,* Chronicle Books, 2004.
Who's Who Among African Americans, 20th ed., Gale, 2007.

Periodicals

Chicago Sun-Times, July 8, 2007.
Chicago Tribune, July 13, 2007.
Ebony, January 1993.
Jet, July 23, 2007, p. 65.
Los Angeles Times, July 12, 2007.

Online

"Buck Brown," *Biography Resource Center,* http://galenet.galegroup.com/servlet/BioRC (accessed December 27, 2007).

"Cartoonist 'Buck' Brown Dies," *Maynard Institute,* http://www.maynardije.org/columns/dickprince/070710_prince/ (accessed December 27, 2007).

"Robert 'Buck' Brown: 1936–2007," *Designboom,* http://www.designboom.com/history/buckbrown.html (accessed December 27, 2007).

"Robert 'Buck' Brown Biography," *The History Makers,* http://www.thehistorymakers.com/biography (accessed December 27, 2007).

—Roger K. Smith

John Compton

1925–2007

Prime minister

Compton, John, photograph. AP Images.

John Compton was serving his third stint as the prime minister of Saint Lucia, the Caribbean island nation, when he suffered a stroke and died a few months later in September of 2007. The longtime head of the United Workers Party, eighty-two-year-old Compton was a veteran of the Saint Lucian political scene and had been instrumental in negotiating its independence from Britain back in 1979. His influence spanned some fifty years of the island's history, and the man dubbed "Pa Pa" or "Daddy Compton" by Saint Lucians had been the most famous figure in the country for several generations. "During his career, in a trajectory familiar to small Caribbean islands, St. Lucia changed from a neglected, semi-feudal backwater with a large, depressed peasantry," wrote Polly Pattullo of London's *Guardian* newspaper, "into an independent state that saw tourism displace agriculture as the economic driving force."

Compton was not a native of Saint Lucia; he was born to a single mother on a small island called Canouan in 1925. Canouan belonged to the Grenadines, a collection of six hundred islands, and later became part of the

island nation known as Saint Vincent and the Grenadines. In 1939 Compton moved in with relatives who lived on Saint Lucia, located north of Canouan, to attend high school there. The members of this Compton branch of the family were known as skilled shipbuilders and boat captains, and during his teens Compton became an experienced sailor in this part of the Caribbean that borders the Atlantic Ocean.

Compton entered adulthood at a time when Saint Lucia was still a colonial possession of Britain. The 240-square-mile island in the eastern Caribbean Sea, with lush rainforest and majestic mountain peaks, was part of the Windward Islands, named so by European sailors because of the prevailing winds in the weather patterns of the West Indies. The other Windward isles were Dominica, Martinique, Saint Vincent, Grenadines, and Grenada, and most had originally been inhabited by the Carib people, who may have originally come from South America. In the 1600s the French, Dutch, and English established settlements on Saint Lucia, but the fertile soil became a battleground for competing British and French interests until 1814, when the last of fourteen wars fought over it ended with a British victory. By then, Saint Lucia had an immense population of African slaves, who had been brought over to work the sugarcane plantations.

Educated in England

After completing high school, Compton headed to Curaçao, an island off the coast of Venezuela, to work at one of its oil refineries. His two-year stint there helped pay the costs he would incur at college in Wales and then England as he pursued a degree in law and economics. After finishing at the London School of Economics, he was called to the bar of Gray's Inn in 1951. Returning home that same year, Compton became an attorney in private practice but also joined a new and thriving political scene in Saint Lucia brought on by the adoption of universal adult suffrage that same year. In 1954 he ran for and won a seat in the legislative council as a representative of the Micoud-Dennery district, a fishing village on the Atlantic side of the island.

Compton initially ran as an independent candidate, but he soon joined the Saint Lucia Labour Party (SLP), an organization that advocated for increased indepen-

dence from British colonial authorities along with better conditions for workers. In 1957 Compton gained a measure of fame when he led a strike by workers at a sugar factory, during which he was arrested. This came because of a confrontation with a white man, either a sugar farmer or factory manager, who brandished a weapon in the heat of argument but froze when Compton pulled out his own in response. Compton was briefly jailed over the incident, but in the end the factory owners were forced to recognize the union.

Compton remained a member of the legislative council during the four-year period when Saint Lucia was part of a new political entity, the Federation of the West Indies, from 1958 to 1962, and served as a government minister after 1957. In 1961 he and two other SLP members broke with the party to found the National Labour Movement, which soon merged with another political party to become the United Workers' Party (UWP). Compton was elected to head it in 1964, and under Saint Lucia's new system of government became chief minister of Saint Lucia in April of that same year after elections. The party held onto power for the next two decades.

Agitated for Full Independence

In the late 1960s Compton led a faction of Saint Lucian politicians who pushed for full independence from Britain, but their plan was rejected. They were instead granted "associated statehood" status, which meant that they were free to rule at home, but Britain would oversee Saint Lucia's defense and foreign affairs. Compton famously quipped at the time that "the colour of our skins is against us," according to the *Daily Telegraph,* "and a government, even one that professes democracy, is pleased to legislate and propound the doctrine of second-class citizenship for people of another colour." People of African ancestry made up more than 90 percent of the island's population.

Compton took up the cause again after the 1974 general election, and this time Britain agreed to the opening of independence talks. Five years later, those negotiations concluded with Saint Lucia's independence day, February 22, 1979, and the ceremonies and festivities were presided over by Compton, whose title of chief minister now evolved to that of prime minister. The sole remaining tie to Britain was Saint Lucia's membership in the British Commonwealth of Nations, whose members recognize the British monarch as the head of state; traditionally, the king or queen is represented locally by an appointed governor-general.

Saint Lucians went to the polls again in July of 1979, and in a surprising turnaround Compton and the UWP were ousted by the SLP. Compton remained politically active, however, and in 1981 attained a long-sought achievement for greater regional cooperation with the formation of the Organization of Eastern Caribbean States (OECS), with Saint Lucia joined by six other founding member nations. A year later, Compton returned to power with the UWP in elections held in May of 1982, when he and his party colleagues took fourteen of the seventeen seats in the House of Assembly. He served as prime minister for the next fourteen years, a period of impressive economic growth for the island.

In 1983 the normally placid atmosphere of the Windward archipelago was shattered by an uprising in Grenada that prompted a U.S. military invasion to oust Marxist rebels. The foreign intervention came at the request of the OECS, whose members had immediately stepped forward and suggested the deployment of a multinational Caribbean force, backed by outside assistance, to quell the trouble in Grenada. President Ronald Reagan agreed, and on October 25, 1983, Americans were greeted by the headlines that a contingent of U.S. Marines and Special Forces had invaded a small Caribbean island most had never heard of until then. "Compton was by now recognised as a conservative figure, with a strong belief in capitalism and the competitive economy," noted his *Times* of London obituary. "He spoke out strongly against the coup in Grenada, seeing it as a threat to the stability of all the neighbouring small island states."

Returned to Office

In April of 1996 Compton resigned as head of the UWP and stepped down as prime minister in favor of Vaughan Lewis, his handpicked successor. In May of 1997 the UWP was badly beaten in the general election, taking just one of seventeen House of Assembly seats. This turn of events actually mirrored similar changes in other parts of the Caribbean, with the ouster or natural deaths of longtime political leaders who had held power since independence, often for decades by that point. "In many respects, political leaders like Mr. Compton, who first came to power in 1964, can be seen as victims of their own success," explained *New York Times* correspondent Larry Rohter. "Throughout the Caribbean, the governments that took power after independence invested heavily in education. As a result, the generation that is now coming to maturity and is voting for the first time is both more worldly and more demanding, unwilling to accept high rates of unemployment, corruption and the other ills that are typical of developing societies."

Compton retired to a banana, coconut, and cocoa farm he had in the Micoud area, and he took legal consulting jobs when not busy with his farm. In March of 2005 he made a surprising comeback when he was elected to head the UWP again, and in the general election on December 11, 2006, the party regained several seats and Compton began his third stint as prime minister. The following March he greeted scores of international visitors and VIPs who came for the cricket World Cup, held in Saint Lucia's capital of Castries. A month later, however, Compton suffered a stroke while in New York City, and in mid-May he transferred his powers to Saint Lucia's minister for health and labour relations, Stephenson King, who became acting prime minister. On September 7, Compton died at a hospital in Castries at the age of eighty-two. Survivors include his wife of thirty-nine years, Janice Clarke Compton, one son, four daughters, and several grandchildren.

Compton's *Times* of London obituary cited his somewhat unique low-key political style in listing his contributions to Caribbean politics over the decades. "Though not blessed with the power to move men by rhetoric, Compton became in effect the chief civil servant of the island," the tribute noted. "He grew increasingly impatient with the personality conflicts and verbiage of local politics and became firmly convinced that only free enterprise could deliver modernisation. A plain man, he could at times be brutally outspoken. There was no cult of personality—he always drove his own car, refusing police outriders or guards." Shortly before taking office in 2006, Compton gave an interview to Donna Sealy from the Barbadian newspaper *Nation* in which he remarked that "the day a prime minister has to get a bodyguard to walk around in his own country, that is the day he needs to go."

Sources

Periodicals

Daily Telegraph (London, England), September 10, 2007.
Guardian (London), September 10, 2007.
Nation (Barbados), December 15, 2006.
New York Times, July 27, 1997.
Times (London, England), September 10, 2007.

—Carol Brennan

Lee Dorsey

1926–1986

Singer

Lee Dorsey was a rhythm and blues (R&B) singer who topped the pop music charts during the 1960s with a series of songs that communicated the relaxed, ebullient spirit of New Orleans, Louisiana. New Orleans plays a unique role in American culture and American music in particular. Out of its multicultural gumbo have come jazz, blues, Cajun and Creole music, R&B, soul, funk, and other genres of African-American music touched by Caribbean influences. Perhaps no musician of the rock and roll era personified the city's spirit with more charm than Dorsey, whose fame was brief but whose influence has reached beyond R&B music to diverse acts such as the Beastie Boys and the Clash.

Irving Lee Dorsey was born into a musical household in the historic Ninth Ward of New Orleans on December 4, 1926. One of his childhood friends was another future exponent of New Orleans music: Antoine "Fats" Domino. His family moved to Portland, Oregon, when Dorsey was ten, and he developed a liking for country music. Coming of age during World War II, he was drafted and saw action in the Pacific as a gunner on a navy destroyer.

Turned from Boxing to Music

After the war the diminutive but muscle-bound Dorsey returned to Portland and began prizefighting, under the nickname "Kid Chocolate." He told interviewer Jeff Hannusch, "I knew some guys who went to the gym to box, so I just started goin' with 'em. Once I saw I could whip some of 'em, I started gettin' fights too." He became one of the region's top boxers, with an un-beaten record as a featherweight and lightweight. However, in 1955 he hung up the gloves and moved back to New Orleans.

With the help of the G.I. Bill, he learned a trade and landed a job in an auto body shop. He would sing while banging out dented fenders, and one day a scout named Reynauld Richard heard his voice and invited him to make a record. Dorsey recorded several 45 rpm singles in 1957 and 1958. "Rock Pretty Baby" got some attention around New Orleans. "Lottie-Mo" was picked up for national distribution and won Dorsey a television appearance on Dick Clark's dance show *American Bandstand*.

"Lottie-Mo" began Dorsey's long association with Allen Toussaint, the young pianist who produced the record. Toussaint and Dorsey began performing together at the Dew Drop Inn and other New Orleans night spots, while Dorsey continued to work days in the body-and-fender business, eventually opening his own shop. Toussaint began to direct his efforts toward writing, arranging, and producing. He quickly became the hit maker of New Orleans R&B, largely responsible for launching the careers of numerous artists; he was inducted into the Rock and Roll Hall of Fame in 1998. The vehicle for Toussaint's greatest success, and his most consistent musical partner, was Dorsey. "If a smile had a sound, it would be the sound of Lee Dorsey's voice," Toussaint was quoted as saying in *Stars of Soul and Rhythm and Blues*. "It's no wonder that he inspired so many of my favorite songs; songs that, if not for him, I would never have written."

At a Glance . . .

Born Irving Lee Dorsey on December 4, 1926, in New Orleans, LA; died on December 1, 1986, in New Orleans, LA.

Career: U.S. Navy, 1944–45; professional prizefighter until 1955; auto body mechanic, 1956–86; singer and recording artist, 1957–81.

When Marshall Sehorn, a record promoter for the Fire/Fury label, heard "Lottie-Mo," the vocalist reminded him of Ray Charles. Sehorn's boss, Bobby Robinson, came to New Orleans in 1961, found Dorsey, and signed him to a recording contract. Dorsey had no original material to record, but while the two men sat on Dorsey's front porch, an idea came wafting their way: a catchy nursery rhyme sung by children on the street. Dorsey replaced the scatological lyrics with nonsense words: "Sittin' in la-la / Waitin' for my ya-ya." Toussaint arranged the number and taught the piano part to another musician because he was under contract to another label. "Ya Ya" was a smash hit, reaching the number-one position on the national R&B charts and number seven on *Billboard*'s Hot 100 in late 1961.

Evolved from Soul to Funk

Dorsey's second Fire/Fury release, "Do-Re-Mi," also landed on the charts, and the singer began touring the R&B circuit full time with a backing band. He appeared with James Brown, Chuck Berry, Aaron "T-Bone" Walker, and other artists. His next few singles were less successful, however, and by 1963 he had lost his recording partners; Toussaint had been drafted into the army, and the Fire/Fury label had gone out of business. Dorsey, unfazed by his success, simply returned to his other line of work in the automotive business. He told Hannusch, "I was just a regular guy. I didn't know much about show business…. I never had any trouble getting body and fender work. I had the tools and I knew the work. I love it. I never knew if I was a better body-and-fender man or a vocalist."

Toussaint returned from military service in 1965 and picked up where he had left off with Sehorn and Dorsey. They rode right back onto the pop charts with "Ride Your Pony," the first of a string of hits distributed by Amy Records. Dorsey had four hit singles in 1966. The first was the bluesy "Get out of My Life, Woman." Next came the tune that would be most identified with him throughout his career, "Workin' in a Coal Mine," another top-ten pop hit and Dorsey's second gold record. He followed up with "Holy Cow," and scored a hit in the United Kingdom with "Confusion." By this point, Toussaint was writing most of Dorsey's material and arranging all of it. The backing musicians, including Leo Nocentelli on guitar and Art Neville on keyboards, evolved into the band the Meters, who went on to a stellar career of their own. Sehorn and Toussaint teamed up to record many other New Orleans artists, building a stable of local talent, and together created Sea-Saint studios.

Dorsey toured for three months in England at the peak of his popularity, performing dates with the Beatles and the Rolling Stones. He continued producing a stream of singles into 1967, but the hits came more slowly. His last chart success came in 1969 with "Everything I Do Gohn Be Funky (From Now On)." By that point, Toussaint and Dorsey were shifting from the relaxed vibes of New Orleans soul into the more dynamic sonic territory of funk. The vocalist's "Shake-a-make-a-make-a-shake-a-hula!" riff in the frenetic dance number "Four Corners" revealed this new intensity.

Acquired a Devoted Following

Dorsey's 1970 album *Yes We Can* was not a commercial success, but many of his fans consider it his greatest work and a highlight of 1970s soul music. Reminiscent of Marvin Gaye and Curtis Mayfield, *Yes We Can* featured anthems of black pride, songs addressing hardship and poverty ("Who's Gonna Help Brother Get Further," "When the Bill's Paid"), and other progressive material penned by Toussaint, backed powerfully by the Meters, and delivered with Dorsey's characteristic optimism. The title track later became the Pointer Sisters' first hit single.

By 1972 Dorsey's recording career had begun to taper off. Again, he retreated contentedly to his body and fender shop, performing occasionally in New Orleans clubs and at its annual Jazz and Heritage Festival. He still had a devoted fan base on both sides of the Atlantic, including many other musicians. He resurfaced in 1976, with a cameo appearance on the debut album by the rock-soul band Southside Johnny and the Asbury Jukes. A new contract with ABC/Polydor Records followed, leading to Dorsey's last album, *Night People,* in 1978.

Dorsey suffered severe injuries in a motorcycle accident in 1979. A year later, he had recovered sufficiently to tour as an opening act for the Clash, the British punk sensation. It was his final tour as a musician. He spent his final few years working in his body and fender shop, alongside his son Irving. There are some who believe that Dorsey's smoking habit and automotive work, and his indifference toward protecting himself from fumes and toxins, contributed to the ill health that shortened his life. He died of emphysema on December 1, 1986.

Selected discography

Albums

Ya Ya, Relic, 1962.
Lee Dorsey, Amy Records, 1966.
The New Lee Dorsey, Amy Records, 1966.
Ride Your Pony, Amy Records, 1966.
Working in a Coalmine, Charly, 1966.
Yes We Can, Polydor Records, 1970.
Night People, ABC/Polydor Records, 1978.

Singles

"Rock Pretty Baby," 1957.
"Lottie-Mo," 1958.

Sources

Books

Hannusch, Jeff, *I Hear You Knockin': The Sound of New Orleans Rhythm and Blues,* Swallow Publications, 1985.

Hildebrand, Lee, *Stars of Soul and Rhythm and Blues,* Billboard Books, 1994.
Koster, Rick, *Louisiana Music,* Da Capo Press, 2002.
Lichtenstein, Grace, and Laura Dankner, *Musical Gumbo: The Music of New Orleans,* Norton, 1993.
Santelli, Robert, *The Big Book of Blues,* Penguin, 1993.

Online

"Article of the Month: Lee Dorsey" *The Geoffrey Himes Home Page,* http://members.aol.com/GEOFFHIMES/homepage.htm (accessed December 27, 2007).
"Friday Flashback 3: Everything I Do Gohn Be Funky," *Funky 16 Corners,* http://funky16corners.word press.com/2007/04/06/friday-flashback-3-funky 16corners-radio-v13-everything-i-do-gohn-be-funky/ (accessed December 27, 2007).
"Lee Dorsey: Biography," *Billboard.com,* http://www.billboard.com/bbcom/bio/index.jsp?pid=44 88&aid=30062 (accessed December 27, 2007).

—Roger K. Smith

Manuel Francisco dos Santos

1933–1983

Soccer player

Manuel Francisco dos Santos, better known as "Garrincha," wowed Brazilian soccer fans and even world audiences with his amazing athletic talents. Considered one of the best players the country ever produced, the diminutive right wing was an impressive, evasive dribbler as well as a shot-scorer despite—or perhaps because of—the bent legs with which he had been born. Widely known by his one-name moniker that means "little bird" or "little wren" in Portuguese—Brazil's main language—Garrincha played a key role in Brazil's first-ever World Cup victory in 1958 and helped his national team retain that title four years later.

Like many Brazilians, Garrincha was of mixed-race heritage. The country was one of the last places in the world to outlaw slavery, which happened less than fifty years before he was born in 1933. He was part black and part Fulnio Indian. This was one of the two-hundred-plus indigenous Indian tribes of Brazil, but the Fulnio Indians were known as genetic carriers of a birth defect that caused infants to be born with bent legs like Garrincha's. Orthopedic braces might have corrected this, but Garrincha's family was too poor to afford them. His right leg bowed inward, while the left leg bent outward and was two inches shorter than the right one, though he later had surgery to correct that. The future soccer star "grew up looking as if a gust of wind had blown his legs sideways, as in a cartoon," wrote Alex Bellos for London's *Guardian* newspaper. He was a sweet, good-natured child, which prompted his older sister Rosa to dub him "Garrincha."

Garrincha grew up in a town called Pau Grande located in the state of Rio de Janeiro. A textile factory was the main employer there, and he went to work at the site at the age of fourteen. He was fired for his poor job performance but then rehired because the company soccer team realized what a talented player he was. Urged to try out for the quartet of professional teams that dominated the state of Rio de Janeiro, he finally agreed but was turned away once for not having the proper shoes; at another tryout he left before it was completed. When he went to audition for Botafogo, he was teamed with one its best players on the pitch, and, when dribbling the ball, he actually passed it through the other man's legs.

Taunted His Opponents

Garrincha was signed to Botafogo, which means "(he who) sets fire" in Portuguese and was also the name from a beachfront neighborhood in the city of Rio de Janeiro, and he made his game debut in July of 1953. In that match he scored a hat trick, the term given to three consecutive goals, which is somewhat of a rarity in soccer. He emerged as the newest star in the game and was to become famous for his specialty kicks and fantastic dribbling abilities, though he also committed his share of fouls and could be merciless in his taunting of an opposing player. "Garrincha seemed to play for the fun of it," noted Bellos. "He relished fooling defenders with his skilful moves, taunting them like a champion toreador taunts a bull. On one occasion he deliberately forgot the ball and carried on running. His opponent, the Argentinian defender Vairo, followed the player without realising the ball was left behind."

At a Glance . . .

Born Manuel Francisco dos Santos on October 28, 1933, in Pau Grande, Rio de Janeiro state, Brazil; died of cirrhosis on January 20, 1983, in Rio de Janeiro, Brazil; married Nair Marques, 1952 (separated, 1965); partner of Elza Soares, 1966–77; married again, early 1980s; children: (with Marques) eight daughters; (with Soares) Manuel Garrincha dos Santos Jr.; possibly five more children.

Career: Botafogo de Futebol e Regatas, 1953, right wing; member of the Brazilian national team, 1958–66; traded to the Sport Club Corinthians Paulista, São Paulo, 1966; also joined Atlético Junior of Barranquilla, Colombia, 1968, and later that same year the Clube de Regatas do Flamengo, and played with Olaria Atlético Clube, until 1972.

Officials of the Brazilian national team decided against giving Garrincha a place on the roster in the lead-up to the 1954 World Cup, believing he did not yet have enough experience, but he continued to impress during regular-season and championship play over the next few years. The team won the 1957 national championship, and both Garrincha and another new star of Brazilian soccer, Pelé, were not put in a game together until a fourth-round match-up against the Soviet Union. "The onslaught of the opening three minutes," wrote Bellos, "showed an audaciousness and skill not seen before in international football. They are considered by many as Brazilian football's greatest three minutes of all time." Brazil went on to beat the host team, Sweden, in the final by 5–2.

The victory of the World Cup—then, as now, believed to be the most-followed sporting event on the planet—ushered in a new, dominant era for Brazilian soccer on the world stage. Suddenly, the hardscrabble South American country known more for its beaches, samba music, pre-Lenten Carnivale, and endemic poverty was producing champions of the game. Garrincha's best World Cup moments came in the 1962 event, which was held in Chile. His teammate Pelé was injured early on, but Garrincha and another Brazilian star, Vavá, led the way to a stunning victory against England in the quarterfinals. In the second of Garrincha's two goals in a game that Brazil won 3–1, he made a curved shot known as the "banana kick." The Brazilians repeated that score when they beat Czechoslovakia in the final for the World Cup victory that year. Garrincha fared less well in the 1966 World Cup, with Brazil losing its title to Hungary.

Sidelined by Injuries and Alcohol

By then, Garrincha was in his thirties, and his physical defects were beginning to hamper him. By 1963 the cartilage in one of his knees was so damaged because of his bent leg that it had to be drained regularly, and he was rarely able to play two regularly scheduled games in a row. The condition would have occurred regardless of his choice of career, and finally in 1964 he underwent surgery to fix the problem but never fully recovered. Garrincha also drank prodigiously, and lived somewhat recklessly; he and his wife often stashed his salary in cupboards at home, and one of his World Cup bonuses was hidden under the mattress in their children's bedroom. When they remembered to look for it later, the bills were ruined because some of the younger of their eight daughters had wet the bed so often. But Garrincha was also victim of club management, who considered him uneducated and easily duped, and on a few occasions the club actually gave him blank contracts to sign; Botafogo management would fill in the amount of his salary later.

Garrincha's final World Cup appearance was at the 1966 games, an event hosted by England. When Hungary beat Brazil 3–1 early on, it was Garrincha's sixtieth game with the national team, but the first one they had ever lost when he was playing. That same year, Botafogo sold him to another team, the Corinthians of São Paulo, and he later played for a Colombian team briefly before returning to Brazil to play with Flamengo, one of Botafogo's Rio rivals. His final professional stint was with Olaria, another Rio team, with which he remained until 1972. After that he played the occasional exhibition match.

Garrincha's personal life continued to be tumultuous. His first marriage, to fellow factory worker Nair Marques in 1952, produced eight daughters, but he had several liaisons outside of the marriage and other children. In the mid-1960s he famously left Marques for Elza Soares, a well-known samba singer. Garrincha's drinking caused several automobile accidents, including one that killed Soares's mother in 1969. Following that tragedy, his drinking worsened, and he reportedly attempted suicide. He and Soares nonetheless had a son in 1976, but Soares left him a year later when he became physically abusive. Garrincha's final years were spent in reduced circumstances, for his salary was gone and he was unable to hold down even the most basic of jobs. Once, Brazil's coffee trade group recruited him to serve as a goodwill ambassador, which required him to merely show up at industry events, but he was a perennial no-show. He wed again in the early 1980s, and in January of 1983 his wife called for help when he passed out after a day of heavy drinking. He never came out of the alcohol-induced coma and died several hours later, on January 20, from cirrhosis of the liver. He was just forty-nine years old.

Garrincha had been forgotten for several years, but news of his death prompted an outpouring of national grief. The funeral procession from the Estádio do Maracanã in Rio back to his birthplace of Pau Grande drew thousands of mourners. A soccer stadium in Brazil's federal capital, Brasilia, is named Estádio Mané Garrincha in his honor; "Mané" is short for his given name, Manuel, and he was commonly called "Mané Garrincha" during the height of his fame in Brazil. Some twenty years after his death, he was the subject of renewed interest, with a biography written that even appeared in English translation. Brazilian academic José Sérgio explained to the *Guardian*'s Bellos about the enduring appeal of Garrincha, noting that he "was identified with the public. He never lost his popular roots. He was also exploited by football, so he was the symbol of the majority of Brazilians, who are also exploited."

Sources

Periodicals

Guardian (London, England), April 27, 2002; August 14, 2004.
Times (London), June 11, 1962.

—Carol Brennan

Joe Dumars

1963—

Basketball player

Joe Dumars set out to become a football player as a child, following in the footsteps of his brothers. However, after being roughly tackled in junior high school, he decided to pursue basketball, which proved to be a very wise move. In eighth grade, Dumars was able to secure pick-up games with nearby Northwestern State University students. During his youth, Dumars's favorite basketball player was Julius Irving, whom Dumars had the good fortune of playing against in his second NBA season and Irving's last. While Dumars felt he had more ability in football, he excelled in basketball, enjoying the fact that he could play it alone.

As the youngest of seven children, Dumars recalls his parents requiring certain behaviors, such as common courtesy and respect for others, and he always considered his parents heroes. Dumars's mother was a custodian and his father a truck driver. Young Dumars walked to and from elementary school with his siblings in southern Louisiana, where he discovered his love of reading. Dumars's basketball talent blossomed along with his reading and, by the time he reached high school, he was a solid team player.

Dumars, Joe, photograph. AP Images.

College recruiters spotted Dumars, and many large schools offered him a chance to play; however, Dumars chose nearby McNeese State University, where he majored in business management and remained close to his family. Dumars also played on the McNeese basketball team, where he started as a guard and quickly established himself as the team's best player, winning the Southland Conference Rookie of the year in 1981–82.

Recruited by the Detroit Pistons

Dumars's consistent college record for game points and team wins resulted in his being drafted as the eighteenth pick in the first round for the Detroit Pistons in 1985. He left McNeese as the eleventh-leading scorer in National Collegiate Athletic Association history. However, the Pistons did not draft Dumars to score, but as a back-up to point guard Isiah Thomas. Even though Dumars wanted to score, he graciously filled the position where he was most needed. Because the Pistons needed a defensive player, Dumars focused on that as a rookie, though he knew it would take him longer to realize his own dreams in the National Basketball

At a Glance . . .

Born Joseph Dumars on May 23, 1963, in Natchitoches, LA; son of Ophelia, father deceased (1990); married Debbie; children: Aren, Jordan. *Education:* McNeese State University, 1981–85.

Career: Detroit Pistons, guard, 1985–99, vice president of personnel, 1999–2000, president of operations, 2000—; Joe Dumars Fieldhouse, owner, 1995—; Joe Dumars Foundation, charity founder, 1993; Detroit Technologies, founder and president, 1996–2006.

Awards: Sporting News NCAA All-America Second team, member, 1985; NBA All Rookie Team, member, 1986; member, National Basketball Association (NBA) Championship Teams, 1989, 1990; named most valuable player of the 1989 NBA finals; tri-captained 1989 Dream Team II at the 1994 World Championships; five-time NBA All-Star and Pistons captain; NBA Defensive First Team, member, 1989–90, 1992, 1993; NBA All Third Team, member, 1990, 1991; member NBA All-Star Team, 1990–93; NBA All Defensive Second Team, member, 1991, 1993; Citizenship Award, 1994; NBA Sportsmanship Award, 1996; Basketball Hall of Fame, 2006.

Addresses: *Office*—Detroit Pistons, 2 Championship Drive, Auburn Hills, MI 48326-1752.

Association (NBA). By the start of the 1988–89 season, the Pistons were ready for all of Dumars's abilities, and he passed, played, and scored as good as any player in the league. While playing against the Cleveland Cavaliers, which proved to be one of his best games in his early professional career, Dumars scored forty-two points, twenty-four of which were in the third quarter, making seventeen consecutive points.

Though touted as one of basketball's top defensive guards, Dumars soon received increased attention for his offensive abilities. By the 1988–89 season, the Pistons made it to the NBA Finals, where Dumars, sporting number 4 on his uniform, was largely responsible for the team's 1989 championship win against the Los Angeles Lakers. In Los Angeles, Dumars shifted into overdrive, winning the third game for the Pistons, where, during the third quarter of the game, he scored seventeen points in a row. Detroit swept the series in four straight games, with Dumars averaging 27.3 points per game. This was Detroit's first NBA title, for which Dumars was named the most valuable

player. To win this NBA title, the Pistons needed someone to step forward on offense to take some of the pressure off of Thomas, and this someone proved to be Joe Dumars. Thereafter, the Pistons were known as "The Bad Boys," though Dumars humbly played oftentimes without the fame and glory received by some of his teammates, much to the chagrin of his fellow players. Thomas once complained that the credit was given to other guards in the league, while failing to mention Dumars, whom Thomas felt was one of the best guards in the league. Indeed, Dumars scored almost as many points per game as Thomas during the 1988–89 season.

Joe Dumars and the Pistons went on to another league title in 1989–90, this time with Thomas starring in the defeat of Portland. No longer seen just as a defensive player, Dumars showed his talent and firepower in the offense as well. As an established star, Dumars again succeeded in scoring and guarding, helping the Pistons to win this second championship, resulting in Dumars's being selected for the All-Star team, a first in his career.

Loyal to his teammates and his profession, and despite his strong family ties, Dumars decided to remain with his team in Portland, Oregon, for two games of the NBA Finals before flying home for his father's funeral, who died of congestive heart failure in June 1990. Triumphantly, the Pistons went on to win the championship against Portland while there. The night Dumars learned of his father's death, he had just finished scoring 22 points in the fourth quarter against Portland, making 12 points in a row as the Pistons rallied from a 111–106 deficit with 3 minutes remaining to a 118-115 lead with 18.6 seconds left.

Recognized as a Major Player

In 1991 he assisted Detroit in lead scoring for the first time. In 1994 he tied the record of Orlando's Brian Shaw for the most three-pointers in a regular NBA season with ten three-pointers in a November game against the Minnesota Timberwolves. Dumars won a gold medal as captain of the Dream Team at the 1994 World Championship. He again tied the NBA record with seven three-pointers in one-half of a game against Orlando Magic in April of 1995.

Dumars consistently pulled through in a crunch, as stated by opposing teammate Chris Webber of the Washington Wizards for the *Washington Post*, "I grew up watching Joe play…. I hope one day I'll have that same type of effect on a game." After winning the 1995 NBA championship, Dumars told the *Washington Post*, "We just kept digging and digging. We used the trap and made them shoot long jumpers. We went helter skelter. That's not going to work for 82 games, but it worked tonight. We didn't play well, but we kept fighting. You never lay down because you can never tell what will happen." This final sentence pretty much summed up the overall belief and performance of Dumars, who was better known for his calm demeanor, especially in comparison with his flamboyant teammates.

According to the *New York Times*, "Wherever he goes, Dumars draws praise from the opposition.... Brad Daugherty, Cleveland's center, ... said that Dumars is the heart and soul of [the] team and that there is no other player he would rather have on his side.... Dumars is more a player's player than a fan favorite or a news- media celebrity, and in many ways, that's fine with him." Dumars's teammates referred to him as Joe Cool, J.D., G.I. Joe, or, most important, Mr. Dumars. Dennis Rodman of the Chicago Bulls shared with the *New York Times* that Dumars was a "peaceful, humble person who doesn't feel too much pressure. Dumars has taken control of his game and of the atmosphere of the team, but he does damage in a quiet way. He's always going to hit the big shots."

Having earned considerable respect in the profession, Dumars made it his goal to help the Pistons continue in the right direction. He was largely responsible for defending against top shooters, and he typically arrived hours ahead of time for games. As a top NBA defender, he was both swift and sure, conscientiously maintaining a positive attitude that kept him focused on the game.

In 1984 Dumars ranked sixth in the country with 26.4 average points per game, and he remains listed among the top twenty all-time college scorers. By 1995, Dumars had played in the NBA All-Star game five times and made the NBA All-Defensive Team four times, playing a total of 762 games from 1985 through 1995, during which he made nearly 85 percent of his 3,391 attempted free throws. He scored a total of 13,079 points in that ten-year span, with an average of 17.2 points per game; in the 1992–93 season alone, he averaged over 23 points per game.

Dedicated to Family and Community

With eighty-two NBA games per season, appearances, charitable activities, and family life, Dumars has mastered good time management. He is happily married to Debbie, and they have one girl, Aren, and one boy, Jordan, named after Michael Jordan. Dumars has always been a family man, and says that his brother Mark was his best friend growing up. Enormously respected by teammates, opponents, and coaches for his unassuming, yet sure demeanor, Dumars was considered like a second coach, having tutoring former rookies such as Grant Hill, Allan Houston, and Lindsey Hunter.

Besides the time he devoted to the game, Dumars shared his success with thousands of others. He started the Joe Dumars Foundation in 1993, which raises money for the Children's Hospital of Michigan. On behalf of this foundation, Dumars has hosted the Joe Dumars Celebrity Tennis Classic since 1993, which attracts tennis pros and has raised over $1,000,000 for the Children's Hospital of Michigan. He also hosts a luncheon each year for one hundred Detroit-area students who have excelled in school.

In February of 1995 Dumars opened the Joe Dumars Fieldhouse, a $2.4 million, seventy-thousand-square-foot facility in Shelby Township outside of Detroit. Youngsters play sports and attend free basketball clinics. Dumars often drops by to play pick-up games with the kids at the facility, which has basketball and volleyball courts, an in-line hockey rink, restaurant/sports bar, and weightlifting and cardiovascular equipment. One of Dumars's favorite activities is his summer basketball camp for kids at the fieldhouse. Dumars told a reporter for *Boys Life* in 1996, "I see myself in a lot of kids at our camp....This kind of program would really have helped me and the other kids when I was growing up."

In 1994 Dumars won basketball's J. Walter Kennedy Citizenship Award for community service, and he recalled that, during his childhood, he learned the value and importance of giving and sharing with others. Named as one of the NBA's "classiest players" by *Sport* magazine, Dumars would rather be known for his work off the court, especially with Detroit's young people. It is easy to see why the title applies to him. Also, rather than taking sole credit for his athletic talents, Dumars attributed the winning of two NBA championships by the Pistons to successful teamwork and emphasized this concept to kids in his basketball camp. In 1996 Dumars became the first recipient of the NBA Sportsmanship Award, which is also called the Joe Dumars Trophy in his honor. The trophy acknowledges players who exemplify ethical conduct, fair play, and integrity.

Shifted from Leading On-Court to Off-Court

Following his retirement in 1999, Dumars was asked to become the vice president of player personnel for the Pistons in 1999. In 2000 he became the president of basketball operations for the franchise. He was honored with the NBA's Executive of the Year Award in 2002 for his success in improving the Piston's roster. It was under Dumars's leadership that the team acquired Ben Wallace, Chauncey Billups, and Richard Hamilton, who later became central figures in the Piston's rise to prominence during the 2003–04 season. In the 2004 NBA championships, the Pistons surprised analysts and fans by winning the series against the heavily favored Los Angeles Lakers. The 2004 victory was the first for the Pistons since the 1990 championships. Dumars led the Pistons to become the Eastern Conference Champions in 2005, though the team eventually lost four games to three against the San Antonio Spurs. In 2007 the Pistons made their fifth consecutive appearance in the NBA finals, only to be eliminated by the Cleveland Cavaliers.

In 2006 Dumars achieved one of the highest honors in professional basketball when he was named to the Basketball Hall of Fame. His enshrinement, alongside Charles Barkley and Dominique Wilkins, served as a final recognition of his career as a player, even though his professional career continued as a manager and executive. In interviews, Dumars expressed the hope that he would be remembered as much for his community and social activity as for his time as a player. As an executive, player, and manager, Dumars has proven himself worthy of being remembered as one of basketball's finest.

Sources

Books

Rambeck, Richard, *Detroit Pistons*, Creative Education, 1993.
Sachare, Alex, ed., *The Official NBA Basketball Encyclopedia*, 2nd ed., Willard Books, 1994.
Stewart, Mark, *Joe Dumars*, Children's Press, 1996.
Thomas, Isiah, *Bad Boys: An Inside Look at the Detroit Pistons' 1988–89 Championship Season*, Masters Press, 1989.
Who's Who in America, 50th ed., 1996.

Periodicals

Boys' Life, Vol. 86, November 1996, p. 9.
New York Times, February 17, 1991.
Sports Illustrated, April 24, 1995, pp. 40–43; February 10, 1997, p. 66.
Sports Illustrated for Kids, August 1995, p. 21; February 1997, p. 18.
USA Today, April 26, 2002.
Washington Post, June 12, 1990; February 8, 1995.

Online

"HoopsHype General Managers," *HoopsHype.com*, http://www.hoopshype.com/general_managers/joe_dumars.htm (accessed December 18, 2007).
"Joe Dumars Biography," *NBA Online*, http://www.nba.com/history/players/dumars_bio.html (accessed December 18, 2007).
"Piston's Joe Dumars Named Today to the Naismith Memorial Basketball Hall of Fame," *NBA Online*, http://www.nba.com/pistons/news/dumars_hof_060403.html (accessed December 18, 2007).

—Marilyn Williams and Micah L. Issit

Edward Dwight

1933—

Sculptor

Edward Dwight Jr.'s diverse talents have brought him success in several highly specialized careers. As a young man, he achieved a boyhood dream by becoming an air force pilot. He gained celebrity status when President John F. Kennedy selected him to become the space program's first African-American astronaut. He grew wealthy as a real estate developer. Then, in his early forties, he began to work professionally as an artist and became one of America's leading sculptors. He has created many works of public art celebrating black heritage and its contributions to American life.

Headed for the Skies

Edward Dwight Jr. was born on September 9, 1933, in Kansas City, Kansas. He was the only boy among the five children born to Edward Dwight, a professional baseball player, and Georgia Baker Dwight, a housewife who passed on to her son a love of art. Dwight's father was an infielder with the Kansas City Monarchs of the Negro Leagues and later worked as a chemist for the state of Kansas. Early on, Dwight showed strong artistic, mechanical, and intellectual gifts. His devoutly religious parents placed him in Catholic schools, including Kansas City's Bishop Ward High School, from which he graduated in 1951.

The Dwight family lived near Kansas City's municipal airport. During World War II, the U.S. Army Air Force used the airfield as a base. As he spent time watching takeoffs and landings, Dwight's ambitions shifted from art to aviation. He saw a fighter plane crash and explode when he was ten, but the incident did not derail his dreams; it only strengthened his determination to learn to fly. During his adolescence, he worked odd jobs on the airfield and spent free time studying pilot tests in the library. He earned academic honors in high school and excelled in athletics, including track, football, and boxing.

When Dwight visited his local recruiting office to ask about enlisting for the air force, he was turned away more than once on account of his race. Nevertheless, when recruiters came to Kansas City Junior College, where he was enrolled, he was allowed to take the pilot's exam. His years of studying paid off when he passed it. He joined the U.S. Air Force in 1953, training in Texas and Missouri. Two years later, he was commissioned as a second lieutenant; he had earned his wings.

Trained for Space Flight

Also in 1955, Dwight married Sue Lillian James, a young woman he had known since high school. The marriage produced a son and a daughter, but ended in divorce years later. His air force career brightened when he undertook jet aircraft training at Williams Air Force Base in Arizona. He became a test pilot and flight instructor at the base, while taking night courses to complete a bachelor's degree in aeronautical engineering at Arizona State University. Subsequent assignments took him to Japan, where he piloted a B-57 bomber, then back stateside to Travis Air Force Base in California, where he trained pilots for the Strategic Air Command.

At a Glance . . .

Born on September 9, 1933, in Kansas City, KS; son of Edward and Georgia Baker Dwight; married Sue Lillian James, 1955 (divorced); married Barbara; children: (with James) Tina Sheree and Edward III; (with Barbara) three children. *Education:* Arizona State University, BA in aeronautical engineering, 1961; University of Denver, MFA, 1977.

Career: U.S. Air Force, pilot, 1953–66; National Aeronautics and Space Administration, astronaut trainee, 1962–63; engineer, aerospace consultant, 1963–67; Jet Training School, cofounder, 1967; restaurant owner, real estate developer, 1967–74; sculptor, 1974—.

Addresses: *Office*—Ed Dwight Studios, 3824 Dahlia St., Denver, CO 80207.

By 1961 Dwight had logged over two thousand hours of flying time. His credentials were strong enough to earn him a plum assignment: to train for the U.S. space program. The administration of President John F. Kennedy, at the suggestion of Whitney Young of the National Urban League, selected Dwight to become the first black astronaut trainee. His training began in 1962, and by the following year, Dwight's participation in National Aeronautics and Space Administration publicity had made him a household name. He appeared on the cover of *Ebony, Jet,* and other magazines and gave dozens of speeches. To young African-American boys, he was a particular role model.

Sadly, discrimination was an obstacle to his success in the space program. Dwight recalled in the *Providence American,* "My classmates were told not to socialize with me and for my instructors to limit their instruction to me. No extra assistance was offered to me like my white counterparts." At the time, Dwight complained about his treatment to the White House and to the press, bringing negative publicity to the space program

In the end, the outspoken Dwight lost his prime sponsor when Kennedy was assassinated in November of 1963. With no allies to support his continuation in astronaut training, Dwight was transferred briefly to Germany, then to Dayton, Ohio, out of the limelight. Even though he had graduated seventh out of seventeen students in his training course, by 1964 he was no longer a candidate to participate in aerospace missions.

Making matters worse, Dwight was a target of racial harassment in Dayton. His effort to buy a house for his family met with one obstacle after another. When he finally found a home, somebody threw a rock through his window, injuring his daughter. His marriage to Sue Lillian James collapsed under these stresses. He later remarried.

Dwight resigned his air force commission in 1966. He moved to Denver and began a series of speculative business ventures, including a restaurant chain and real estate sales. He also established a Jet Training School with some partners, a project that literally went up in flames when six of his colleagues were killed in a plane crash. Dwight himself would have been on board the aircraft had he not tarried on the telephone trying to close a real estate deal. The tragedy ended his flying days for good.

Became a Professional Sculptor

For several years, Dwight worked in a variety of fields without a central focus. He worked as an engineer and as a consultant for IBM. During the early 1970s, he prospered, briefly, as a real estate developer and construction entrepreneur, building condominiums and luxury housing in the Denver metropolitan area. He later lost much of this property through a combination of unwise investments and poor market conditions.

By his own account, the year 1974 marked a new beginning in Dwight's professional life. He returned to another of his childhood passions: art. He had made sculptures as a hobby, and now decided to pursue the craft further. For his first professional project, he received a commission to produce a sculpture of George Brown, the first African-American lieutenant governor of Colorado. He followed this with an ambitious work called *Black Frontier Spirit in the American West,* casting thirty bronzes that depicted African-American explorers, settlers, buffalo soldiers, and other unheralded pioneers. He completed a master's degree in fine arts at the University of Denver in 1977 and joined the faculty there for a time.

His early work, especially the *Black Frontier Spirit* series, won acclaim for its originality. Soon, Dwight was in demand as a creator of public art commemorating the African-American experience. He undertook a series of more than seventy bronze pieces portraying the history of jazz from its roots in African tribal culture to the memorable performers of the classic and contemporary jazz eras. Some individual works from this series, *Jazz: An American Art Form, are now on permanent display at the National Museum of American History in Washington, D.C.*

Created Public Artworks

Dwight now owns a large studio in Denver that is devoted exclusively to his own artwork. He is considered an innovator in the use of negative space in sculpture; that is, the empty spaces surrounding and between elements in an artwork. Dwight's pieces are displayed in many institutions, museums, and private collections. Other major works in his catalog include statues of Martin Luther King Jr. and Hank Aaron, both in Atlanta; a more complex, twenty-six-foot-tall tribute to King in Denver; the Frederick Douglass Memorial in Washington; the Kunta Kinte–Alex Haley Memorial at the City Dock in Annapolis, Maryland; and two monuments honoring the Underground Railroad, one in Detroit and the other across the Detroit River in Windsor, Ontario. He has been working for several years on a ninety-foot-long sculpture honoring the thousands of enslaved Africans and free blacks who fought in the American Revolution. This work will be sited on the Washington Mall, between the Lincoln Memorial and the Washington Monument.

Dwight has been involved in plans for another major installation in Washington: the Martin Luther King Jr. National Memorial. He stirred up some controversy in 2007 by suggesting that he had been unjustly passed over as the monument's artist of record, in favor of the Chinese sculptor Lei Yixin. Dwight was hired as a consultant on the project in 2004 and contributed a small model that he believed would become the basis of the memorial's design. According to the *New York Times*, Dwight was a member of the panel that selected Lei to complete the project, on the strength of Lei's work in the medium of granite. However, Dwight subsequently voiced misgivings about Lei's fitness for the project. To some, the incident raised ironic echoes of Dwight's bitter public complaints about discrimination in the space program four decades earlier.

Nevertheless, the larger picture of Dwight's life is of a multitalented individual who has risen to prominence in a remarkable variety of endeavors. As an artist, he has helped cement public understanding of the contributions of African Americans to American culture and history.

Sources

Books

Gubert, Betty Kaplan, et al., *Distinguished African Americans in Aviation and Space Science,* Oryx Press, 2002.

Periodicals

New York Times, September 24, 2007.
People, May 25, 1987, p. 115.

Online

"About Ed Dwight," *Ed Dwight Sculptor,*http://www.eddwight.com/about_eddwight/index.htm (accessed December 27, 2007).

"Ed Dwight, Jr. Biography," *The History Makers,* http://www.thehistorymakers.com/biography (accessed December 27, 2007).

"Edward Dwight," *Biography Resource Center,* http://galenet.galegroup.com/servlet/BioRC (accessed December 27, 2007).

"Rhode Island Black Heritage Society Hosts Nationally Acclaimed Artist Ed Dwight," *The Providence American* http://www.providenceamerican.com/news.cfm?article_id=1647 (accessed December 27, 2007).

—Roger K. Smith

Israel L. Gaither

1944—

Religious leader

Gaither, Israel L., photograph. Bill Greenblatt/Landov.

On May 1, 2006, Israel L. Gaither became the first African American to assume national leadership of the Salvation Army, a religious denomination with a predominantly white membership. For Gaither, it was only the latest in a long string of similar firsts. He has spent more than forty years—his entire career—as an officer of the evangelical Christian organization known worldwide for its charity work. A talented administrator and motivational speaker, he has steadily ascended the ladder of leadership within the Army, serving in England and South Africa as well as in the United States.

Heeded the Call of Service

Gaither was born on October 27, 1944, in New Castle, Pennsylvania. Both his father and grandfather were Baptist ministers. The eldest of five children, he grew up heavily steeped in Christian values and moral teachings. Both his parents offered role models of dignity and responsibility. Young Gaither made friends with a boy whose parents were Salvationists and began attending Salvation Army youth activities and Corps Cadet Bible Study classes. An Army summer camp "was the hook God used to attract me," he recalled in the *Washington Post*.

During his teens, Gaither continued to attend his father's Union Baptist Church while his involvement with the Salvation Army grew. Finally, he broke away from the church to become a soldier in the Salvation Army's New Castle Corps. Feeling called to a career in the Salvation Army, he applied to its School for Officer Training in New York. He was commissioned as an officer in the Salvationist clergy in 1964 and appointed to a pastorship at Pittsburgh Northside Corps.

Graduating in the same year was a fifth-generation Salvationist, Eva Shue of Sidney, Ohio. She was also appointed to a position in Pittsburgh, and their collegial relationship soon developed into something more. In 1967 Gaither's father presided over the first racially integrated marriage between two officers of the Salvation Army USA. The couple met with some hostility early on, especially from the white community. Gaither has said that he did not experience open racism within the Army, but he believes that certain paths of advancement were closed to him early in his career. Over time, however, he overcame those obstacles.

At a Glance . . .

Born on October 27, 1944, in New Castle, PA; son of Israel L. Gaither Sr. and Lillian Gaither; married Eva Shue, 1967; children: Michele, Mark. *Education:* Salvation Army School for Officer Training, 1964; attended Pittsburgh Theological Seminary.

Career: Salvation Army, USA Eastern Territory, held various positions, including pastor, divisional youth leader, divisional secretary, and divisional commander, 1964–86; field secretary for personnel, 1993–97; chief secretary, 1997–99; territorial commander, Southern Africa, 1999–2002; territorial commander, USA Eastern Territory, 2002; chief of the staff, International Headquarters, 2002–06; national commander, USA, 2006—.

Awards: Asbury College, Honorary Doctor of Humane Letters, 2005.

Addresses: *Office*—Salvation Army National Headquarters, 615 Slaters Lane, PO Box 269, Alexandria, VA 22313.

Ascended Through the Ranks

Joining forces, Israel and Eva Gaither went on to serve in a variety of leadership roles within the Salvation Army. They soon moved from Pittsburgh to the Bedford-Stuyvesant neighborhood of Brooklyn, where they worked as divisional youth leaders. Gaither advanced to the position of divisional secretary for greater New York, then general secretary for western Pennsylvania. He became the first African American to reach the position of divisional commander; along with his wife, he led the Army's efforts in southern New England and later in western Pennsylvania. The couple was then appointed to administrative positions for the eastern United States, culminating in the senior position of territorial commander. Both Gaithers attained the Salvation Army's highest rank, that of commissioner. No African American had previously risen to any of these levels of leadership within the Army.

In 1999 Israel and Eva Gaither were chosen to head Salvation Army operations in southern Africa. Again, Gaither was breaking a color barrier; his was the Army's first appointment of an African American to any overseas post. Working from the Army's headquarters in Johannesburg, South Africa, the couple administered the organization's extensive famine relief, AIDS-related health services, and other programs in South Africa, Mozambique, Lesotho, and Swaziland.

After three years in Africa, Gaither moved to the Army's international headquarters in London, serving as chief of staff and second in command under the Army's worldwide leader, General John Larsson. Eva Gaither assumed the title of World Secretary for Women's Ministries, with responsibilities in the area of women's advancement, notably in the developing world. The Gaithers traveled to more than thirty countries during their four years working for the Army internationally.

Named National Commander

Following General Larsson's retirement, Gaither returned to the United States as national commander. The office gives him executive leadership of one of the nation's largest organizations, with over sixty thousand employees, four hundred thousand members, and three and a half million volunteers. The Salvation Army oversees an array of social services in the United States, including medical facilities, disaster relief, women's shelters, transitional housing centers, services for the elderly, health education, day care centers, summer camps, thrift stores, and drug rehab programs. In addition, each of the Army's corps community centers maintains an active evangelical religious mission.

The organization performs this slate of programs with military efficiency. As national commander, Gaither's duties are similar to those of a Fortune 500 chief executive—except that instead of the bottom line, Salvationists measure their success in terms of their mission "to preach the gospel of Jesus Christ and to meet human needs in His name without discrimination." Asked by *USA Today* for the secrets of his success in management, Gaither said, "I happen to believe that the way to the best leadership is modeling after Jesus."

The notion of mission is important to Gaither, and the heart of that mission is to spread the spiritual values that have guided him since his childhood. As quoted on the Salvation Army Web site, Gaither believes, "Americans, generally, are growing discontented with the artificial … we want authenticity!… We need to be authentic Christians in an artificial world."

The challenges facing the Salvation Army today put these values to the test. The Army is financially secure as a result of an astonishing $1.5 billion bequeathed to it by Joan Kroc, the widow of McDonald's founder Ray Kroc. The money is being used to build several dozen new community centers around the country. Some of these complexes, like the one in Kroc's home of San Diego, California, are considerably more upscale than any facilities the Army has used in the past. Furthermore, operating the Kroc Centers will require the Army to raise millions of dollars annually through user fees, forcing administrators to develop profit-oriented programs. Gaither, however, remains dedicated to protecting the core values of the organization. He told an interviewer in the *New York Times*, "We are at a crossroads, and the challenge for us is to remain true to our mission."

Sources

Books

Gariepy, Henry, *Israel Gaither: Man with a Mission*, Crest Books, 2006.

Periodicals

Ebony, September 2006, p. 32.
Jet, May 29, 2006, p. 16.
New York Times, August 4, 2006.
USA Today, November 20, 2006.
Washington Post, May 12, 2006.

Online

Donnell, Kat, "On the Hunt for the Soul of America," *Philanthropy World*, http://www.philanthropy magazine.com/Articles/12-3-IsraelGaither.html (accessed December 27, 2007).
"Israel L. Gaither," *Biography Resource Center*, http://galenet.galegroup.com/servlet/BioRC (accessed December 27, 2007).
"Israel L. Gaither: Man with a Mission," *Salvation Army USA*, http://www.salvationarmy.org/ihq/www_sa.nsf/vw-dynamic-arrays/88853B08ED29DE658025711E004D0142?openDocument (accessed December 27, 2007).
"Salvation Army National Commanders," *Salvation Army USA*, http://www.salvationarmyusa.org/usn/www_usn.nsf/vw-sublinks/85256DDC007274DF85256C670067BDC8?openDocument (accessed December 27, 2007).

—Roger K. Smith

Chris Gardner

1954—

Stockbroker, philanthropist, author

Chris Gardner is a stockbroker and philanthropist whose rise to prominence provided the basis for both his memoir, *The Pursuit of Happyness,* and a successful Hollywood film of the same name. From a poor background, Gardner endured a year on the streets of San Francisco as a homeless single father and came out the other side a multimillionaire financial manager. However, he insists the meaning of his life is no mere fulfillment of the American dream of financial success. In an interview included on the DVD release of *The Pursuit of Happyness,* he said, "My story has been portrayed in certain media outlets as a rags-to-riches story. That ain't important. The important thing is the commitment to my children, to be there."

Overcame a Difficult Childhood

Gardner was born in Milwaukee on February 9, 1954. He had a harrowing childhood, with an absentee father and a violently abusive stepfather, Freddie Triplett. In his youth, his mother, Bettye Jean Gardner, was incarcerated twice: once when Triplett reported her for working while on public assistance, and later for attempting to set fire to the house with Triplett inside. Each time, Gardner and his older sister were shuttled between relatives and foster homes.

Gardner credits his mother, despite her misdeeds, with transmitting to him the "spiritual genetics" that guided him through the traumas of his upbringing. She instilled in him a sense of self-reliance and awareness of his unlimited potential. Gardner's three uncles provided him with his most positive male role models. Emulating his uncle Henry, he enlisted in the navy after he graduated from high school. He served as a hospital corpsman and made the acquaintance of a heart surgeon, Dr. Robert Ellis, who offered him employment as a civilian. Following his discharge in 1974, Gardner moved to San Francisco and became a laboratory assistant to Ellis.

While employed in the medical field, Gardner married Sherry Dyson in 1977 after a long-distance courtship. Their relationship was ill-fated; Sherry conceived a child, but had a miscarriage. Gardner began having second thoughts about his ambition to become a doctor, but his decision to abandon that option put further strain on his marriage. He had an affair with another woman, Jackie Medina, who was studying dentistry. When Medina became pregnant, he left his wife and moved in with her, although he and Sherry did not legally divorce for another nine years.

Undertook a Dramatic Career Change

Gardner's son, Chris Jr., was born in early 1981. The young father struggled to make ends meet. He left a position at a Veterans Administration hospital to work as a medical supply salesman. Around this time, a pivotal event in his life occurred after a routine sales visit to San Francisco General Hospital. In the parking lot, he saw a well-dressed man in a red Ferrari. Gardner offered the man his parking space in exchange for the answers to two questions: "What do you do and how do you do it?"

At a Glance . . .

Born Christopher Paul Gardner on February 9, 1954, in Milwaukee, WI; son of Thomas Turner and Bettye Jean Gardner; married Sherry Dyson, 1977 (divorced); Jackie Medina (partner); children: (with Medina) Chris Jr., Jacintha.

Career: U.S. Navy, 1972–74; medical research assistant, 1974; medical supply salesman; Dean Witter Reynolds, stock broker, 1981–83; Bear Stearns & Co., 1983–87; Gardner Rich & Co., founder and chief executive officer, 1987–2006; Christopher Gardner International Holdings, founder and chief executive officer, 2006—.

Memberships: National Fatherhood Initiative, board member; National Education Foundation, board member.

Awards: National Fatherhood Initiative, Father of the Year, 2002; Los Angeles Commission on Assaults Against Women Twenty-fifth Annual Humanitarian Award, 2006; Continental Africa Chamber of Commerce, Friends of Africa Award, 2006.

Addresses: *Office*—Christopher Gardner International Holdings, 401 S. Financial Place, Chicago, IL 60605.

The gentleman was a stockbroker named Bob Bridges, and he arranged for Gardner to make initial contacts at several brokerage firms. Attracted by the financial world, Gardner put his sales job on the back burner while he applied to training programs in San Francisco's financial district. His car languished on the street, collecting parking tickets. When a man at E. F. Hutton offered him a position, he quit his sales job right away. Unfortunately, the man who hired him lost his own job before Gardner arrived for his first day.

This bad break came at a tense time in his relationship with Medina. They had a fight, and she called the police. He was arrested and, because he owed $1,200 in parking fines, sentenced to ten days in a county jail. He came home to an empty apartment; Medina had taken Chris Jr. and fled. His possessions had been cleaned out—and he had an appointment the next morning at the Dean Witter Reynolds brokerage house. With no alternative, he showed up for his interview wearing the clothes in which he had been arrested. Despite the sartorial transgression, he was offered a six-month traineeship.

Kept Homelessness a Secret at Work

For four months, Gardner did not know where his child was. Then one day Medina appeared at his boarding house to hand over their son: she had had enough, and now it was his turn. He was glad to take custody of his son. He had vowed, during his own troubled childhood, never to leave his own children without a father. However, the boarding house did not allow children, and he could not afford an apartment with his trainee stipend. So began the period of a homeless, working single father that is the centerpiece of the book and film *The Pursuit of Happyness*.

Gardner and his toddler son slept some nights at a cheap hotel, under his office desk, in the park, or—on a couple of occasions—behind a locked bathroom door in a Bay Area Rapid Transit station. He told his colleagues nothing about his situation. Finally, he persuaded the Rev. Cecil Williams, pastor of Glide Memorial Church in San Francisco's Tenderloin neighborhood, to let him stay in the church's shelter for homeless women. Gardner left a strong impression on Williams, as the minister told the magazine *Jet*: "Every day he was the only man in line—and I'm talking about a long line of people—who had a child with him. He came and ate and volunteered ... even then he was different, different from any person I had ever met, or seen in line seeking help."

The Glide shelter was a step up from the street, but it required the two Gardners to arrive at the church before the doors closed at six in the evening, and to leave by eight in the morning, taking their possessions with them. Gardner recounted the experience in the *Chicago Sun-Times*: "For a year, I'd take my son, his stroller, a big duffle bag with all his clothes in it, my briefcase, an umbrella, the biggest bag of Pampers in the world, one suit on my back and one suit in a hanging bag and we'd hit it *every* day."

Even amid these intensely arduous circumstances, Gardner was committed to learning his new trade. His determination paid off: he passed his licensing exam on the first try, and he was the only one in his training program offered a permanent position at Dean Witter. Even with his increase in salary, it took several months before he could save enough money to afford an apartment. He and Chris Jr., who was now two and a half years old, slept on the floor the first night in their new place in North Oakland. Gardner told *Reader's Digest* that when the next morning came, Chris Jr. said in alarm, "'Dad, we need to take our things.' ... I told my son, 'No, boy. We have a key now. We are home.' We skipped to the train that day."

Earned His Fortune in Business

With his darkest days behind him, Gardner could finally devote his full efforts to his work in the business world.

When he did, he advanced quickly. He left Dean Witter in 1983 for a job with Bear, Stearns & Company in San Francisco and became one of the firm's top earners. Medina came to visit her son and his father in their new home, and during her brief stay she and Gardner conceived their second child. Jacintha Gardner was born in Los Angeles in 1985. Chris Jr. spent a period living there with his mother and new sister, while his father worked in New York at Bear Stearns's Wall Street office.

Two years later, Gardner took custody of both his children and moved to Chicago, where he opened his own brokerage firm, Gardner Rich and Company. The company specializes in debt, equity, and futures transactions for public and private institutions. Gardner owned a controlling interest in the firm until he sold his stake in a multimillion-dollar deal in 2006. He then founded Christopher Gardner International Holdings and became its chief executive officer.

His new company maintains offices in New York, San Francisco, and Chicago. Inspired by a visit he took to South Africa in 2003, which included a private meeting with Nelson Mandela, Gardner launched an initiative to raise $1 billion in investment capital for South Africa, hoping to create jobs and opportunities there.

There can be no doubt that Gardner has earned his tremendous wealth, and that he has enjoyed it. Never forgetting his fateful encounter with Bob Bridges and his Ferrari, he acquired a customized Ferrari of his own from its previous owner, the basketball superstar Michael Jordan. Gardner owns several residences, including a condominium in New York's Trump Tower. His Chicago office sports a custom desk made from the tail wing of a DC-10 jet.

He has also donated his money and his time to a variety of causes, especially those serving homeless and at-risk urban populations. One recipient of his philanthropic endeavors is Glide Memorial Church. A quarter century after his time of need, he has repaid his debt by sponsoring the Cecil Williams Glide Community House, a nine-story complex in the Tenderloin. Gardner also donates clothes and shoes to the church and comes periodically to volunteer. He offers career counseling and job placement assistance to needy communities in Chicago through the Cara Program.

Immortalized on the Big Screen

Gardner currently serves on the boards of numerous nonprofit organizations, including the National Education Foundation and the National Fatherhood Initiative. The latter group named him Father of the Year in 2002. Other honors he has received include the Humanitarian Award given by the Los Angeles Commission on Assaults Against Women and the Friends of Africa Award from the Continental Africa Chamber of Commerce, both in 2006.

Gardner has become a sought-after public speaker. His own experience conveys powerful messages about breaking destructive cycles, commitment to parenting, and achieving goals through perseverance. He told *Jet* that he disdains the phrase "motivational speaking": "I see it as a matter of shared empowerment because I'm getting as much from the audiences as I am giving to them, and one of the things I've learned is that men are in so much pain. At the end of every speech I'm signing books and a guy comes up, he's got this look in his eye, all I've got to do is stand up and open my arms and he'll fall in them crying like a baby."

Gardner's life story has now reached millions of people. After he was featured on the television program *20/20* in 2002, he realized that his story contained the elements of a heartwarming narrative. His autobiography, *The Pursuit of Happyness,* went to the top of the *New York Times* and *Washington Post* best-seller lists in 2006. Later that year, Columbia Pictures released the film by the same name, directed by Gabriele Muccino and starring Will Smith and his son Jaden in the leading roles. Gardner joined the film crew during production as an associate producer. He was initially unsure about how Smith would portray his life's most trying moments, but in the end, as he remarked to *People* magazine, he felt that Smith "played Chris Gardner better than Chris Gardner ever did. He got paid better, too."

Selected writings

Books

The Pursuit of Happyness, Amistad, 2006.

Sources

Periodicals

Black Enterprise, January 2007, p. 112.
Chicago Sun-Times, May 28, 2006.
Jet, December 18, 2006.
People, January 8, 2007.
Reader's Digest, December 2006.
USA Today, May 23, 2006.

Online

Christopher Gardner: The Official Site, http://www.chrisgardnermedia.com/ (accessed December 27, 2007).

Other

Gardner was interviewed on video in "The Man Behind the Movie: A Conversation with Chris Gardner" on the DVD of the film *The Pursuit of Happyness.*

—Roger K. Smith

Petey Greene

1931–1984

Radio host

Ralph Waldo Greene—better known as Petey Greene—was a pioneer in African-American radio as the host of a popular call-in show in Washington, DC, in the 1960s and 1970s. Greene's frank, on-air opinions spurred listeners to contribute their own thoughts and gripes, and he sought to admit his own shortcomings—which included a stint in prison for armed robbery—as a way to inspire others. He was one of the first personalities created by talk radio, which would become an enduring staple of urban radio well into the twenty-first century, and he remained such a compelling figure after his untimely death in 1984 that a 2007 film was made loosely based on his life story. *Talk to Me* starred actor Don Cheadle as the ebullient, sometimes combative personality, along with Chiwetel Ejiofor as Dewey Hughes, the straitlaced boss who hired the former convict at the DC radio station.

Greene was born in 1931, and according to a 1971 interview he gave to National Public Radio (NPR) journalist Gwen Hudley, his father was incarcerated in the federal prison at Alcatraz Island in the San Francisco Bay at the time. His mother had several other children to care for and feed, so Greene was raised by his grandmother, Maggie Floyd, known as "A'nt Pig." He grew up in the Georgetown section of Washington, DC, which was then a run-down, predominantly African-American neighborhood. In the interview with Hudley, Greene described Floyd as an excellent role model who tried to set him down the right path in life, "but I had to be one of the fellas, you know. And being one of the fellas can get you in the penitentiary so

quick, or get you to have confrontations with the law so fast that you won't even know what happened to you."

Before he reached his teens, Greene had spent time in a juvenile home, and as a young man he developed a problematic and multifaceted substance abuse habit. He quit school at the age of sixteen and eventually wound up in the U.S. Army at the height of the Korean War in the early 1950s but was discharged for drug use. He returned to Washington, DC and in 1960 was convicted on an armed robbery charge for holding up a grocery store. Sentenced to ten years at the Lorton Reformatory in Virginia, he finally found his calling as a popular disc jockey on the prison radio station, thanks in part to the hit records his grandmother would send him. He even managed to reduce his sentence through good behavior. Before his release, he was introduced to Dewey Hughes, the program director for a Washington, DC, radio station, in the visitors' room. Hughes's brother, a Lorton inmate, spoke enthusiastically about Greene's talents and recommended him for a job.

Lit up Phone Lines

Few people were willing to hire a recently discharged convict, but once he was released from Lorton, Greene visited WOL 1450-AM, the leading black-music radio station in DC. He convinced Hughes and station owner E. G. Sonderling to give him a tryout, and the caller lines lit up in response. Soon, his Sunday-evening show, *Rapping with Petey Greene,* was one of the most talked-about programs in the city. Greene's emergence as a media personality in the late 1960s dovetailed with an important shift in African-American political consciousness, when the promises of the civil rights movement gave way to a new militancy coalescing under the banner "Black Power." Just ten years earlier, in some parts of the country not far from the nation's capital, speaking one's mind and calling attention to racial injustice was a dangerous act, one that might even result in death by mob violence. Times had changed, however, and Greene urged his listeners to voice their concerns about the pace and tenor of those changes. He added his own voice to protesting against the deep institutional bias many still experienced in schools and on the job. His well-known catchphrase was "I'll tell it to the hot. I'll tell it to the cold. I'll tell it to the young. I'll tell it to the old."

Greene was active in his community, working with the United Planning Organization (UPO) and founding Efforts for Ex-Convicts, both of which provided jobs and training for those recently released from prison. The 1971 NPR interview focused on these efforts by Greene. Speaking with Hudley for *All Things Considered,* he recounted the story of what his parole officer told him when he was first released from Lorton. The officer said that he did not need to worry too much about Greene, because ex-cons like him were habitual offenders and Greene would soon be locked away again. Greene recalled the words as hurtful and potentially ruinous to any hope of a fresh start he might have felt, but he privately vowed to prove the man wrong. Later, after Greene became famous, the same officer came up to him at a social event, greeting him warmly and saying he knew all along he would succeed in life. Greene said that he wanted to give the man a piece of his mind but instead just thanked him. "You can fight better when you can smile, because people don't know when they got your back to the wall," he explained to Hudley about how he had learned to battle others'

diminished expectations. "Once you let people hold you back, then you're defeating your own self. You have got to be able to say, 'Can't nobody help me but me.'"

In April of 1968 Greene took to the air and pleaded with his listeners to remain calm in the wake of rioting prompted by news of the assassination of Martin Luther King Jr. in Memphis, Tennessee. He emerged as one of the best-known media figures in the city, and reportedly Hubert H. Humphrey, vice president under Lyndon B. Johnson from 1965 to 1969, was among Greene's listening audience. His popularity led to the television show *Where It's A,* followed in 1976 by the debut of *Petey Greene's Washington,* which aired on WDCA-TV 20. His famous opening catchphrase this time was "Adjust the color of your television!" and the show was picked up for national broadcast in 1980 by a fledgling Black Entertainment Television (BET) cable network. He was even invited to the White House during the administration of President Jimmy Carter, for a March of 1978 state dinner in honor of visiting Yugoslav president Josip Broz Tito.

Booked on the Tonight Show

Greene and Hughes became close friends at WOL 1450-AM, despite their dissimilar backgrounds and personalities, with Hughes serving as his manager and pushing him into a stand-up comic career at the same time that another frank-speaking black comedian, Richard Pryor, was becoming famous. The record remains unclear whether Greene's appearance on the hugely popular *Tonight Show* with Johnny Carson ever actually happened: Reportedly, Greene was leery about how well his jokes would go over with a largely white studio audience made up mainly of tourists and done for national television, and he told his biographer that he never showed up for the booking; other sources report that he bombed, badly, and may have been under the influence of drugs, alcohol, or both.

Greene died of cancer on January 10, 1984, at age fifty-two. Thousands came to pay their respects at Union Wesley African Methodist Episcopal Zion Church in Washington, DC, but his achievements faded from memory over the next two decades until Hughes's son wrote a screenplay about the friendship between his father and Greene. The script attracted serious interest in Hollywood, with names such as Martin Lawrence reportedly interested in taking on the role, but the job eventually went to Don Cheadle. *Talk to Me* earned mixed reviews from critics, but one reviewer, Gail Mitchell in *Billboard,* called it impressive as a "historical snapshot of black radio and its potent, engaging mix of community service and entertainment." Mitchell continued, "It was a pre-syndication, pre-satellite world back then, inhabited by individually styled personalities who were just as popular as the artists whose music they played because of their innate ability to relate to their audiences."

Sources

Books

Rackley, Lurma, *Laugh If You Like, Ain't a Damn Thing Funny: The Life Story of Ralph "Petey" Greene as Told to Lurma Rackley,* Xlibris Corporation, 2003.

Periodicals

Billboard, July 21, 2007.
Entertainment Weekly, July 20, 2007.
Essence, February 2007.
Jet, July 23, 2007.
Washington Times, January 27, 2004; July 13, 2007.

Online

Mondello, Bob, "'Talk to Me': The Mouth That Roared in '60s DC," *All Things Considered,* http://www.npr.org/templates/story/story.php?storyId=11957643 (accessed December 26, 2007).

—Carol Brennan

Hill Harper

1966—

Actor, writer

Harper, Hill, photograph. © Allstar Picture Library/Alamy.

Called "one of the more compelling actors of his generation," by Blockbuster.com, Hill Harper, originally named Frank Harper, has become an actor who, according to Blockbuster.com, "has earned a reputation for turning in complex performances defined by equal parts intensity and charisma."

Born on May 17, 1966, in Iowa City, Harper started acting when he was seven, but it was not originally what he intended to do as a career. He graduated magna cum laude from Brown University with a bachelor of arts degree before going on to Harvard University, where he received a JD (cum laude). He also earned a master's in public administration from the Kennedy School of Government, a part of Harvard University. He did, however, continue acting throughout his college career—even becoming a member of Boston's Black Folks Theater Company, an acclaimed theater troupe, when he was attending Harvard—so perhaps it was no surprise that Harper turned to acting in the end. "I'm motivated by something that motivates most men—making your father proud and getting girls," Harper jokingly told *Essence*.

Began Acting Career on Television

Harper began his television career playing Aaron on the hit comedy *Married ... with Children*. From there, he won parts in several feature films, including *Confessions of a Dog* (1993), *Pumpkinhead II: Blood Wings* (1994), and *Zooman* (1995). Also in 1995, he wrote and was seen in the movie *One Red Rose*. It was in 1996, however, that Harper became well known in the film industry for his portrayal of the student filmmaker documenting the Million Man March in Spike Lee's *Get on the Bus*. *Newsweek* said of the film, "A great cast, including ... Hill Harper, breathes life into every scene.... A sermon wrapped in a road movie, at its best it can stir the soul."

The role of Xavier in *Get on the Bus* opened a door for Harper. After the Spike Lee film, he was seen in a slew of feature films, including *Steel* (1997), a comedy about superheroes, *Hav Plenty* (1997), a romantic comedy, and *The Nephew* (1998). The next movie Harper was seen in was *Park Day*. According to *Variety,* the film "concentrates on the lives of ordinary black Americans rather than criminals, drug addicts, recently freed slaves, or other well-worn archetypes." It was exactly the type of film that Harper had always wanted to see more of. Also in 1998, he took a part in another Spike Lee film, *He Got Game,* a movie about basketball that met with mixed reviews.

In 1999 Harper was involved with *Loving Jezebel.* In this movie, Harper played the lead—a man who seemed to have no luck at love because he was always going out with women who ended up getting him beaten, shot at, and threatened. The *Daily Herald* said that *Loving Jezebel* had "a sweet earnestness about it. Plus, it offers one of the most appealing casts ever hired for an independent motion picture." In 2000 Harper was seen in the movie *The Skulls* alongside Joshua Jackson, Paul Walker, and Leslie Bibb. Harper played Jackson's best friend, who tried to convince Jackson not to join the secret Skulls fraternity. The *Seattle Times* said the actors "do their work smoothly" and that, even though Harper's role is underwritten, he "makes the most" of it.

Enjoyed Challenging Characters

His next film, *The Visit,* won much acclaim, and Harper himself won the Audience Award at the Urbanworld Film Festival for his portrayal of a prisoner who was incarcerated for a rape he might not have committed. The movie deals with prisoner Alex, who has been told that he has AIDS, and therefore has begun struggling to reconnect with his family before he dies. Harper chose the role because it was a risk. He has never believed in what he calls, according to *Essence,*

the "Hollywodization" of movies—those movies that "sacrifice quality for commerce."

But whether it was a risk or not, Harper's gamble paid off in the critical acclaim he received. The *New York Times* said of his performance, "Mr. Harper's part is the most challenging; really, it is four or five different parts, since Alex … changes according to his company…. Mr. Harper melds these distinct personas in a moving, understated performance." The biggest challenge in playing this part seems to have been that most of the main character's changes are internal, and yet have to be expressed to the audience.

Next, Harper tried his hand at television in CBS's *City of Angels,* a medical drama in which Harper played a young resident. According to the *Milwaukee Journal Sentinel,* the show was notable because "its cast is largely made up of African-Americans and other minorities, which shouldn't be such a rare thing in a network drama but emphatically is." But the show was soon canceled. In 2000 Harper was awarded the Emerging Artist Award at the Chicago International Film Festival. In 2001 he was awarded the John Garfield Best Actor Award and was also listed as one of the Top 29 Most Eligible Super Bachelors by *Ebony.*

Harper completed two more movies: *Higher Ed* (2001) and *The Badge* (2002). He took part in the March of 2001 play *Dogeaters,* a two-act play about the Philippines in the 1980s in which Harper plays the part of a drug-addicted hustler. He was also seen in the off-Broadway show *Blue,* playing a rebellious son in a Roundabout Theatre Company production. The play received mixed reviews. Called "stale" by *Variety,* a reporter from *The Record* said, "Despite its obviousness, the play does have an old-fashioned sweetness in its affection for its characters and its affirmation of family ties…. [It is the] equivalent of easy-listening music, soothing and undemanding." The cast was African-American, but the audience was not entirely, and that was something that Harper was glad to see. "Scientists proved that human beings are the most alike of all species in the world," Harper told the *New York Post.* "We always want to talk about our differences, but it's sad that we do…. I love that the Roundabout audience is predominantly white and older. To have a 75-year-old white man say, 'That was my mother,' or 'That was my story,' reinforces what I've always believed: That all our stories are universal."

Worked to Break Typecasting of Race

Harper has objected to the disparity between the sorts of films that are being done about African Americans and the ones being done about whites. Harper told the *New York Post* that African-American films are either "comedies or gangsta films; *Pootie Tang* or *Baby Boy.*

There's nothing wrong with those films, but it's wrong to say there's no space for anything else." It is to hoped that a man who has been called "thorough at his craft" by Blackfilm.com will have the chance to do a lot more with his career. "Hollywood needs more Hill Harpers," wrote *Interview*. "He's the kind of actor who will—by the scope of his choices and depth of his characters—force the system, and the viewing public, to abandon typecasting and categorization. Because he has."

In 2004 Harper won a starring role as Dr. Sheldon Hawkes in *CSI: NY*, a television drama detailing the lives and work of a group of forensic detectives and staff in a New York City crime laboratory. Harper won critical acclaim for his role as a child prodigy turned chief medical examiner for the New York forensic unit and was hailed, by fans, as one of the show's most complex characters.

In 2006 he published the book *Letters to a Young Brother: MANifest Your Destiny*, which was intended to serve as an inspirational guide to avoiding the problems and pitfalls facing African-American youth. With the help of friends and colleagues, including Barrack Obama and hip-hop artist Nas, Harper collected a series of inspirational messages on a variety of common issues. Among his chief goals was to help young African-American men avoid the belief that their "self worth is attached to outside things," such as the acquisition of wealth and material possessions. Harper received critical praise for the conversational tone of his writing, which enabled him to make complex concepts accessible to a young, urban audience.

In conjunction with the release of his book, Harper founded the MANifest Your Destiny Foundation, a nonprofit organization helping to fund programs for African-American youth. The foundation functions through a series of scholarships, grants, and mentorship programs, funded in part by proceeds from the sale of Harper's book. "Part of the problem," Harper said in a 2006 interview with National Public Radio, "has to do with how we, ultimately, as African-American men, perceive ourselves." Harper explained that he believes that as more African Americans expand the boundaries set by society, others will take notice and do likewise. "As we really reach out to each other and start to go for elements of self that are more expansive" he said, "you'll see examples everywhere."

Selected writings

Letters to a Young Brother: MANifest Your Destiny, Gotham Books, 2006.

Sources

Periodicals

Atlanta Journal-Constitution, October 27, 2000.

Daily Herald (Arlington Heights, IL), October 27, 2000.

Ebony, June, 2001.

Entertainment Weekly, April 14, 2000, p. 49; May 4, 2001, p. 45; May 11, 2001, p. 54; May 18, 2001, p. 58; November 2, 2001, p. 55.

Essence, January, 2001, p. 54.

Interview, February, 2001, p. 58.

Jet, July 16, 2001, p. 56.

Milwaukee Journal Sentinel, January 16, 2000.

New York Post, July 9, 2001.

Newsweek, October 28, 1996, p. 74.

New York Times, December 15, 2000; March 20, 2006; May 26, 2006.

People Weekly, May 7, 2001, p. 33.

The Record (Bergen County, NJ), June 29, 2001.

Rocky Mountain News, May 1, 1998.

San Francisco Chronicle, October 31, 2000.

Seattle Times, June 19, 1998; August 25, 1999; March 31, 2000.

Variety, August 18, 1997, p. 33; January 11, 1999, p. 116; November 15, 1999, p. 92; March 12, 2001; July 9, 2001, p. 29.

Online

"CSI's Hill Harper: 'Letters to a Young Brother,'" *National Public Radio*, http://www.npr.org/templates/story/story.php?storyId=5358913 (accessed December 19, 2007).

Flint, Rebecca, "Hill Harper," *Blockbuster.com*, http://www.blockbuster.com/catalog/personDetails/182134 (accessed December 19, 2007).

"Hill Harper," *Hollywood.com*. http://www.hollywood.com/celebrity/Hill_Harper/187498 (accessed December 19, 2007).

"Hill Harper," *IMDB.com*. http://imdb.com/name/nm0004991/ (accessed December 19, 2007).

Jones, Shelby, "Actors Making the Grade: Hill Harper Is Fearless in the Active State of Being," *Blackfilm.com*. http://www.blackfilm.com/0305/features/i-hillharper.shtml (accessed December 19, 2007).

—Catherine Victoria Donaldson
and Micah L. Issit

Vy Higginsen

1945(?)—

Playwright, theatrical producer, theatrical agent, performer

The widely varied career of Vy Higginsen reflects her deep commitment to preserving and celebrating the rich heritage of African-American culture. As a radio broadcaster, a magazine publisher, a writer and producer of plays, a founder of a school of musical arts, and much more, Higginsen has repeatedly broken down barriers and set new standards of excellence. With exuberant enthusiasm she has entertained tens of thousands of people with her musical productions, and with tireless effort she has worked to carry on the black cultural traditions of gospel, soul, and rhythm and blues (R&B) music from generation to generation.

Higginsen spent her early years in Harlem, the New York City neighborhood that is one of the oldest centers of African-American culture. Her father, Randolph A. Higginson, an immigrant from the Caribbean island nation of Barbados, was a preacher in a Pentecostal church in Harlem. In 1946 he suffered a sudden massive heart attack while delivering a sermon during a Sunday service. He died almost immediately, leaving behind a wife, Geraldine Payne Higginson, and four children, Doris, Joyce, Randy Jr., and Vy (who later changed the spelling of her last name to Higginsen).

Geraldine supported her young family by working as a real estate agent, becoming one of the few African-American women to earn a broker's license at the time. The family lived just down the street from her mother, who played a large role in raising the four Higginson children. During the 1950s and 1960s, drug use—and the crime that accompanied it—increased in Harlem, eroding the strong, family-based black community

there. Like many other African Americans concerned for the safety of their children, Geraldine moved her family to the nearby borough of the Bronx. However, the children continued to visit their grandmother regularly and still felt part of the cultural life of Harlem. Higginsen's sister Doris, who had sung in the choir in her father's church, began working as an usher in Harlem's famous Apollo Theater and soon started her own music career as a singer under the name Doris Troy.

Higginsen herself demonstrated both creativity and ambition at an early age. She began babysitting for neighbors' children at the age of eleven, but soon set up an in-home childcare business that provided before- and after-school care for the children of working parents. As she grew up, she continued to contribute to the family finances with part-time jobs, such as working as a page in the public library.

Worked in Fashion and Advertising

Higginsen graduated from Theodore Roosevelt High School in the Bronx and entered the Fashion Institute of Technology (FIT) in Manhattan. She studied merchandising and marketing by day, and worked for New York Citibank at night, balancing stacks of checks with an adding machine to pay for her education. After her graduation from FIT, she went to work at Alexander's, a local department store. The daily demands of the retail business taught her a sense of responsibility and diligence that would help her in all of her future jobs.

At a Glance . . .

Born Vy Higginson on November 17, 1945(?), in New York City, NY; daughter of Randolph A. and Geraldine Higginson; married Ken Wydro, 1981; children: Knoelle. *Education:* Fashion Institute of Technology, BA in merchandising and marketing.

Career: Alexander's Department Store, assistant department manager; Snelling and Snelling, Inc., employment counselor; *Boutique* magazine, advertising sales; *Ebony* magazine, advertising sales; WBLS, radio host; *Unique NY,* publisher, 1975–80; NBC-TV, *Positively Black,* coanchor; WWRL, radio host; WRKS, radio host; playwright and theatrical producer, 1983—; Mama Foundation for the Arts, cofounder and chief executive officer, 1998—; Vy Higginsen, Inc./Reach Entertainment and Sports, founder.

Memberships: Harlem Arts Alliance; New York Association of Black Journalists.

Awards: Coalition of 100 Black Women, Candace Award, 1988; New York City Chamber of Commerce, Business Woman of the Year, 1989; *Legacy* magazine, Legacy Award, 2005.

Addresses: *Office*—Mama Foundation for the Arts and Vy Higginsen's School of Gospel, Jazz, and R&B Arts, 149 W. 126th St., New York City, NY 10027.

After leaving Alexander's, Higginsen went to the employment agency Snelling and Snelling, Inc. for help in seeking another job. The interviewer there was so impressed with her that he offered her a position working as an employment counselor for the agency. After a short time, however, she returned to the world of fashion by taking a job in the advertising sales department with a small fashion magazine called *Boutique.*

In 1963 Higginsen's sister Doris Troy performed the soul song "Just One Look" that quickly rose to number one on music charts in both the United States and England, boosting Troy to stardom. During the 1960s Higginsen joined her sister on tour, traveling with her in Europe and meeting many music industry celebrities.

Higginsen worked for *Ebony* magazine in the early 1970s, becoming the first woman to work in that journal's advertising sales department. She found the work rewarding in many ways: she enjoyed promoting

Ebony as one of the major voices of black culture, and, as a marketing expert, she was interested in exploring data about the buying power of black consumers. However, she frequently found dealing with white-owned corporations to be frustrating. Many major advertisers were either ignorant or overtly racist about their African-American customers, and, while Higginsen worked hard to educate them, she eventually decided that she needed to do a different kind of work.

Broke Gender Barrier in Radio

Inspired by her experiences with her sister in the entertainment industry, Higginsen began attending night classes at the Columbia School of Broadcasting. After a period of study she made an audition tape, which she sent to Frankie Crocker, the program manager of the R&B radio station WBLS. Impressed by Higginsen's sophisticated voice, Crocker hired her, not for a fashion and beauty program as she had imagined, but as host and disc jockey of a midday show. Higginsen thus became the first woman to host her own primetime radio program in New York City, and she worked at WBLS for five years, attracting a number of loyal fans.

At the same time she was launching her radio career, Higginsen also decided to start her own magazine, an urban lifestyle journal aimed at an African-American audience. She published *Unique NY* from 1975 to 1980, while continuing to work in broadcasting. Though she loved the camaraderie of working at a black radio station, Higginsen felt that, as a woman, her opportunity for advancement was limited at WBLS. She left her job there and took a position as coanchor on a local NBC television program called *Positively Black.* She also hosted radio shows on New York stations WWRL and WRKS.

In 1981 Higginsen married Ken Wydro. Soon after their marriage, the couple began working on a theater project based on the life of Higginsen's sister Doris Troy. The resulting play, *Mama, I Want to Sing,* told the story of Troy's youth singing in the gospel choir at her father's church in Harlem, her difficulties in persuading her strictly religious mother to allow her to pursue a career in popular music, and her eventual return to her gospel roots. The play was presented in the form of a vintage radio serial, with Vy Higginsen introducing the scenes in her sultriest deejay style. The musical opened at the off-Broadway Heckscher Theater in 1983, becoming an immediate popular success, especially with black audiences.

Produced Successful Series of Musicals

Mama, I Want to Sing ran off-Broadway for eight years, offering twenty-two hundred performances in

New York, then touring the United States and around the world. Higginsen earned critical praise, not only for the play's exuberant gospel music and uplifting message of family solidarity, but also for attracting African-American audiences to the theater in record numbers. Higginsen understood and valued her black audience, and she used all of her marketing skills to promote her play to the people for whom it was written.

Family cooperation was not only one of the themes of *Mama, I Want to Sing* but also was key to the production. Higginsen wrote the play with her husband; her sister Doris joined the cast, playing the part of their mother; and their other sister, Joyce, became company manager. During the following years, other family members also joined the production.

Higginsen and Wydro followed *Mama, I Want to Sing* with two sequels: *Sing! Mama 2* in 1990 and *Born to Sing! Mama 3* in 1996. Each play was both a continuation of Doris Troy's life and career and a celebration of the African-American traditions of gospel, soul, and R&B music. Higginsen continued her role as narrator in each show, and audiences continued to pour in. Critics sometimes faulted the musicals for being unsophisticated and "homemade," but acknowledged that these very qualities made them genuinely intimate and powerful theatrical experiences.

As their reputation for attracting black theater audiences grew, Higginsen and Wydro were called on to produce other plays as well. One of these, August Wilson's *Joe Turner's Come and Gone,* earned a 1988 Tony Award nomination for Best Play. Concerned for the well-being of her actors, Higginsen also formed a talent management company, called Vy Higginsen, Inc./Reach Entertainment and Sports, to offer career management assistance.

Founded School of Theater Arts

Though Higginsen enjoyed creating theatrical events, she wanted to do something more lasting to preserve the cultural history of black music. In 1998 she and Wydro used $35,000 of their own money to found the Mama Foundation for the Arts (MFA), a theater and musical arts school focused on African-American music. Through MFA, which was located in Harlem, in the building next door to Higginsen's childhood home, she hoped to offer training and performance opportunities to young people. One of MFA's most successful projects has been Gospel for Teens, a program of study that teaches both the techniques and historical roots of gospel music to students from thirteen to nineteen years of age.

In 2005 Higginsen's exploration of her African-American heritage took her in an entirely unexpected direction. Anxious to learn which part of Africa her ancestors had inhabited, she obtained an ethnoancestry test. Ethnoancestry is a type of DNA testing that can determine ethnic background and discover relations all over the world by tracing the y-chromosome carried by males in a family. Wydro asked a male cousin for a sample of DNA, obtained by swabbing the inside of the mouth, then sent it to a company that performed ethnoancestry testing. What she discovered surprised and fascinated her. Instead of being almost entirely African-American, with some Native American ancestry, as she had expected, Higginsen found that her background was 64% African, 28% European, and 8% Asian. Besides this startling information, she received a call from an unknown relative who had also done an ethnoancestry test, hoping to find British nobility in his bloodline. Marion West, a white rancher from Missouri, and Vy Higginsen from Harlem were surprised to find that they were related, but both were happy to expand their idea of family once they met.

Higginsen has continued her energetic career of production, management, and promotion of gospel and other black musical heritage. Besides creating a series of gospel musical productions including *I Gotta Praise* and *Let Me off in Harlem,* she has written two children's books: *Mama, I Want to Sing,* published in 1992, and *This Is My Song! A Collection of Gospel Music for the Family,* released in 1995. She continues her role as executive director and chief executive officer of MFA and is an ordained interfaith minister who speaks frequently on a wide range of topics, including gospel music, the role of women in radio, and achieving success. Her daughter, Knoelle Higginson, has followed Higginsen into the entertainment field, acting in several stage productions and slated to star in an upcoming film version of *Mama, I Want to Sing.*

Selected works

Books

(With Tonya Bolden) *Mama, I Want to Sing,* Scholastic Trade, 1992.
This Is My Song! A Collection of Gospel Music for the Family, Knopf Books for Young Readers, 1995.

Plays

(With Ken Wydro) *Mama, I Want to Sing,* 1983.
(With Wydro) *Sing! Mama 2,* 1990.
(With Wydro) *Born to Sing! Mama 3,* 1996.

Sources

Periodicals

Essence, May 1980, pp. 44–46.
Jet, February 1, 1988, pp. 34–36.
New York Beacon, April 26, 2000.
New York Times, March 29, 1988.
Washington Post, February 25, 1985.

Online

Coveney, Janine, and Dana Hall, "Women Speak out on Their Unique History in Male-run Music Industry," *Billboard,* February 21, 1998. Reproduced by *All Business Web Site,*http://www.allbusiness.com/retail-trade/miscellaneous-retail-retail-stores-not/4631808-1.html (accessed December 28, 2007).

"Doris Troy Biography," *Musician Biographies,* http://www.musicianguide.com/biographies/1608004055/Doris-Troy.html (accessed December 28, 2007).

Holden, Stephen, "Love Arrives in 'Mama, I Want to Sing' Sequel," *New York Times,* http://theater2.nytimes.com/mem/theater/treview.html?res=9C0CEFD61E39F93BA15750C0A966958260 (accessed December 28, 2007).

Mama Foundation for the Arts, http://www.mamafoundation.org/ (accessed December 28, 2007).

"Reconstructing the Family Tree," *CBS News 60 Minutes,* http://www.cbsnews.com/stories/2007/10/05/60minutes/main3334427.shtml?source=search_story (accessed December 28, 2007).

Stasio, Marilyn, "Marketing 'Mama': A Little Gospel and a Lot of Savvy," *New York Times,* http://query.nytimes.com/gst/fullpage.html?res=9C0CE0D9153EF937A15755C0A966958260&sec=&spon=&pagewanted=3 (accessed December 28, 2007).

"Vy Higginsen," *Biography Resource Center,* http://galenet.galegroup.com/servlet/BioRC (accessed December 28, 2007).

"Vy Higginsen Biography," http://www.thehistorymakers.com/biography (accessed December 28, 2007).

"Vy Higginsen's Gospel for Teens," *My Space,* http://profile.myspace.com/index.cfm?fuseaction=user.viewprofile&friendID=81641999 (accessed December 28, 2007).

Vy Higginsen Web Site, http://www.vyhigginsen.com/connect.html (accessed December 28, 2007).

Other

Information for this profile was obtained through an interview with Vy Higginsen on October 11, 2007.

—Tina Gianoulis

Anita Hill

1956—

Lawyer, activist, educator

Hill, Anita, photograph. Fernando Salas/Landov.

On October 6, 1991, Anita Hill's life was dramatically and irrevocably changed when her charges of sexual harassment against a former employer, Clarence Thomas, were made public on the eve of his confirmation as a U.S. Supreme Court justice. In the ensuing days, Hill was grilled by the Senate Judiciary Committee about the graphic details of the alleged harassment and about her personal life. Her compelling testimony before the committee was broadcast live around the globe, sweeping her from the quiet obscurity of her life as a professor of law at the University of Oklahoma. Her charges produced a stunning collision of race and gender issues, and reactions to her and her story were highly polarized; some viewed her as a hero and martyr, whereas others vilified her as mentally unstable, a liar, and even a racist.

In the end, the U.S. House and Senate chose to dismiss her allegations, and as a result, Thomas was given a seat on the highest court in the nation. Yet, Hill's appearance in Washington, D.C., had far-reaching effects. Her testimony, and the committee's reaction to it, have since been credited with revitalizing feminism, greatly increasing the public's awareness of sexual harassment, inspiring women to run for office in record numbers, and significantly increasing the numbers of women willing to speak out publicly about their own experiences of sexual harassment when they might otherwise have suffered in silence.

Grew up to Study Law

Nothing in Hill's upbringing could have prepared her for the glare of international publicity that she would eventually face. The youngest in a family of thirteen children, she was raised in a deeply religious atmosphere on her parents' farm in rural Morris, Oklahoma, located forty-five miles south of Tulsa. Sundays were spent at the Lone Pine Baptist Church, while the rest of her week was filled with farm chores and schoolwork.

She attended Okmulgee County's integrated schools, where she earned straight As and graduated as class secretary, valedictorian, and a National Honor Society student. After graduation, she attended Oklahoma State University, where she continued her outstanding academic performance and graduated with a degree in psychology and numerous academic honors.

An internship with a local judge had turned her ambitions to the field of law, and she sought and won admission into Yale University's demanding School of Law, where she was one of 11 African-American students in a class of 160. After graduation in 1980, she took a full-time job as a professional lawyer with the Washington law firm of Ward, Harkrader, and Ross.

Worked for Clarence Thomas

In 1981, after working with the firm for about a year, Hill accepted a job as the personal assistant to Clarence Thomas, who was then head of the U.S. Department of Education's Office of Civil Rights in Washington. It was at this time, according to her sworn testimony, that Thomas made repeated advances toward her. When she rebuffed him, he began to make vulgar remarks to her and to describe in vivid detail pornographic films he had seen. According to Hill, when Thomas began dating someone else, the harassment stopped, and she accepted an offer to follow him to a better job when he was made chairman of the Equal Employment Opportunity Commission. According to Hill's version of the events, the harassment began again, however. In 1983, after being hospitalized with stress-related stomach problems, she left Washington to accept a position as a civil rights professor at Oral Roberts University in Tulsa.

In 1986 she joined the faculty at the University of Oklahoma College of Law, where she became a specialist in contract law. Six years of teaching are usually required before tenured status is granted to a professor there, but Hill was tenured after only four years. Besides her teaching duties, she served on the faculty senate and was also named the faculty administrative fellow in the Office of the Provost, which made her a key voice in all major academic policy decisions.

Such was the state of Hill's life on September 3, 1991, when she was approached by the Senate Judiciary Committee and asked to supply background information on Thomas, who was then being considered as a replacement for Justice Thurgood Marshall of the U.S. Supreme Court. In a news conference given at the University of Oklahoma by Hill, which was excerpted at length in the *New York Times*, Hill elaborated: "They asked me questions about work that I had done there, and they asked me specifically about harassment and issues involving women in the workplace. Those questions, I have heard, were prompted by rumors that individuals who had worked at the agency had understood that I had been subject to some improper conduct." Hill, who had never filed a complaint against Thomas, found herself reluctant to go public with her story ten years after the fact.

Decided to Reveal Harassment by Thomas

Initially, she decided to protect herself and her privacy by remaining silent. On further reflection, however, she felt an obligation to tell the truth as she knew it, no matter how difficult that might be. "Here is a person [Thomas] who is in charge of protecting rights of women and other groups in the workplace and he is using his position of power for personal gain for one thing," she said in an interview with the National Public Radio, also quoted by the *New York Times*. "And he did it in a very ugly and intimidating way."

By September 9, Hill had decided to cooperate in the investigation of Thomas on the condition that her identity be kept confidential. But she was informed on September 20 that the Judiciary Committee could not be told her story unless Thomas was notified of her identity and given a chance to respond to her allegations. Furthermore, if she agreed to cooperate, she and Thomas would both be questioned by the Federal Bureau of Investigation (FBI). Hill pondered these new developments as the confirmation hearings for Thomas, already underway, were about to end. On September 23, she agreed to allow her name to be used in an FBI investigation. She also requested permission to submit a personal statement to the committee.

Hill has since criticized the handling of her complaint, in part because copies of the FBI report were given to just two committee members, and her personal statement also failed to reach all those who should have seen it. Meanwhile, Thomas had issued a sworn statement forcefully denying all of Hill's allegations against him. In his version of the events, he had simply asked Hill out for dates a few times. He and his supporters characterized her eleventh-hour appearance as a ploy designed to keep him off the bench, engineered by liberals opposed to his appointment to the court. Hill answered such suggestions in her press conference at the University of Oklahoma: "There is absolutely no basis for that allegation, that I am somehow involved in some political plan to undermine the nominee. And I cannot even understand how someone could attempt to support such a claim.... This has taken a great toll on me personally and professionally, and there is no way that I would do something like this for political purposes."

After considerable debate, the U.S. Senate decided that new hearings on Thomas's confirmation would be held and that Hill would be called to Washington to testify before the Senate Judiciary Committee—which was made up of fourteen white, male legislators. The televised hearings, which included Hill's and Thomas's appearances, drew an audience of millions, who were riveted by the drama of race and sex unfolding on the screen. Hill remained dignified and composed throughout the proceedings—in the face of repetitive questioning by the senators. Her credibility and character were vehemently attacked by some observers, who questioned why she maintained a speaking relationship with Thomas after the alleged incidents occurred and why she never filed a formal complaint. Republican legislator Arlen Specter went so far as to imply that Hill had fantasized the whole scenario; others suggested that she was acting out of jealousy because Thomas had failed to provide her the attentions she secretly desired from him.

Racial issues were in evidence during the hearings and influenced reaction among both the general public and the Judiciary Committee. Thomas himself fueled that fire when he denounced the proceedings as a "high-tech lynching," effectively accusing Hill of participating in a racist plot to keep him out of the Supreme Court because he is African American. In the book *Race-ing Justice, En-gendering Power: Essays on Anita Hill, Clarence Thomas, and the Construction of Social Reality,* essayist Carol M. Swain discussed another race-related phenomenon that turned the tide of African-American opinion against Hill: "For African Americans generally, the issue was not so much whether Hill was credible or not; she was dismissed because many saw her as a person who had violated the code ... which mandates that blacks should not criticize, let alone accuse, each other in front of whites."

Moved Forward by Focusing on Career

Thomas's nomination was confirmed on October 16, 1991. Hill, who had by then returned to Oklahoma,

accepted the news with the composure that had marked her appearance before the committee. Disregarding all the racial, political, and feminist implications of the decision, she told Roberto Suro of the *New York Times,* "For me it is enough justice getting it heard. I just wanted people to know and understand that this had happened.... You just have to tell the truth and that's the most anyone can expect from you and if you get that opportunity, you will have accomplished something."

Many of Hill's detractors had predicted that she would capitalize on her experience by making high-paid speaking appearances, writing a book, or even selling her story as a television movie-of-the-week, but in the months following her testimony, she proved them wrong. She resumed her usual teaching duties and returned to her regular routine as nearly as was possible, given the reporters and others who constantly sought her out. In time, she took a sabbatical from teaching, using the interlude to study the sociology and psychology of sexual harassment. Aside from an appearance on the CBS News program *60 Minutes,* and, much later, one on the *Today* show, she turned down all interview requests. She made carefully selected appearances on the speaking circuit, often for no fee, and at such appearances she declined to talk in detail about the hearings or her own personal experience, focusing instead on the larger issues of sexual harassment and discrimination in general.

Following the hearings, former Minnesota House representative Gloria M. Segal approached Hill with a plan to establish an endowed fund for a special professorship in her name—devoted to the study of sexual harassment and workplace equity—at the University of Oklahoma. In spite of the fact that half of the $250,000 needed for the project was easily raised, by mid-1993 work on establishing the professorship had stalled, due mainly to the adverse publicity and political fallout felt at the University of Oklahoma. The future of the fund remains in doubt, although several other colleges and universities across the country have reportedly expressed an interest in assuming control of the money and following through on the institution of the professorship.

Affected American Society

The Thomas-Hill hearings continued to resonate long after the headlines had faded. Public opinion polls taken at the time of the Senate hearings showed that a majority of those polled discredited Hill's story. Yet a poll taken one year later showed that twice as many people had come to believe her version of the events. Then, in the spring of 1993, investigative journalist David Brock published his controversial book *The Real Anita Hill,* in which he claimed to offer hard evidence that Hill lied about her relationship with Thomas. Conservative political commentator George F. Will commented in *Newsweek,* "To believe that Hill told the truth you must believe that dozens of people, with no common or even apparent motive to lie, did so. Brock's book will be persuasive to minds not sealed by the caulking of ideology." However, several reviews of the book questioned the reliability of Brock's assertions. As Jacob Weisberg put it in *Entertainment Weekly,* "*The Real Anita Hill* has yet to produce many converts."

Still, Hill has, for many, become a symbol of a new and powerful wave of feminism. Women's groups continue to credit Hill's appearance before the Senate Judiciary Committee with vastly increasing the public's awareness of sexual harassment and making it much less tolerated in the workplace. In an Associated Press news story dated October 11, 1992, Helen Neuborne, executive director of the National Organization for Women's Legal Defense and Education Fund, stated, "A lot of women had felt so isolated and perhaps couldn't even define sexual harassment…. The hearings made an enormous difference even though they were horrible."

The Equal Employment Opportunity Commission, where Hill and Thomas once worked, reported a 50 percent increase in complaints filed for harassment in the year following Hill's testimony. Additionally, in the aftermath of the hearings, numerous women ran for and won election to government office for the first time, citing their dissatisfaction with the all-male Senate Committee's response to Hill's allegations as their primary reason for doing so. And debate about the truth or falsity of Hill's allegations went on. Tonya Bolden, a *Black Enterprise* contributor commenting on the various analyses of the Hill-Thomas affair, suggested that the entire incident may have sparked a vital understanding of broader issues, "At the end you care less about who was lying and more about what you can do to counter racism and sexism."

Addressed Critics Skepticism

In 1994 journalists Jill Abramson and Jane Mayer published the book *Strange Justice: The Selling of Clarence Thomas,* which purported to be a thorough account of the events and controversies surrounding the Thomas case, his nomination, and eventual acceptance to the bench. Abramson and Mayer's book was criticized by some as an attempt to pander to feminist outrage, whereas others felt the book was an honest effort to uncover the pertinent facts behind the controversy. Even though opinions varied, Abramson and Mayer's work was widely cited by journalists and writers investigating the issue and was nominated for a National Book Award.

In 1997 Hill released her biography *Speaking Truth to Power,* in which she addressed the events leading up to the Clarence Thomas controversy and the ongoing effects of the incident on her life and career. Critical

response to Hill's biography was mixed, but many felt it was a fitting for Hill to respond to the many character attacks lodged against her during and after the Senate hearings. Some critics felt that the book was too late to have a major impact, whereas others responded positively and praised Hill for providing an inside look at events that were, ultimately, an important milestone in bringing public scrutiny to sexual harassment issues.

For a decade after the release of her book, Hill disappeared from the public eye and focused on her work at Brandeis University, where she teaches social policy, women's studies, and law. In 2007 Thomas released an autobiography containing passages in which he criticized Hill and her legal team for engaging in a liberal character assault against him. During Thomas's promotional tour, he repeated his accusations against Hill and the members of the media who supported her. Hill responded to Thomas's statements in a series of media interviews and also decided to publish an op-ed article in the *New York Times,* in which she reaffirmed her accusations and expressed surprise that Thomas was still defending his actions by defaming his accusers. "In the portion of his book that addresses my role in the Senate hearings into his nomination," Hill wrote in her article, "Justice Thomas offers a litany of unsubstantiated representations and outright smears that Republican senators made about me when I testified before the Judiciary Committee."

In the wake of Thomas's biography, Hill expressed hope that her experience and actions have contributed to positive developments for working women in the United States. As she stated in the conclusion to her article, "My belief is that in the past 16 years we have come closer to making the resolution of these issues an honest search for the truth, which, after all, is at the core of all legal inquiry." Speaking in her biography about the importance of the Thomas trials for women's rights, Hill said, "More than anything else, the Hill-Thomas hearing of October 1991 was about finding our voices and breaking the silence forever."

Selected writings

Speaking Truth to Power, Doubleday, 1997.

Sources

Books

Abramson, Jill, and Jane Mayer, *Strange Justice: The Selling of Clarence Thomas,* Houghton Mifflin, 1994.

Black Scholar staff and editors, *Court of Appeal: The Black Community Speaks Out on the Racial and Sexual Politics of Thomas vs. Hill,* One World/Ballantine, 1992.

Brock, David, *The Real Anita Hill,* Free Press, 1993.

Morrison, Toni, ed., *Race-ing Justice, En-gendering*

Power: Essays on Anita Hill, Clarence Thomas, and the Construction of Social Reality, Pantheon, 1992.

Periodicals

American Spectator, March 1992.
Associated Press wire report, October 11, 1992.
Black Enterprise, April 1993, p. 12.
Boston Globe, October 3, 2007.
Entertainment Weekly, June 18, 1993, p. 53.
Essence, March 1992, pp. 55–56, 116–117.
Ms., January–February 1992.
Nation, November 4, 1991.
National Law Journal, January 20, 1992.
Newsweek, December 28, 1992, pp. 20–22; April 19, 1993, p. 74.
New York Times, October 7, 1991; October 8, 1991; October 9, 1991; October 10, 1991; October 11, 1991; October 14, 1991; October 16, 1991; October 17, 1991; November 2, 1991; December 18, 1991; February 3, 1992; April 26, 1992; October 7, 1992; October 17, 1992; October 19, 1992; October 26, 1997; October 2, 2007.
New York Times Book Review, October 25, 1992.
Oakland Press (Oakland County, MI), October 11, 1992; April 24, 1993.
Time, October 21, 1991; October 19, 1992; June 28, 1993.
U.S. News & World Report, November 2, 1992.
Working Woman, September 1992, p. 21.

Periodicals

"Then and Now: Anita Hill," *CNN Online,* http://www.cnn.com/2005/US/01/03/cnn25.tan.anita.hill/index.html (accessed December 18, 2007).

—Joan Goldsworthy and Micah L. Issit

Barbara Hillary

1932(?)—

Nurse, athlete

Hillary, Barbara, photograph. AP Images.

In 2007 Barbara Hillary, a retired nurse from New York City, achieved a historic first when she became the first African-American woman ever to reach the North Pole. Hillary had begun taking physically challenging vacations after surviving a bout with lung cancer several years earlier, and she trained intensely for her North Pole excursion, an adventure that would involve an hours-long cross-country ski trek. Hillary claimed to be in no hurry "to meet the Grim Reaper," she said when interviewed by *Newsweek*'s Karen Springen and asked about the risks involved in a journey that would daunt many. "However, if I'm going to die, I want to go doing something I enjoy."

Hillary is a native of New York City and spent her earliest years in the area of Manhattan called San Juan Hill, which until the 1950s was a predominantly African-American area of the city. Its unsafe tenement houses were demolished to make way for the performing arts complex of Lincoln Center. She never knew her father, who died when she was still an infant, and her mother, who worked as a domestic, later moved the family to Harlem. Hillary recalled that as a child she was enchanted by books featuring extreme adventure tales, such as *Robinson Crusoe,* Daniel Defoe's 1719 novel about a man stranded on a tropical island for twenty-eight years.

As a young woman, Hillary trained to become a nurse, and she never married. She was active in community organizations in the New York area and made her home in the beachfront community of Arverne, in the borough of Queens. At the age of sixty-seven, she was diagnosed with lung cancer but recovered. The brush with mortality jarred her, and she began taking vacations in places that were far from the traditional tourist destinations. She went dog-sledding in northern Quebec, and she took part in a photography expedition to another Canadian province, Manitoba, to photograph polar bears. When she learned that there was no record of a black woman ever reaching the North Pole, she decided to make that her next goal.

The first humans on record to reach the North Pole did so in 1909 in a well-publicized event. The National Geographic Society–sponsored trip was led by American adventurer Robert Peary and included four Inuit men and Matthew Henson, an African-American explorer who had traveled with Peary on several other

At a Glance . . .

Born c. 1932 in New York, NY. *Education:* Trained as a nurse.

Career: Worked as a nurse.

Addresses: *Home*—Queens, NY. *Office*—PO Box 920174, Arverne Station, New York, NY 11692.

expeditions. Peary fell ill as they neared the pole, however, and sent Henson ahead to plant the U.S. flag at the geographic top of the Earth. But Henson's role was ignored for many years, with Peary receiving the majority of honors and accolades.

In 1986 Ann Bancroft, a physical-education teacher from Minnesota, became the first woman ever to reach the North Pole. By then there were regular expeditions that ferried scientists and adventuresome types back and forth, usually from a base in Norway within the Arctic Circle. There were two methods of reaching the Pole: either by cross-country skis or being dropped off by a helicopter. A company called Eagles Cry Adventures Inc. took North Pole visitors to and fro, but the cost of such a journey was $16,000 when Hillary first inquired. She began saving and training for the trip and seemed undaunted by the fact that she had never skied in her life. "It wasn't a popular sport in Harlem," she was quoted as saying by Meghan Barr in the *Seattle Times*. Hillary's North Pole trip would involve hauling a sled while on cross-country skis, and to prepare herself she began working out with a personal trainer. She even dragged a plastic sled along the beach near her home, with a bag of sand atop to simulate the weight of the supplies she would need, but the sled quickly fell apart.

Another complication arose once Hillary's preparations were fully underway, when Eagles Cry Adventures was forced to implement a major price hike to $21,000 because of currency fluctuations and other factors. Hillary began soliciting donations to meet the additional costs, and she even contacted the New York City Mayor's Office. "Mayor Bloomberg referred me to the Department for the Aging, which sent a form letter of things I could do in the senior center," she recounted in an interview with Lauren Collins for the *New Yorker*. "Mister, don't you get it? If I'm going to the North Pole, why ... do I need a senior center?"

Collins's article appeared in late March, just a few weeks away from Hillary's planned departure date, and readers began sending donations in to the magazine. One was from an eleven-year-old boy who wrote, according to Collins's follow-up article in May, "You have had a great life." On April 16, 2007, she arrived in Longyearbyen, Norway, and underwent a mandatory fitness test. She was elated to pass it, but Robert Russell, the owner of Eagles Cry Adventures, convinced her it would be more prudent to do just a one-day trip, instead of the original plan to ski for three days to reach the pole, with eight to ten hours of skiing required daily. On April 23, she and two guides were dropped off by helicopter on an ice floe called Base Camp Barneo, about sixty miles from the North Pole, where she was required to wait for the right moment to depart, because reaching the pole safely depends on weather and ice conditions. The camp at Barneo was a large one, with dozens of heated red tents and a runway for aircraft, and serves as the main base camp for the polar-bound. The tents were unisex, however, and for Hillary this was the most alarming part of her journey. "In the middle of the night, some burly Russian gentleman comes walking in, lies down, and starts snoring," she told Collins in the *New Yorker* follow-up. "You don't have any choice but to adjust or go sleep outside, where it's twenty to forty below."

Finally, Hillary boarded another helicopter, and, after landing, she and her guide began skiing toward the pole. When she finally reached it, a number of immediate thoughts crossed her mind, she told Collins: "Part of you is saying, 'I can't believe I made it this far'; another part is saying, 'Let this thing be over with'; another part, 'Damn, it's cold.'" In the elation of the moment, Hillary removed her gloves and suffered minor frostbite on her fingers. She became the first African-American woman to reach the North Pole, but was also one of the oldest people ever to make the trek. Her adventure had turned her from a community activist into a global one, as she learned about the effects of global warming on polar ice. She hoped to use her newfound fame "to go and lecture to different groups on what they can do on a grass-roots level" to stall potentially disastrous climate change, the *Seattle Times* report by Barr quoted her as saying. She was also considering another trek, as she told Collins. "All the people who didn't believe in me—I'd like to go to the South Pole and give 'em the one-two punch!"

Sources

Periodicals

Houston Chronicle, May 7, 2007.
Newsweek, March 5, 2007.
New Yorker, March 26, 2007.
Seattle Times, May 7, 2007.

Online

Collins, Lauren, "Top of the World," *NewYorker.com,* http://www.newyorker.com/online/2007/05/28/070528on_onlineonly_collins (accessed December 26, 2007).

—Carol Brennan

Brenda Holloway

1946—

Singer

Brenda Holloway was a California teen who recorded for the legendary Motown label in the 1960s. A noted beauty, she joined the Detroit label and released her first single in 1964, just before the explosive success of label-mates Diana Ross and the Supremes. Though she later faded into obscurity, Holloway actually wrote some of her own songs—a rarity for a female rhythm and blues (R&B) performer at the time—and is also noteworthy as the first West Coast act that Motown ever signed. Less than a decade later, the company abandoned its Detroit roots and moved its headquarters to Southern California.

Holloway was born in 1946 in Atascadero, a town in San Luis Obispo county, and moved with her family to Los Angeles when she was still a toddler. The Holloways, which would soon grow to include her younger brother and sister, settled in the Watts neighborhood in South Los Angeles—by this point a predominantly African-American community—in a house on Bandera Street near Ninety-second. Demonstrating an early aptitude for music, Holloway began taking violin lessons at the age of seven and learned several other instruments, including the piano, cello, and flute. She also began composing melodies at a young age, and though she was thoroughly immersed in the classical genre as part of her musical training, she gravitated toward pop music in her teens. In middle school, she sang in an early version of the Whispers, an enduring R&B act that had hits until the 1980s, but she soon teamed with her younger sister, Patrice, to sing together. Holloway was fourteen years old and Patrice was twelve when they recorded their first single, "Do

the Del Viking." Over the next three years, a solo Holloway recorded a number of songs that were released on local Los Angeles labels and were minor radio hits in Southern California.

Holloway was a senior at David Starr Jordan High School in Watts in 1964 when Hal Davis, her manager/producer, booked her for an appearance at a national convention of radio disc jockeys held at the Ambassador Hotel in Los Angeles. Davis knew that Berry Gordy, founder of Motown Records, was likely to turn up at the convention at some point and hoped that he could engineer a meeting between the vivacious and talented Holloway and the Detroit record mogul who was rapidly changing both the sound and the look of African-American music in the United States. Holloway's gig at the convention involved singing "My Guy," which was Motown's newest hit for its top female soloist, Mary Wells, over a six-hour period. "Later I was talking to this gentleman. I said, 'You know, I'm getting tired, because I'm supposed to be singing for Berry Gordy. I wish he would hurry up and come,'" Holloway recounted in a lengthy interview with Kimasi Browne for the book *California Soul: Music of African Americans in the West*. "He left. After about forty minutes, he came back and said, 'I like the way you sing.' I said, 'I'm glad that you like the way I sing, but I'm supposed to be here to sing for Berry Gordy.' He said, 'I am Berry Gordy.'" The Motown chief told Holloway he wanted to sign her, to which she replied, "'Call my mom. Tell her to come, to put on the best clothes she has and let's sign this contract.'"

At a Glance . . .

Born on June 21, 1946, in Atascadero, CA; daughter of Wade and Johnnie Mae Holloway; married, 1968; children: three daughters. *Education:* Attended Compton Community College, c. 1964–65.

Career: Recorded first single, "Do the Del Viking," c. 1960; cut other singles that were issued on Los Angeles labels, 1961–64; signed to Motown imprint Tamla, 1963; first Motown single, "Every Little Bit Hurts," peaked at number thirteen on *Billboard's* Hot 100 chart, 1964; opening act for the Beatles on their 1965 U.S. tour; retired from performing, c. 1968–80; returned in 1980 with the gospel album, *Brand New*; began performing again, 1995—.

Addresses: *Agent*—Richard de la Font Agency, 4845 S. Sheridan Rd., Ste. 505, Tulsa, OK 74145.

Became Motown's Newest Star

Holloway was the first West Coast artist ever signed by Motown, and her first Motown single was recorded in a Los Angeles–area studio and released in May of 1964. The song was the ballad "Every Little Bit Hurts," written by Ed Cobb, and peaked at number thirteen, making it the first Motown hit produced outside of its legendary Hitsville, U.S.A. studio in Detroit. Even though the hit would be a career chart high for Holloway, she was unhappy with the song choice. After dropping out of Compton Community College's music program, she began traveling to Detroit to record at the Motown studios. The process proved difficult, and she was dismayed to learn that her ideas and suggestions were unwelcome by Motown's team of songwriters and producers.

Holloway was briefly the newest Motown sensation in the period just before the Supremes, a female trio, had their first number-one hit with "Where Did Our Love Go?" later in 1964. The Supremes would go on to have a string of hits, and they became the label's most lucrative act for the rest of the decade. Holloway felt shunted aside, though she did open for the Temptations, Motown's other hugely successful act, and even played her violin to a standing ovation. But she was warned by one Temptations member not to return for an encore, despite the crowd's cheers. "It seemed like I was a threat to them because I was a different type of act," she said in the *California Soul* chapter. "I think that they saw my potential even more than I saw my potential." She also noted that among the rough-and-tumble teens and young adults who had grown up in

Detroit, her Los Angeles background and classical musical training set her apart from the others, who wrongly perceived her as coming from a more middle-class background than their own. Her diction was also flawless, and Gordy reportedly had Diana Ross listen to tapes of Holloway to hone her own pronunciation.

Holloway's next hits, 1965's "When I'm Gone" and "Operator," were written and produced by Smokey Robinson and made respectable showings on *Billboard's* R&B chart. She was home with her family in Watts in August of 1965 when the infamous Watts riots erupted, and she recalled that the family literally barricaded themselves inside the house. She told Browne in the *California Soul* interview that those days "seemed like the end of the world. Tanks were driving down our streets, no cars—just National Guards with guns. We were so afraid that the National Guardsmen would kill us. I didn't feel like a star. I felt like dead meat." She finally phoned Gordy and told him she could not live there any longer, and he gave her the down payment for a house in Los Angeles's quieter Westside neighborhood. Three days after the riots, she joined that year's biggest tour as an opening act for the Beatles and earned a spot in music history as the only solo female act ever to open for the British band on tour.

"I Just Walked Out"

Holloway had a few more minor hits for Motown, including "You've Made Me So Very Happy" in 1967, which she cowrote with her sister Patrice. Two years later, it was covered by the rock act Blood Sweat & Tears and reached number two for them. She and her sister also sang backup on the famous Joe Cocker hit "With a Little Help from My Friends," a cover of a Beatles tune, in 1968. That same year, her second album, *The Artistry of Brenda Holloway*, was finally released after a long delay by Motown executives. Holloway felt pushed aside as Diana Ross and the Supremes racked up hit after hit for the label, but then Gordy told Holloway that he wanted to ready her for a regular gig in Las Vegas. "I had a lot of fears about Vegas, because that was an area and a territory that no one at Motown had been into," she told Browne. "I didn't know who Brenda was or the potential that I had in me. It could be because I came from Watts, and I didn't put enough value on me."

In 1968 Holloway finally decided to leave Motown. The decision was made one day when she was in Detroit, following a telephone call to her mother back in Los Angeles, during which she fumed once again about her treatment by label executives. "I just walked out," she told Browne. She married a minister and had three daughters, and Holloway returned to the music business briefly in 1980 with a gospel album on Birthright Records. Later that decade, she made some recordings in Britain and finally began performing again in the mid-1990s. She released her fifth album, *My Love Is Your Love*, in 2004. Other artists later covered her hits as well as the songs she wrote, beginning with "Every Little Bit Hurts"—her first single and the ballad she loathed—which has been recorded by George Clinton's Funkadelic, the Clash, the Jam, and Alicia Keys.

Selected discography

Albums

Every Little Bit Hurts, Motown, 1964.
The Artistry of Brenda Holloway, Motown, 1968.
Brand New, Birthright Records, 1980.
It's a Woman's World, Volt Records, 1999.
My Love Is Your Love, Bestway Records, 2004.

Singles

"Hey Fool," 1962.
"Game of Love," 1962.
"I'll Give My Life," 1962.
"Every Little Bit Hurts," 1964.
"I'll Always Love You," 1964.
"When I'm Gone," 1965.
"Operator," 1965.

"You Can Cry on My Shoulder," 1965.
"Together 'til the End of Time," 1966.
"Hurt a Little Everyday," 1966.
"Just Look What You've Done," 1967.
"You've Made Me So Very Happy," 1967.
"Give Me A Little Inspiration," 1987.

Sources

Books

Browne, Kimasi, "Brenda Holloway: Los Angeles's Contribution to Motown," in *California Soul: Music of African Americans in the West,* edited by Jacqueline Cogdell DjeDje and Eddie S. Meadows, University of California Press, 1998.

Online

"Brenda Holloway," *Richard De La Font Agency,* http://www.delafont.com/music_acts/Brenda-Holloway.htm (accessed December 26, 2007).

—Carol Brennan

Ayanna Howard

1972—

Robotics engineer

Ayanna Howard was a child with science-fiction fanta-sies. When she encountered the 1970s' television series *Bionic Woman*—in which a severely injured woman was outfitted with robotic limbs and thus en-dowed with superhuman powers—Howard was less interested in becoming a super heroine then she was in understanding how the show's fictional scientists man-aged to create the robotic limbs that gave the bionic woman her powers. Howard was in elementary school at the time, but this early inspiration motivated her through years of hard work and meticulous research to become one of the twenty-first century's leading robot-ics engineers, helping to design the next generation of robots and making yesterday's science-fiction fantasies a modern reality.

Howard was born in 1972 in Providence, Rhode Island, but spent most of her childhood in California. Her family relocated to Inglewood, California, when Howard was between two and three years old and later to the Altadena/Pasadena area, where Howard's mother, Johnetta, and father, Eric, owned and oper-ated a small company that manufactured parts for railroad signal stations. Howard's parents fostered and encouraged an early interest in machines and engineer-ing.

Howard attended public schools in Pasadena, where she excelled in math and physics. Though she had an obvious aptitude for working with computers, ma-chines, and electronics, she also recalls wanting to take a different path from that of her father. "My father was an engineer," Howard told *Contemporary Black Biog-raphy* (*CBB*), "so I knew I didn't want to do that." From age eleven, Howard believed she knew the course of her career: she would attend medical school, become a doctor, and specialize in limb replacement. However, her biology class during her freshman year in high school changed her mind about the future. "After taking biology, I realized that what I loved was math and physics and that what interested me about robotics was the mechanics and control, not the human physiol-ogy," Howard recalled in a 2002 interview with Ima-giverse.org. By the time she was ready for college, she had decided, like her father, that her talents and interests were more geared toward engineering.

Returned to Providence

When Howard was applying to universities, her parents told her that they would only pay for her education if she left California, both for the experience of living in another state and because, as Howard told Stephen Cass of IEEE Spectrum Online, "They felt California was too laid back!"

Howard chose to attend Brown University in Provi-dence, Rhode Island, because, as she told *CBB*, "Brown didn't use the grade system. I had always been competing for grades just to get into college and so, when I got to college, I didn't want to do that any-more." Freed from the constant concern of maintain-ing a grade point average, Howard allowed herself the freedom to explore Brown's liberal arts classes, taking dance and literature courses to supplement her core curriculum. Though Brown was a liberal university, the

At a Glance . . .

Born Ayanna MacCalla in 1972 in Providence, RI; daughter of Eric and Johnetta McCallum; married 2002 (divorced); child: Zyare Howard. *Education:* Brown University, BS computer engineering, 1993; University of Southern California, MS electrical engineering, 1997, PhD electrical engineering, 1999; Claremont University, MBA, 2005.

Career: National Aeronautics and Space Administration, Jet Propulsion Laboratory (JPL), computer information internships, 1993–97, information systems engineer, 1997–99, senior robotics researcher, 1999–2005; Georgia Tech University, associate professor, 2006—.

Awards: JPL, Lew Allen Award for Excellence in Research, 2001; Massachusetts Institute of Technology's *Technology Review* Top 100 Young Innovator of the Year, 2003; LA Council of Engineers and Scientists, Engineer of the Year Award, 2004; Allstate Insurance Distinguished Honoree for Achievement in Science, 2004; Young Global Leaders Award, 2006.

Addresses: *Office*—Van Leer Electrical Engineering Building, 777 Atlantic Dr. NW, Atlanta, GA 30332-0250.

school offered a number of classes in technology and computing, and Howard decided to pursue a bachelor of science in computer engineering.

During her summer break in 1990, Howard returned to Pasadena, where she was accepted for an internship at the National Aeronautics and Space Association's (NASA) Jet Propulsion Laboratory (JPL). Howard enjoyed the JPL program and returned in 1991 and 1992 to help JPL engineers design a database. While at the JPL, Howard learned how to function in the applied research community and was exposed to new ideas and research interests in disparate fields. During her senior year internship, she began working with the JPL robotics group.

Entered the Robotics Field

Howard returned to Pasadena after graduation and entered the University of Southern California (USC) at Los Angeles for graduate studies. In 1994, during her second semester at USC, Howard was offered a position in the JPL's computer science department to work on software applications. Her work at NASA complemented her studies as she worked toward a master's in electrical engineering. While at USC, Howard became fascinated with the concept of artificial intelligence (AI). By 1997, when she began her PhD program in USC's engineering department, Howard was working on developing software for AI applications.

In 1999, the same year she received her PhD, Howard joined the JPL's Telerobotics Research and Information Group. Though her initial interest was in building the mechanical components used in robotics, Howard's experience with AI and programming led her to the Dynamic Programming Group, where she was introduced to nonlinear algorithms and neural network programming.

While working as a junior robotics researcher, Howard began publishing papers on robot "thinking" and the use of software systems in directing navigational systems. From 1993 to 2005, Howard's research was featured in over sixty articles. In 2001, she was honored by the JPL with the Lew Allen Award for Excellence in Research, which recognizes success in research and effectiveness as a teacher and leader in the field. In 2002, Howard was named as a senior robotics researcher.

Developed a Variety of Technologies

While working with the JPL, Howard's research was used for a number of different projects, of which space exploration and military applications absorbed most of her time. From 1998 to 2005, she spent some of her time working on software for military projects. Though Howard is now able to discuss some of the military projects she worked on at the JPL, some of her research applications are still classified as military secrets. One of Howard's declassified military projects was an application that uses visual recognition software to help identify dangerous elements on the battlefield.

"We were working with [Principal Component Analysis]," Howard told *CBB*, "a tool that picks out dominant features of an object or potential enemy and then classifies them as, for example, a jet, helicopter or missile." To create an automated program that could identify potential threats, researchers first needed to train their neural network by showing it thousands of examples of different objects that fall into target categories. Using a system similar to the way humans identify and classify objects, the computer learns to identify key features—such as the shape of the object's body or the presence or absence of wings and/or rotor blades—to classify the object into one of several predetermined classes. "We eventually achieved about a 96 percent recognition rate," Howard said. Visual recognition software can be used to identify the locations of enemy equipment and troops and from there scientists can use additional computational systems to infer information about enemy strategy.

The majority of Howard's time at the JPL was focused on developing technology for robotic exploration of extreme environments, such as those found on other planets. Howard was a leader of the Safe Rover Navigation Task, a project aimed at building robots that can navigate independently on the Martian landscape. The rocky terrain of Mars makes navigation difficult, and Howard and her colleagues realized that, to navigate successfully, robot rovers will need the capability to evaluate the terrain visually, using a system superficially similar to that of a human explorer.

Howard explained in an interview with *Time*'s Dan Cray, "People always look for the straightest, clearest path, so that's what we map to the robot." The goal is to create robots that can function with relative autonomy. Howard's neural network programming enables the robots to integrate new data into an evolving behavioral scheme, thereby allowing adaptation. Though the process is different from that used by humans, Howard's robots are "thinking" machines. "They recognize things like rock distribution, slope, and the presence or absence of cliffs and depressions," Howard told *CBB*. "It's a fuzzy logic engine that says, for instance, 'If rock distribution is high but the slope is low and there are no cliffs, then the terrain is navigable.'"

The ultimate goal is to free the operators from having to direct the robots' every movement, which is the system used for the current Mars rovers *Spirit* and *Opportunity*. In an interview with IEEE Spectrum Online, Howard said, "I want to plop a rover on Mars and have it call back when it finds interesting science." In Howard's estimation, it will eventually be possible to design robots that are capable of mineralogical analysis while moving through the environment. The rover will investigate rocks and samples that appear interesting, and will then use its initial analysis to determine whether further investigation is warranted.

Howard's designs will feature prominently in NASA's planned exploration of Mars, set to begin in December of 2009 and land on the Martian surface in 2010. The project will be part of NASA's Mars Science Laboratory, a moving laboratory that will collect geologic samples and eventually send samples back to Earth during future missions. Howard's designs for neural networks and automated navigation are at the forefront of robotics research and have applications beyond space exploration. In 2003, Howard was named as one of the world's top innovators by the Massachusetts Institute of Technology's *Technology Review* in recognition for her pioneering work in AI.

Expanded Focus to Community and Academia

As Howard gained recognition as a leader in her field, she began taking a role as a community leader, helping

to disseminate information about science and engineering to young women in the Altadena community. Howard was a frequent guest at Southern California schools, where she gave speeches about employment opportunities in engineering. "So many of our girls get persuaded to pursue other career choices at a young age and become discouraged with math and science," Howard said in an interview with Imagiverse.org. "By the time robotics is thought of as a career choice, they have already been left behind in the game." From 2001 to 2003, Howard started a mentoring program for young women in the Altadena area, focusing on encouraging achievement in science and mathematics.

While working for the JLA, Howard began pursuing an master in business administration (MBA) in hopes of eventually transitioning into the administrative aspects of the research community. Howard felt that her MBA training was an immediate benefit because it helped her to learn skills that were not common among researchers, such as how to deal with the public or handle relational issues among employees and associates. "I have a bigger vision in terms of what I want to do when I'm 50," she said to Cass. "It's about being strategic in what you want to do."

In 2005, Howard left the JPL for an associate professor position at Georgia Tech University. The decision to leave the JPL was partially based on a massive restructuring at NASA, after which Howard found that the organization was no longer able to provide the compensation and research environment she desired. However, at Georgia Tech she found an environment conducive to research and was able to remain involved in helping young people develop an interest in technology.

After joining the university's Systems and Controls Group, she founded the Human Automation Systems Laboratory. One of Howard's primary goals is to work on technological innovations that help the field of robotics transition from strictly scientific applications to more general industrial functions. Howard believes that industrial robotics will grow rapidly in the twenty-first century and that AI research will play a major role in the future of robotics application.

Beginning in 2006, Howard spent some of her time at Georgia Tech working on social assistance applications. One of her goals is to develop neural networks that can learn from human demonstration. Howard wants to design a simple interface that will allow users with no experience in technology or robotics to train domestic robots. "Say you want a robot to help clean up the children's toys in the morning or feed your grandmother breakfast," Howard said to *CBB*. "We're now at a stage where simple robot technology is available, like the Roomba [a robotic vacuum cleaner that navigates a home while cleaning carpets]. Now we have to go beyond that." Howard is certain that assistive technology will be the most important field of robotics in the coming years.

Besides working with assistance technology, in 2007 Howard was also collaborating with NASA researchers on a project that has immediate applications for research on global warming. The project has allowed Howard and her colleagues to work with a new set of variables using groups of robots to navigate inhospitable areas, such as the polar ice caps, and cooperate to retrieve information about global warming. After reaching a target location, the probes will use visual cues to determine the best locations to look for data. By sharing information and comparing data, a group of robots will have a better chance of maximizing time spent looking for fruitful data collection areas. In the future, Howard hopes that robots of this kind will retrieve data that will be impossible or impractical for humans to obtain and will free operators to work on data analysis rather than on the mechanics of data collection.

Besides contributing to the development of robotics science, Howard hopes to continue working in the community. After obtaining a grant from the National Science Foundation in 2007, Howard began working on a program to create video games aimed at underrepresented students, such as women and minorities, to create interest and understanding in technology careers. The games will use simulations, such as space exploration and tracking fugitives as a law enforcement officer, to teach students about data retrieval and analysis. "They will be doing data mining," she said to *CBB*, "but they don't know it. If you have a bunch of data, how do you find something interesting and relevant?"

As of 2007, Howard was considered one of the nation's leading experts in robotics and AI. Working on pioneering projects in a number of fields, Howard has also become a leader in helping engender interest in science for the next generation of students. Her own experience as an African-American woman in a typically white male field helps her to understand the struggles that many young women endure. When Imagiverse.org asked her what advice she would give to students interested in engineering, she replied, "Don't let anybody persuade you to give up. Know that some things may be difficult and others may cause you to struggle, but deal with it and keep trying."

Selected writings

Nonfiction

(With Curtis Padgett) "A Generalized Approach to Real-Time Pattern Recognition in Sensed Data," *Pattern Recognition,* Vol. 32, 1999, pp. 2069–2071.

(With George A. Bekey) "Intelligent Learning for Deformable Object Manipulation," *Autonomous Robots,* Vol. 9, 2000, 51–58.

(With Homayoun Seraji and Edward Tunstel) "Safe Navigation on Hazardous Terrain," *International Conference on Robotics and Automation,* 2001, pp. 3084–3091.

(With Seraji and Tunstel) "A Rule-Based Fuzzy Traversability Index for Mobile Robot Navigation," *International Conference on Robotics and Automation,* 2001, pp. 3067–3071.

(With Curtis Padgett) "An Adaptive Learning Methodology for Intelligent Object Detection in Novel Imagery Data," *Neurocomputing,* Vol. 51, 2003, pp. 1–11.

Sources

Periodicals

Time, June 6, 2004.

Online

Cass, Stephen, "Ayanna Howard: Robot Wrangler," *IEEE Spectrum Online,* http://www.spectrum.ieee.org/feb05/2268 (December 11, 2007).

Cray, Dan, "The Bionic Engineers: Driving School on Mars," *Time,* http://www.time.com/time/2004/innovators/200406/story.html (December 11, 2007).

"An Interview with … Ayanna Howard," *Imagiverse.org,* http://www.imagiverse.org/interviews/ayannahoward/ayanna_howard_16_08_02.htm (December 11, 2007).

Kerr, Andrew, "Georgia Tech's Bionic Woman," *CEISMIC Gazette,* http://www.ceismc.gatech.edu/gazette/2006_11/2006_11_howard.aspx (December 11, 2007).

Other

Additional information for this profile was obtained through an interview with Ayanna Howard on October 17, 2007.

—Micah L. Issitt

Ryan Howard

1979—

Professional baseball player

Howard, Ryan, photograph. Tim Shaffer/Reuters/Landov.

Ryan Howard emerged in 2005 as one of the top rookies in the National Baseball League. In 2006, his first full season with the Philadelphia Phillies, Howard played as a first baseman and was voted the National League's Most Valuable Player (MVP) and won the Hank Aaron Award as the most successful "slugger" in the league. Howard has become one of Major League Baseball's (MLB) most promising figures in terms of developing the kind of star power necessary to maintain and increase public interest in MLB.

Howard was one of four children born and raised in the suburbs of St. Louis, MO, by Ron and Cheryl Howard, formerly of Birmingham, Alabama. Howard and his fraternal twin brother Corey, older brother Chris, and sister Roni Karen were active children whose parents encouraged participation in sports and other extracurricular activities.

Cheryl Howard, a former marketing manager, and Ron Howard, who works as an engineer for IBM Corporation, instilled in their children the idea that hard work leads to success, a lesson they both relate to their experience with the Alabama civil rights movement of

the 1960s. In a 2006 interview with Derrick Goold of the *St. Louis Post Dispatch*, Howard quoted his father's message: "Don't focus on the blockers, on the challenges, if you have a chance to be what you want to be, be the best, be the pinnacle." The Howard children all cite their parents' unwillingness to accept mediocrity as a key, motivating factor in their initial and continuing successes. Howard told *Philadelphia Daily News* reporter Rich Hofmann that his mother taught him "common sense, being courteous," while his father gave him "aggressiveness, that fire to want to be the best."

Besides playing baseball, basketball, soccer, and football, Howard played trombone in the Lafayette High School marching band. He managed to excel in his athletic and musical interests without sacrificing academic progress. As he began to recognize that baseball was his favorite sport, his father installed a batting cage in the basement, helping Howard to learn the skills necessary to become a home-run hitter. Howard earned all-conference honors while playing baseball for Lafayette High, but he was not considered a major prospect until the end of his high school playing career. Howard set a home-run record during his senior year

At a Glance . . .

Born Ryan James Howard on November 19, 1979, in Saint Louis, MO; son of Ron and Cheryl Howard; children: Darian Alexander. *Education:* Lafayette High School, Saint Louis, MO, 1994–98; attended Southwest Missouri State University, 1999–2002.

Career: Philadelphia Phillies Minor League, first base position, 2001–05; Philadelphia Phillies, first base position, 2005—.

Memberships: Major League Baseball Players Association; Negro League Hall of Fame.

Awards: National League Rookie of the Year, 2005; Philadelphia Chapter of the Baseball Writers' Association of America, Mike Schmidt Most Valuable Player (MVP) Award, 2006; Sporting News Player of the Year, 2006; Negro League Hall of Fame and Museum, Oscar Charleston Legacy Award, 2006; Hank Aaron Award, 2006.

Addresses: *Office*—Philadelphia Phillies, One Citizens Bank Way, Citizens Bank Park, Philadelphia, PA 19148.

and as a result received an offer to play a first-base position for Southwest Missouri State (SMS) University.

Howard entered SMS without a scholarship for his first year but was informed that if he performed well he would be eligible for funding for his last three years. Howard was named Freshman of the Year by the Missouri Valley Conference Association, after hitting nineteen home runs in his first season. In the interview with Hofmann, Howard described his first years playing for SMS as an important stage in his development. "College was important for me. College allowed me to mature, not only as a baseball player but also as a person."

After his sophomore season, Howard was invited to the U.S. Junior Nationals Team, where he traveled extensively and made his first international excursions. While on tour with the Nationals Team, he had the chance to meet coaches, professional scouts, and seasoned veterans, all of whom gave him advice that he remembered long after succeeding to the major leagues. Though Howard was clearly a prospect for the junior league drafts, his draft appeal declined significantly after a relatively poor junior season. Howard was

drafted in the fifth round by the Philadelphia Phillies, who chose him because the managers and coaching staff believed he had the potential to develop into a first-tier player. Howard left SMS at the end of his junior year, finishing his college career with a total of fifty home runs.

Played in the Phillies Junior Leagues

Howard's first position as a professional player was with the New York–Philadelphia league. After an impressive early performance, he was transferred to the Lakewood A League, where he continued his excellent batting record to become the leader in home runs among all Phillies minor league players. At this time, Howard was still learning to handle different pitchers and had a high strikeout average during his first and second years. Though his flaws led some analysts to ignore Howard as one of the minor league's potential stars, Phillies managers and coaches were certain that he would overcome his difficulties. Howard was promoted to the Phillies Florida League team in 2003, where he excelled with twenty-three home runs and eighty-two runs batted in (RBIs) to win the MVP Award for the Florida League. Howard participated in the 2003 Futures All-Star Game, where U.S. Minor League players play against teams from other countries.

In 2004 Howard was invited to attend the major league spring training, where he relished in the opportunity to play with and learn from members of the Phillies major league roster. Though it appeared that Howard was being groomed for a spot on the major league team, the Phillies decision to recruit Jim Thome, another prominent left-handed first base player, for a six-year contract indicated to some sports analysts that Howard had no place on the major league roster.

At the start of the 2004 season, Howard was placed on the double-A Reading Pennsylvania team. Howard broke the team's single-season home-run record, with 50 home runs and also scored 102 RBIs. Howard was then promoted to the triple-A team, playing from the Scranton, Pennsylvania, area, and finished the season with the Arizona Fall League, playing with the Phoenix Desert Dogs, where he increased his season RBI record to 160. As a crowning achievement to his minor league career, Howard was named by *USA Today* as the top minor league player of 2004, and he received the Paul Owens Award from the Phillies as the club's leading minor league player.

Because Thome was performing well as the team's first baseman, the Phillies management wanted to keep Howard playing with the club's triple-A team in 2005, a decision that led Howard to request a potential trade. However, when Thome suffered from injuries in 2005 and was eventually placed on the disabled list, Howard was given an opportunity to fill in for Thome in his first major league appearance.

Played in the Major League

Howard was initially transferred to the major league squad in May of 2005, where he fared poorly in his first games with the team. Thome returned from injuries in June, and Howard was again sent to the triple-A team. When Thome's injuries recurred, Howard was brought back to the major league to finish the season in Thome's absence. Howard's performance, which included twenty-two home runs and sixty-three RBIs in the last eighty-eight games of the season, impressed analysts and the coaching staff and solidified his position on the team. Howard was given the National League Rookie of the Year Award as a crowning acknowledgment for his performance in 2005.

In the off season, the Phillies made the decision to trade Thome and keep Howard as their permanent first baseman. In 2006, during his first full season as a major league player, Howard exceeded expectations with 58 home runs and 149 RBIs, winning the National League MVP Award for 2006, and becoming only the second player in baseball history to win the Rookie of the Year and MVP awards in successive seasons. Howard capped the season by winning the home-run competition at the 2006 All-Stars Game.

To begin the 2007 season, the Phillies renewed Howard's contract with a significant pay increase to an annual $900,000. Howard performed well in the early 2007 season but suffered an injury in May that placed him temporarily on the disabled list. When Howard returned in late May, his performance remained strong through the remainder of the series and helped his team to win the National League Eastern Division, the first time the Philadelphia squad has reached the division championships since the team's 1993 appearance against the Toronto Blue Jays. Howard's final statistics for the regular season were 47 home runs and 136 RBIs.

Though the Phillies had a relatively successful 2007 season and achieved the goal of playing in the postseason championships, the team also achieved the dubious honor of setting a major league record when they lost their ten-thousandth game to the St. Louis Cardinals on July 15. Regardless, the Phillies performed well in the closing half of the season and, with Howard's return to the roster, they gained the National League East Title. However, the team was swept in the first four out of seven games to lose the title to the Colorado Rockies. Howard had a disappointing performance in the four-game series, scoring only one home run and one RBI. Despite the disappointing end to the season, Howard continued to be one of the best players in the league and was ranked second in both home runs and RBIs for the 2007 season.

Howard is one of the most important players on the Phillies and has rapidly become one of MLB's rising stars. His effect on the Phillies is more significant because of the team's history. The Philadelphia Phillies were one of the last teams in the National League to sign an African-American player for their team, and the addition of Howard has been an important step in establishing the popularity of MLB among Philadelphia's African-American community. The Philadelphia Phillies ball club has long had a reputation of being unwelcoming toward African-American players and many of the club's former African-American players suffered abuse at the hands of the city's fans. However, Howard's rise in popularity, to become one of Philadelphia's most beloved athletes, signaled to many fans and sports analysts the beginning of a new era for the franchise.

Sources

Periodicals

New York Times, July 11, 2006; November 21, 2006; March 4, 2007.
Philadelphia Daily News, August 27, 2006.
Philadelphia Inquirer, October 3, 2007.
St. Louis Post Dispatch, January 15, 2006; April 7, 2006; September 29, 2006; October 26, 2006; November 21, 2006.
USA Today, September 13, 2006.

Online

Amaro, Ruben Jr., "High Above Home Plate," *Courier Post Online,* http://www.courierpostonline.com/blogs/2007/03/amaro-interview-on-howard-deal.html (December 12, 2007).
Hollander, Dave, "Beast Burdens," *Philadelphia City Paper,* http://www.citypaper.net/articles/2006-03-23/cover.shtml (December 12, 2007).
Mandel, Ken, "Notes: Howard Receives Honor," *Philadelphia Phillies Official Site,* http://philadelphia.phillies.mlb.com/news/article.jsp?ymd=20060922&content_id=1676747&vkey=news_phi&fext=.jsp&c_id=phi (December 12, 2007).
"Player Profile," *MLB Official Site,* http://mlb.mlb.com/team/player.jsp?player_id=429667 (December 12, 2007).
"Ryan Howard Biography," *Ryan Howard Official Site, Philadelphia Phillies,* http://www.ryanhoward.info/biography/ (December 12, 2007).
Santoliquito, Joseph, "Notes: Howard Makes a Memory," *Major League Baseball Online,* http://mlb.mlb.com/news/article.jsp?ymd=20060423&content_id=1414701&vkey=news_phi&fext=.jsp&c_id=phi; (December 12, 2007).

—Micah L. Issitt

Vernon Irvin

1961—

Chief marketing officer

Growing up near Pittsburgh, Pennsylvania, Vernon Irvin did not receive encouraging career advice from his high school teachers and guidance counselors. They assumed that he would follow his father into the steel mills that provided work for many of the city's working-class African Americans. However, his mother believed in her son's potential and encouraged him to complete his education by attending college. After obtaining a degree in computer science, Irvin understood that this new technology heralded a digital revolution that could transform people's lives around the world. Armed with technical knowledge, highly developed management and communication skills, and an unwavering drive to succeed, Irvin gained executive positions in several respected corporations.

As a successful business leader, Irvin contributed to the growth of the organizations he worked for by under-standing and responding to customer needs. As an African-American executive in a largely white industry, he has also devoted himself both to mentoring young people of color working in the field of information technology and working to make sure that low-income people of all races have access to that technology.

Vernon Irvin Jr. was born on December 31, 1961, in Braddock, Pennsylvania, on the eastern edge of the city of Pittsburgh. Braddock was a working-class sub-urban community, whose economy depended largely on the Edgar Thomson Steel Works, which had been constructed by Andrew Carnegie in 1873. Like many Braddock citizens, Irvin's father, Vernon "Jock" Irvin worked, first in the steel mill, then, as the U.S. steel

industry declined, in an oil refinery. His mother worked at a school of cosmetology, the Pittsburgh Beauty Academy.

Irvin attended St. Anselm's, a Catholic elementary school in the nearby, largely white suburban town of Swissdale. It was not easy being one of very few black students in his school, and it was even harder riding the bus home to Braddock wearing the jacket and tie of his school uniform. However, the taunts and beatings he received merely inspired him to learn to defend himself and to study hard so that he could build a different life.

Began Career in Computer Science

Irvin's parents encouraged him to follow his ambition. Working several jobs each, they saved money to help him attend college, and Irvin contributed by working nights while attending classes during the day. After his graduation from high school in 1979, he entered California State University, San Bernardino, in south-ern California. He chose to study computer sciences, not because he enjoyed working with computers, but because he recognized that the newly developing field would offer a wide range of career opportunities. At night he worked in the data processing department of the Sisters of Charity Hospitals.

Irvin soon found that he had been right about the expanding job possibilities available to those familiar with computers and information systems. The Sisters

At a Glance . . .

Born Vernon Irvin Jr. on December 31, 1961, in Braddock, PA; married Erica; five children. *Education:* University of Cincinnati, BS in computer science, 1989.

Career: Star Bank, director of telecommunications, 1982–85; MCI, 1985–91; Ameritech Small Business Services, vice president of strategy, business development, and product management, 1990–92; MFS/UUNET, senior vice president, 1992–93; eSpire, advanced data services division, senior vice president of marketing, executive vice president of corporate development and strategy, chief financial officer, 1993–95; WorldCom, 1995–99; British Telecommunications Worldwide, senior vice president of marketing and Internet, 1999–2002; American Management Systems, global communications, media, and entertainment division, executive vice president and general manager, 2002–03; VeriSign Telecommunication Services, executive vice president and general manager, 2003–06; XM Satellite Radio, chief marketing officer, 2006—.

Memberships: Center for Telecommunication Management, board of directors; CTIA, The Wireless Association, board of directors; William and Mary School of Business, board of directors; Wireless Foundation, board of directors.

Awards: National Eagle Leadership Institute, Eagle Award, 2004; 50 Most Important African Americans in Technology, Pinnacle Award, 2006.

Addresses: *Office*—XM Satellite Radio, Office of the Vice President and Chief Marketing Officer, 1500 Eckington Pl. NE, Washington, DC 20002.

supervisors at MCI advised him that he could advance much farther if he returned to college to finish his degree work. He took their advice and graduated from the University of Cincinnati in 1989 with a BS in computer sciences. During his career, he became convinced that he had made the right decision, and he would frequently advise young computer-science students to resist the temptation to leave school to take an attractive job offer. Though jobs are available to nongraduates, Irvin warned, real advancement can be limited without a college degree.

Irvin worked at MCI for six years, moving from Cincinnati to Chicago and Atlanta to the corporation's centers there. After transferring back to Chicago, he left MCI to take administrative positions in a number of other companies. From 1990 to 1992 he served as vice president of strategy, business development, and product management at Ameritech Small Business Services. He then became senior vice president of MFS Communications, presiding over that company's takeover of Internet service provider UUNET. He left MFS/UUNET in 1993 to take a position as president of the advanced data services division at eSpire, an information technology investment company. He advanced to become chief marketing officer at eSpire before leaving in 1995 to take a job at WorldCom.

Assumed International Role in Telecommunications Industry

In 1999 Irvin was hired away from WorldCom by another international telecommunications leader, British Telecom (BT). To take the position of senior vice president of marketing and Internet with BT, Irvin moved to London. Even though the job required a grueling commute across the Atlantic every other week to see his family and work at the BT North American center in northern Virginia, Irvin loved living in London and enjoyed traveling around the world as a representative of BT's international network. Through his job he met world leaders such as the French president Jacques Chirac and Jiang Zemin, president of the People's Republic of China. He especially enjoyed visiting Africa, where he met the South African Archbishop and activist Desmond Tutu.

Irvin left BT in 2002. After a year as executive vice president and general manager of the global communications, media, and entertainment division of American Management Systems, he was hired as executive vice president of VeriSign Telecommunication Services. Irvin's innovative work at VeriSign helped the corporation to double its earnings in just two years, boosting its gross income to $850 million. One of his biggest contributions to the telecommunications company was the concept of easily downloadable cellphone ringtones taken from popular songs. Irvin initiated VeriSign's acquisition of a German company

of Charity transferred him to Houston, Texas, where he continued his education at the University of Houston, earning an associate's degree while continuing to work in the field. In 1982 he took a job in the telecommunications division of Star Bank, heading their ATM and computer operations. After three years with Star Bank, he moved to Cincinnati, Ohio, and took a job with the telecommunications giant MCI.

Irvin found that his knowledge of computers had enabled to find him good jobs with prestigious companies even without a bachelor's degree. However, his called Jamsa that had created a number of downloadable options for cell phones, such as games, wallpaper, and ringtones. Expanding Jamsa's idea, Irvin created Jamster, which offered cell-phone users access to a wide variety of ringtones.

However, Irvin's contribution to VeriSign and to the mobile phone industry in general went beyond the addition of a few ringtones. Aware that cell-phone options were especially appealing to young audiences, he worked with music industry leaders to make the connection between cutting-edge hip-hop artists and the individual mobile phone. The broad marketing vision he had developed during his varied corporate career enabled him to understand that the telecommunications industry and the entertainment industry could develop a mutually beneficial relationship. He could not only use popular music to sell ringtones, he could use the sale of ringtones to promote rising musical stars, such as rapper Mike Jones, whose early career was boosted by Jamster. In addition, Irvin began to envision immediate mobile phone connections to music, photographs, and even television broadcasts. Irvin's innovations in telecommunications earned him the nickname of "ringtone czar."

In 2006 Irvin left VeriSign to take a position at XM Satellite Radio, where he has continued uniting technology and entertainment. As chief marketing officer for XM, he is responsible for market research, retail sales, and advertising. He has continued to reside in northern Virginia, where he spends rare leisure moments with his family. An avid golfer, he is also an amateur artist, creating sketches in charcoal and pastels.

Sources

Periodicals

Black Enterprise, July 2006, p. 65.
Inter@ctive Week, December 6, 1999, p. 18.
Pittsburgh Post-Gazette, February 7, 2006.
Telecommunications Reports, June 5, 1995, p. 36.
Wireless News, September 13, 2006.

Online

Bolden, Janeé, "Vernon Irvin: Ringtone Czar," *SOHH.com,* http://www.sohh.com/articles/article.php/8757 (accessed December 28, 2007).
"Convergence of Communication," *IT Conversations,* http://itc.conversationsnetwork.org/shows/detail1543.html (accessed December 28, 2007).
"Vernon Irvin," *Tavis Smiley Show,* http://www.pbs.org/kcet/tavissmiley/archive/200609/20060921_irvin.html (accessed December 28, 2007).
"Vernon Irvin," *Urban Influence Magazine,* http://www.urbaninfluencemagazine.com/Men%20of%20Influence_Profiles.pdf (accessed December 28, 2007).
"XM Satellite Radio Names Vernon Irvin as Chief Marketing Officer," *Orbitcast,* http://www.orbitcast.com/archives/xm-satellite-radio-names-vernon-irvin-as-chief-marketing-officer.html (accessed December 28, 2007).

Other

Information for this profile was obtained through an interview with Vernon Irvin on October 18, 2007.

—Tina Gianoulis

Al Jarreau

1940—

Vocalist

Jarreau, Al, photograph. Mike Stotts/WENN/Landov.

Al Jarreau became one of the world's foremost vocalists in the mid-1970s and continued to give crowd-pleasing performances into the twenty-first century. While his eclectic style is difficult to categorize, he has won fans of various genres, including rhythm and blues, jazz, and pop. Borrowing from the scat tradition that evolved out of the bebop style of the 1940s, Jarreau became known as the "Acrobat of Scat." His unique vocal delivery, combined with his creative fusion of diverse musical genres, has earned him many awards and contributed to his longevity as a recording artist.

Majored in Psychology

Jarreau was born Alwyn Lopez Jarreau on March 12, 1940, in Milwaukee, WI. His father was a minister and his mother played piano in church. Jarreau was the fifth of six children, and he became involved in music early on in life, singing at the age of four. The family lived across the street from a Catholic church, and even though the family was not Catholic, the music Jarreau heard from the church influenced his love of music. "I'm not a Catholic, but I felt real close to it," he told the

Chicago Tribune in 1992. "On Sunday mornings I was just hanging out with the paperboys, eating a sweet roll and drinking coffee. I heard the music of the Catholic church, and in parts of my music, it's in there."

Jarreau began singing in his own church and with neighborhood street harmony groups, filling whatever part was open. He sang in jazz bands in high school, but even then his musical repertoire was quite eclectic. "I know the lyrics to more polkas than most German and Czech people," he told the *Chicago Tribune*. "It's all in those wrinkled folds of gray matter."

While he never turned his back completely on his music, Jarreau put it on the back burner for a time after high school. He earned a degree in psychology from Ripon College in Wisconsin in 1962, and followed that with a master's degree from the University of Iowa in 1964. He then moved to San Francisco, where he worked as a rehabilitation counselor.

During his time in the Bay Area, music began to creep back into Jarreau's life. He began singing in nightclubs with a band called the Indigos, then landed a regular gig singing for the George Duke Trio three nights a week in clubs such as the Jazz Workshop, the Half Note, the Troubadour, and the Bitter West End. "I knew I would be doing music the rest of my life at some level, even if it was after work in a cocktail lounge in some Holiday Inn," he told the *Chicago Tribune.* In 1968 he finally achieved enough success to quit his day job. "I was just not ready for that kind of work," he told the *Tribune.* "I was inefficient or something. I got overwhelmed by it all…. After some talks with my supervisors, I told them, 'I'm off to join the circus,' and that was it."

Landed His First Record Contract

Jarreau's nightclub work began to expand, eventually branching out to include engagements in New York City. He crisscrossed the country for the next six years and performed on television variety shows on occasion. Jarreau was discovered in 1974, when he opened a show for Les McCann at the Troubadour in Hollywood. Several record company executives were in the audience, and his performance earned him a record contract. Two weeks later, he was in the studio recording his debut album.

That first album, *We Got By,* introduced the style that fans would expect from Jarreau over the years. Jon Hendricks and Dave Lambert have most often been identified as Jarreau's primary influences, but his scat style is very eclectic, with some of his vocals being described as sounding African, Oriental, or Arabic. It includes tongue clicks, gasps, and nonsense syllables. Some of his vocals do not fall within a jazz framework at all, but sound unmistakably like rhythm and blues or soul.

In 1976 Jarreau released his second album, *Glow*, and he toured Europe for the first time. That tour was a watershed event in his life, for it was on that continent that he would enjoy some of his most enduring popularity. His third album, *Look to the Rainbow* (1977), was a live album recorded in Europe, and it included a song that would become one of his trademarks, a vocal version of the Dave Brubeck standard "Take Five." This album won Jarreau his first Grammy.

Two more Grammy Awards followed in 1977 and 1978, when he was named Best Jazz Vocal Performance. His 1980 album, *This Time,* brought in a new producer, Jay Graydon, and a focus on the material over Jarreau's personal style.

In 1981 Jarreau saw his breakthrough as a commercial pop artist. His album that year produced his fourth Grammy and two hit singles: "We're in This Love Together," which emphasized his pop singing ability more than his jazz style, and the title cut, "Breakin' Away." The following year saw another hit single, "Teach Me Tonight." He continued to record and tour throughout the 1980s and enjoyed an unusual amount of commercial success for a jazz artist.

Was Successful Because He Toured

His commercial success, though, came primarily from his singles, and not, despite the platinum status of *Breakin' Away,* from his albums. "I'm not one of those fortunate recording artists who have the luxury of continually producing big-selling albums," he admitted to the *Los Angeles Times* in 1986. "I really have remained alive as a recording artist because I'm out there touring a lot. People come to hear the Al Jarreau live concerts and, fortunately, some of them buy records."

One of the keys to Jarreau's commercial success was his appeal to music fans who were younger than the typical jazz fan. His fusion of other contemporary styles into his music brought him popularity with people who were not, strictly speaking, jazz fans. But as the 1990s dawned and Jarreau turned fifty, he began having more difficulty selling records to the younger demographic, and his sales began to slump. Four years passed between his last album of the 1980s, *Heart's Horizon,* and his first of the 1990s, *Heaven and Earth,* which won him his fifth Grammy Award in 1992. He kept busy in the interim by contributing songs to the films *Skin Deep* and *Do the Right Thing.* On *Heaven and Earth,* he tried to reclaim his share of the youth market by, as he told the *Chicago Tribune,* leaning "hard on my R&B side. I see that the R&B scene is changing. It's a revolution.... The music is live and angry. I see my fans saying, 'What in the world is going on?' I say to them, 'While you listen to rap and scratch, take this album along with you as an alternative.'"

Misfortune struck Jarreau in late 1995, when his home in Encino, California, was damaged by an earthquake. It was also about this time that his contract with Warner Brothers ran out after twenty years. He recorded a few new songs for a greatest hits package in 1996, but it was unclear whether the contract would be renewed, and the impasse led to some hard feelings on Jarreau's part. "They sit there and throw handfuls of artist mud against the wall," he complained about the record business to the *Los Angeles Times.* "And what sticks they go and build a frame around for a few minutes. And I can tell you it's not a gilded frame in which they've invested a whole lot. What they really want is these still wet-behind-the-ears people who will color their hair a strange color, turn their lives over to some hot producer, be there for five minutes of airplay in a year, get their pictures in a magazine and then be gone. They don't want to deal with someone who understands the mechanism of this madness."

Preferred Live Performances to Recording

Jarreau had never been completely comfortable with the recording process, and he gave the impression that it would not be the worst thing for him if he had to return to making a living doing one-nighters across the country. He told the *Los Angeles Times,* "Everything that's happened for me up to now has worked because I go out there and I do a good show. I've been doing that for more than 20 years, and that's got nothing to do with the record company. I've stayed alive in the record business because I've been out there being a salesman, telling people, 'Listen to this.' They listen and bring a friend back, and that friend goes and buys a record and that's my new customer. I'll keep pounding on people's doors, and just keep on doing what I've been doing, asking them to listen to the songs I have to sing."

Jarreau also told the *Los Angeles Times* that he remained optimistic about his future. "It's been a good career," he asserted. "Am I concerned about where things now stand with my recordings? Sure. I'm as nervous as a frog on a freeway. I keep waiting for one of the shoes to fall. But I have high hopes, high apple pie in the sky hopes, and I'm still thinking that there's

some serious success ahead of me."

In 2000 Jarreau began recording music for GRP Records, a subsidiary of the Universal Music Group, with whom he produced two highly successful albums: *Tomorrow Today* (2000) and *All I Got* (2002), which debuted at number three on *Billboard*'s Contemporary Jazz Album rankings. In 2001, in acknowledgment of his lifetime achievement in music, Jarreau received a star on the Hollywood Walk of Fame. Even though Jarreau was forced to take a hiatus from touring in September of 2002, for surgery related to a compressed spinal column, he soon returned to the stage and completed a European tour in 2003.

In 2004 he released *Accentuate the Positive,* which diplayed Jarreau's lyricism set to sparse accompaniment. The album received critical praise and was nominated for a Grammy Award for best jazz vocal album in 2005. In 2006 Jarreau teamed with jazz guitarist George Benson for *Givin' it Up,* which became one of Jarreau's most popular albums. At the Forty-ninth Grammy Awards in 2006, Jarreau and Benson shared the award for Best Traditional R&B Vocal Performance for the song "God Bless the Child."

After winning his sixth Grammy Award in 2006, Jarreau continued traveling and performing across the United States and abroad. During a busy 2007 touring season, Jarreau visited Denmark, Germany, and France. As he has transitioned from popular music through jazz and R&B to adult contemporary, Jarreau continued to gain fans with his enthusiasm and infectious energy. When asked about his feelings on being a vocal artist in a 2005 interview with Ed Gordon of the National Public Radio, Jarreau said he wanted to impart a positive message telling each member of his audience, "You are a child of god and you can have a good day if you work on it."

Selected discography

Albums

We Got By, Warner Brothers, 1975.
Glow, Warner Brothers, 1976.
Look to the Rainbow, Warner Brothers, 1977.
All Fly Home, Warner Brothers, 1978.
This Time, Warner Brothers, 1980.
Breakin' Away, Warner Brothers, 1981.
Heart's Horizon, Warner Brothers, 1988.
Heaven and Earth, Warner Brothers, 1992.
Tenderness, Warner Brothers, 1994.
Tomorrow Today, GRP Records, 2000.
All I Got, GRP Records, 2002.
Accentuate the Positive, Verve Records, 2004.
Givin' it Up, Concord Music, 2006.

Sources

Books

Kernfeld, Barry, ed., *The New Grove Dictionary of Jazz,* Volume 1, St. Martin, 1994.

Larkin, Colin, ed., *The Guinness Encyclopedia of Popular Music,* Volume 3, Groves Dictionaries, 1995.

Nite, Norm N., with Charles Crespo, *Rock On: The Illustrated Encyclopedia of Rock 'n' Roll—The Video Revolution,* HarperCollins Children's Books, 1978.

Salzman, Jack, David Lionel Smith, and Cornel West, eds., *Encyclopedia of African-American Culture and History,* Volume 3, Macmillan Library Reference, 1996.

Periodicals

Billboard, September 13, 2002; August 1, 2004.

Chicago Tribune, July 30, 1992.

Los Angeles Times, December 26, 1986; August 31, 1989; May 29, 1997.

Online

Gordon, Ed, "Al Jarreau: 'Accentuate the Positive,'" *National Public Radio,* http://www.npr.org/templates/story/story.php?storyId=4494961 (accessed December 19, 2007).

—Mike Eggert and Micah L. Issit

Edith Mae Irby Jones

1927—

Medical doctor

Almost a decade before the civil rights movement began gathering strength, a dedicated young African-American woman from Arkansas challenged the system of segregated education in the southern United States. Edith Irby Jones made headlines in newspapers across the nation in 1952, when she became the first black woman to graduate from a white medical college in the South. In the face of such obstacles as poverty, prejudice, and institutional racism, Jones had achieved her goal of becoming a doctor, driven by a determination to increase access to medical care for the poor and people of color. By quietly refusing to accept the limits put on her life by a segregated society, she not only built a successful medical career but also used the fruits of her success to establish clinics in areas crushed by poverty and set up a scholarship fund to help other young people enter the field of medicine.

Edith Mae Irby was born on December 23, 1927, in Conway, Arkansas, the daughter of Robert Irby and Mattie Buice Irby. Her mother worked as a cook and housecleaner, and her father was a sharecropper, a kind of tenant farmer common among former slaves and their descendants in the post–Civil War South. Sharecroppers were allowed to live on and farm land they did not own in exchange for a share of the crops they produced. It was typically an insecure and unbalanced situation for the sharecroppers, as the landowners kept most of the profit and shared little with those who actually worked the farms.

Determined to Become a Doctor

Jones's childhood was marked by sadness and loss. She survived a severe illness at the age of five to lose her older sister a year later to typhoid fever. Even at the age of six, Jones noticed that in the homes of her neighbors who could afford medical care, those who had the fever often survived. She began to believe that her twelve-year-old sister had died because her own family could only pay for one visit from the doctor. She decided then that she would become a children's doctor and treat everyone who needed her, regardless of race or ability to pay. Several other members of Jones's family died of typhoid during her childhood, strengthening her resolve to be a doctor.

Robert Irby accompanied his family to church and taught his children about the importance of contributing to their community. Though his lessons would remain important to her throughout her life, Jones lost her father, too, at an early age. She was only eight years old when he was killed in a riding accident. Mattie Irby moved her family to the resort city of Hot Springs, Arkansas, where she found work as a cook.

Jones began attending segregated black public schools in Hot Springs at the age of ten. Before that, she had been educated at home, where she became an avid reader, finishing the encyclopedia and the works of William Shakespeare, John Milton, and Robert Louis Stevenson. She loved Stevenson's writing so much that, when she was allowed choose names for her two

At a Glance . . .

Born Edith Mae Irby on December 23, 1927, in Conway, AR; daughter of Robert and Mattie Buice Irby; married James Beauregard Jones, 1950; children: Gary, Myra, and Keith; seven grandchildren. *Education:* Knoxville College, BS in biology, chemistry, and physics, 1948; University of Arkansas School of Medicine, MD, 1952.

Career: University of Arkansas Hospital, intern, 1952–53; private medical practice, Hot Springs, Arkansas, 1953–59; Baylor College of Medicine Affiliated Hospitals, resident in internal medicine, 1959–62; private medical practice, Houston, Texas, 1962—; Universal Healthplan, Inc., medical director, 1997—; Jones, Coleman, and Whitfield, partner; Jones Properties, co-owner, chief executive officer.

Memberships: American Medical Women's Association; National Council of Negro Women; National Medical Association, president, 1985–86; Planned Parenthood, Physicians for Human Rights.

Awards: National Council of Negro Women, Houston Section, Distinguished Service Award, 1972; National Black College Alumni Hall of Fame, 1985; Delta Sigma Theta, Award for Outstanding Accomplishments, 1998; United Negro College Fund, Award for Contribution to the Health of Haiti, 2000; University of Arkansas, Fayetteville Campus, Silas Hunt Legacy Award, 2006.

Addresses: *Home*—3402 S. Parkwood Dr., Houston, TX 77021.

baby brothers, she named them Robert and Louis. She loved school, and, besides excelling in her regular classes, she learned shorthand and became an expert typist, able to type 120 words per minute. By the time she was fourteen, she was able to contribute to the family's income with a secretarial business, offering transcription and typing services to the vacationers who came to Hot Springs for the healthful mineral baths.

When Jones graduated with honors from Langston High School in 1944, a supportive teacher helped her obtain a scholarship to Knoxville College, a historically black college in Tennessee. Still driven by her ambition

to practice medicine, she mastered an unusually heavy course load to major in biology, chemistry, and physics. In 1948 she earned a bachelor's degree and graduated with high honors. She took the medical college admissions tests and placed among the top thirty applicants in the nation. She then took a historic step: applying for admission to the all-white University of Arkansas School of Medicine.

Broke Barriers of Race and Gender

Though the University of Arkansas School of Medicine had never had a black student, the board of admissions complied with a recent decision of the U.S. Supreme Court against segregated education. They accepted Edith Irby's application, and in the fall of 1948 she became the first African-American student to enter a southern university since the Reconstruction period following the Civil War. The university's decision made national news, and Jones found out about her acceptance when a reporter from *Time* magazine called to ask for her reaction.

When Jones was accepted for admission, tuition at the University of Arkansas was $500 per semester, an astronomical sum for a young woman from a poor family. However, her community was behind her, and, through the efforts of teachers and alumni of her former high school, friends, neighbors, and a Little Rock black newspaper called the *Arkansas State Press,* money was raised to pay her academic fees and living expenses. She arrived for her first day in medical school with her first semester's tuition money in nickels, dimes, and quarters, the way it had been collected from people who wanted to contribute, but had little to give. It was this support from her community that gave Jones the courage to face the difficult years ahead, as the only black and one of very few women studying medicine in Arkansas.

Though the university had accepted Jones as a student, its facilities were still segregated, and, as the only black student, she faced isolation in a separate dining room, bathroom, and study area. However, even in this atmosphere of prejudice, there were gestures of support. The mostly black custodial staff cheered Jones by placing flowers each day in her segregated dining area, and some white students befriended her and shared her separate restroom and study area. One white woman in Jones's class rode with her to school on the bus each day, standing with Jones so they could ride together and talk without violating the segregated seating policy. Jones's hard work and openness made her so popular with her classmates that, after graduation, she was named alumni contact person for her year. During her second year of medical school she met and married James B. Jones, a college professor who became one of her most devoted supporters.

Jones graduated from the University of Arkansas School of Medicine in 1952, in the top half of her class.

She worked at the university hospital for a year as a pediatric intern, fulfilling her childhood desire to become a children's doctor. Following her internship, she returned home to Hot Springs and set up a private practice. While working as a doctor in Hot Springs, Jones also became involved in the growing civil rights movement, working with such well-known leaders as Martin Luther King Jr. With three attorneys, she became part of a group of speakers known as the "Freedom Four," who traveled throughout the South, encouraging African Americans in their struggle for civil rights. During the late 1950s, increasing racial tension in Arkansas prompted the Jones family to move to Houston, Texas.

Opened Private Practice in Houston

After six years in her own medical practice, Jones developed a strong interest in internal medicine, the field of general adult medicine. Once again breaking barriers, she applied and was accepted for a residency to study internal medicine at the all-white Baylor College of Medicine in Houston, becoming that institution's first black resident. She was assigned to work at a segregated hospital, where she once again found herself a victim of isolation and discrimination. Finally frustrated, she transferred to the Freedman's Hospital, an African-American hospital established in 1863 in Washington, D.C., where she finished her residency.

After completing her training in internal medicine in 1962, Jones established a private practice in Houston's third ward, a largely black, low-income inner city area. True to her childhood vow, she devoted her career to those who could least afford medical care. While tending to her patients, she took an active part in many organizations, becoming, in 1975, the first woman to chair the National Medical Association's (NMA) Council on Scientific Assembly. The NMA was founded in 1895 as a support organization for African-American physicians. In 1985 Jones became the first woman president of the NMA, where she worked to make black doctors more visible and accessible in the larger society. Jones has also had a distinguished career as a staff doctor at several Houston hospitals, including St. Elizabeth's, where she served as chief of cardiology, and Riverside General Hospital, where she was both associate chief of medicine and chief of medical staff. She also worked as medical director for the health management organization Universal Healthplan of Texas.

Remembering her father's early lessons in giving back to her community, Jones has always shared her success. Along with the Edith Irby Jones Healthcare Center in Houston, which has many programs for underserved communities, Jones created the Edith Irby Jones Foundation to provide scholarships for those who, like her, dream of becoming a doctor, but cannot afford tuition to medical school. In 1986, as chief of a U.S. Task Force on Health, she visited the Caribbean island nation of Haiti to pinpoint causes and solutions for severe health problems there. As a result of that visit, she not only established a health clinic for impoverished patients but also arranged for the drilling of several wells to provide much-needed drinking water. She also set up and continues to support urgent care clinics in Veracruz, Mexico, and in the African nation of Uganda.

Not content merely to contribute in the field of health, Jones has also devoted her energy to the issue of affordable housing. With her husband, she started a real estate business to buy and renovate homes, then make them available to low-income families at very low rent. The Joneses have also been involved with Habitat for Humanity, a community-based program that builds affordable housing.

Jones's multifaceted career has won recognition and respect from many different organizations. Besides honors in the field of medicine, such as being named Internist of the Year in 1988 by the American Society of Internal Medicine and earning recognition for leadership support from the Association of Black Cardiologists in 1992, she has received numerous awards for community service. In 1979 the state of Arkansas proclaimed Edith Irby Jones Day, and in 2000 she received the first ever Volunteerism and Community Service Award from the Texas Academy of Internal Medicine. Jones remains in Houston and continues her active medical practice into her eighties.

Sources

Books

Brew, Lydia E., *The Story of Edith Irby Jones, M.D.,* NRT, 1986.

Pierce, P. J., "Edith Irby Jones," in *Texas Wisewomen Speak: Let Me Tell You What I've Learned,* University of Texas Press, 2002, pp. 136–139.

Periodicals

Arkansas Democrat-Gazette, April 29, 2006; September 13, 2007.

Ebony, June 1986, pp. 90–96; July 2000, p. 35.

Jet, January 27, 1986.

Life, January 31, 1949.

Online

"Dr. Edith Irby Jones," *National Library of Medicine,* http://www.nlm.nih.gov/changingthefaceofmedicine/physicians/biography_175.html (accessed December 28, 2007).

"Edith Irby Jones," *Notable Black American Women,* Book 2, Gale Research, 1996. Reproduced in *Biog-*

raphy Resource Center, http://galenet.galegroup.com/servlet/BioRC (accessed December 28, 2007).

"Edith Irby Jones, M.D.," *National Library of Medicine,* http://www.nlm.nih.gov/locallegends/Biographies/Jones_Edith.html (accessed December 28, 2007).

"Edith Mae Irby Jones," *Notable Black American Scientists,* Gale Research, 1998. Reproduced in *Biography Resource Center,* http://galenet.gale group.com/servlet/BioRC (accessed December 28, 2007).

Park, Carolyne, "Fayetteville: Law, Medicine Pioneers Reflect on Early Struggles," *NWANews.com,* http://www.nwanews.com/adg/News/201298/ (accessed December 28, 2007).

—Tina Gianoulis

Elijah Kelley

1986—

Actor, singer, dancer

Kelley, Elijah, photograph. PHOTOPRO/Landov.

Actor Elijah Kelley was born into a family grounded in both religion and music. His performing career, which started at the age of three when he joined a family gospel group, has grown and developed quickly. Only a few years after arriving in Los Angeles looking for work as an entertainer, Kelley made his mark in Hollywood with a role in the 2007 hit film *Hairspray*. His talent, versatility, and unaffected good sense contribute to the likelihood that Kelley's rapid climb marks the beginning of a memorable career.

Kelley was born on August 1, 1986, in LaGrange, Georgia, a small town not far from the Alabama state line in the northwestern part of the state. His family had a deep interest in gospel music, a type of Christian music characterized by powerful vocals and complex harmonies. Gospel music is heavily influenced by African-American spirituals, which in turn owe a debt to the rhythms and shouts of African music. Gospel is frequently also a family tradition, with many singing groups made up of members of the same family. Elijah Kelley joined his family's gospel quartet, the Leonard Family, when he was only three years old.

Performed in Commercials, Television During Childhood

By the time he was seven years old, Kelley knew that he wanted to be a performer, not only a singer but also an actor. His mother, Evalene Flournoy, encouraged and supported her son's ambition. When Kelley was eleven, she took him to the nearby city of Atlanta to answer a newspaper advertisement seeking talented youth. An agent gave Kelley a piece of chewing gum and challenged him to create a commercial for it on the spot. His original improvisation led to a contract with a theatrical agent, his first paid acting jobs in soft drink commercials, and roles in two made-for-television films. In 1998 he played Young Willie in the 1998 movie *Mama Flora's Family,* directed by Peter Werner and based on an Alex Haley novel about several generations in a postslavery African-American family. The following year he took the role of Clarence in Joseph Sargent's 1999 film *A Lesson Before Dying,* a sensitive look at the effects of racism in the American South during the 1940s. He made his film debut in the

Betty Thomas film *28 Days* (2000), starring Sandra Bullock. Kelley played the role of Darnell in the film, which chronicles a celebrity's experience in a drug and alcohol rehabilitation program.

Though Kelley was well on his way to a successful acting career before he had finished middle school, he also began to display qualities of forethought and responsibility. At the age of fourteen, he backed away from a professional performing career in favor of finishing high school at LaGrange's Troop County High School. After his graduation in 2004, he decided to move to the entertainment industry center of Los Angeles, California, to continue developing his acting career. To help their youngest child and ensure that he had family support and love surrounding him during his search for success, his parents decided to move to California with him.

Kelley's many talents and engaging personality began to win him roles almost as soon as he arrived in Los Angeles. In 2005 and 2006 he was hired to appear in several episodes of the cable police drama *The Shield,* the CW network situation comedy *Everybody Hates Chris,* and the CBS criminal investigation series *Numb3rs.* Showing a persistent energy and drive, he also managed to perform in three different films in 2006: the Charles T. Kanganis update of William Shakespeare's *Romeo and Juliet,* titled *Rome and Jewel*; Liz Friedlander's story of ballroom dance in the inner city, *Take the Lead*; and *Heavens Fall,* a dramatization of a true story of racism and the justice system, directed by Terry Green.

Besides his rapidly rising acting career, Kelley also began to cultivate a career as a singer, songwriter, and record producer. He performed as a singer in Las Vegas, Nevada, wrote and produced songs for such well-known singers as Omarion and Diana Ross, and began planning his own rhythm and blues album.

Gained Recognition for Role in Hairspray

Kelley's breakout role came when he was cast to play Seaweed J. Stubbs in the 2007 film *Hairspray,* directed by Adam Shankman. A musical version of the 1988 John Waters film, *Hairspray* is a zany satire about racism, prejudice, and forbidden love in 1960s Baltimore. Kelley's audition so impressed the filmmakers that they gave him the part even before they had cast the lead role. After opening in thousands of theaters across the United States during the summer of 2007, *Hairspray* received positive reviews and went on to become one of the most financially successful musicals in movie history. Many critics noted the standout performance of a relative newcomer in the role of Seaweed J. Stubbs, a fast-talking, hot-dancing, black high school student who falls for a white girl in his class. Though Kelley's role is not a starring one, he captured the attention of audiences and critics alike with his show-stopping number "Run and Tell That."

Kelley was delighted to be part of the *Hairspray* cast, working with such veteran performers as John Travolta and Queen Latifah. As much as he enjoyed the chance to demonstrate his skill as a singer and dancer, he also appreciated the film's joyful message of self-acceptance, tolerance, and celebration of diversity. As an African American, he had, of course, felt the effects of prejudice and racism, and, in preparing for his role, he spent time talking to his parents and grandparents about their experiences during the 1960s.

Kelley's role in *Hairspray* pushed his career from success to stardom. Having shown he could captivate a movie audience, he began receiving offers for leading roles in other films, such as a production for New Line Cinema titled *Party Up.* From the beginning of his show business career, Kelley has aspired to be an old-style entertainer, versatile, classy, and committed to his craft, in the tradition of such legends as Sammy Davis Jr., Frank Sinatra, and Marvin Gaye.

Even during this early phase of his career, Kelley was committed to sharing his success with others. In 2007 he joined the advisory board of *Variety* magazine's Power of Youth, a charitable organization founded by the entertainment journal.

Selected works

Films

Mama Flora's Family, 1998.
A Lesson Before Dying, 1999.
28 Days, 2000.
Heavens Fall, 2006.
Rome and Jewel, 2006.
Take the Lead, 2006.
Hairspray, 2007.

Sources

Periodicals

Daily Variety, August 21, 2007, pp. 4–6.
Los Angeles Times, July 14, 2007.
Time, July 30, 2007, p. 56.
USA Today, July 23, 2007.

Online

"Amanda Bynes, Elijah Kelley Interview, Hairspray," *Movies Online,* http://www.moviesonline.ca/movie news_12420.html (accessed December 28, 2007).

Barnes, Brad, "LaGrange to Honor Local 'Hairspray' Star," *Ledger-Enquirer,* http://www.ledger-enquirer. com/news/breaking_news/story/89011.html (accessed December 28, 2007).

Boyd, Betsy, "Up Next: Elijah Kelley," *Variety,* http://www.variety.com/article/VR1117973336.html?ca tegoryid=2721&cs=1 (accessed December 28, 2007).

"Elijah Kelley," *My Space,* http://profile.myspace. com/index.cfm?fuseaction=user.viewprofile&frien did=192892011 (accessed December 28, 2007).

Philadelphia, Desa, "Elijah Kelley Has the Total Package," *USA Weekend,* http://www.usaweekend. com/07_issues/070715/070715elijah_kelley.html (accessed December 28, 2007).

—Tina Gianoulis

Reatha Clark King

1938—

Chemist, educator

Reatha Clark King is a chemist whose long scientific career includes breakthroughs in fluoride research that advanced the National Aeronautics and Space Administration's (NASA) space program. She has devoted the second half of her career as an educator and administrator to expanding opportunities for education available to students from poor backgrounds.

Seized Educational Opportunities

Reatha Belle Clark King was born on April 11, 1938, in Pavo, Georgia, one of three children born to Willie and Ola Watts Campbell Clark. Her parents, an illiterate farm worker and a domestic servant, divorced when she was young. King's mother then moved with her children to Moultree, Georgia, where she found work as a maid. King's early life centered around the institutions of church and school, although the family was so poor that she often had to leave school to pick cotton or tobacco for $3 per day. "Those were bitter moments," King recalls in the book *True North: Discover Your Authentic Leadership* by Bill George, "because white children didn't have to leave school. That contrast was so clear and so wrong."

She found strength in the Mt. Zion Baptist Church, where the older women, known as "sisters," were well aware of King's keen intellect and strong work ethic: "They kept an eye on me, and encouraged me to overcome unjust barriers against black people," she told George. King graduated from high school in 1954 as the valedictorian of her class.

King attended Clark College in Atlanta on a scholarship. She planned to become a high school home economics teacher, so she could help her family financially, but her life dramatically changed direction when she enrolled in an introductory chemistry class required for her major. The professor, Alfred Spriggs, was an African-American chemist with a doctoral degree from Washington University. His dynamic teaching style inspired King to change her career path and pursue a doctorate. Her older sister, who had joined the U.S. Army Nurse Corps, offered to support the family so that King could go to graduate school. King majored in physical chemistry at the University of Chicago, focusing on thermochemistry. She received her doctorate in 1963.

Excelled in Academia

After a six-month job search, King accepted a research position with the National Bureau of Standards in Washington, D.C. Her first goal as a team leader was to develop a material able to contain the corrosive compound oxygen difluoride. King's discoveries regarding the effect of heat on metallic alloys—specifically, her invention of a coiled tube that allowed hot liquids such as fuel to cool instead of exploding—were crucial for rocket design in the NASA space program. King was known at the bureau for her dedication and professionalism, often staying at the lab overnight to analyze new data. She was cited with an outstanding performance rating and won the Meritorious Publication Award for a paper on fluorine flame calorimetry (the science of

At a Glance . . .

Born Reatha Belle Clark on April 11, 1938, in Pavo, GA; daughter of Willie and Ola Watts Campbell Clark; married N. Judge King, 1961; children: N. Judge III, Scott. *Education:* Clark College, BS in chemistry and math, 1958; University of Chicago, PhD in physical chemistry, 1963; Columbia University, MBA, 1977.

Career: National Bureau of Standards, researcher, 1963–68; York College, assistant dean of natural sciences and mathematics, 1969–77; Metropolitan State University, president, 1977–88; General Mills Foundation, president and executive director, and General Mills, Inc., vice president, 1988–2002; University of Minnesota, Louis W. Hill Fellow, 2002—.

Memberships: Exxon Mobil Corp., board member; Lenox Group Inc., board member; International Trachoma Initiative, board member; National Association of Corporate Directors, board member; University of Chicago, life trustee.

Awards: Exceptional Black Scientist Award, CIBA-GEIGY Corporation, 1984; Twin Citian of the Year, Minneapolis–St. Paul, Minnesota, 1988; International Adult and Continuing Education Hall of Fame, inductee, 1996; named one of *Ebony* magazine's Top 50 Black Executives in Corporate America, 1992; received honorary doctorate degrees from numerous institutions of higher education.

Addresses: *Work*—Lenox Group Inc., One Village Pl., Eden Prairie, MN 55344.

measuring the heat of chemical reactions). King was keenly aware of the additional hurdles represented by both her race and gender. "You had to reach down deep," she says in *True North*, " to reinforce your courage."

King returned to academia in 1968 to teach at York College, an inner-city school in New York City, where she was soon appointed assistant dean of natural sciences and mathematics. During this time, she also obtained a master's degree in business administration from Columbia University. King left York in 1977 to assume the presidency of Metropolitan State University in Minneapolis, Minnesota. At Metro State, King

worked tirelessly to increase educational opportunities for women and minorities. During her tenure, the college increased its number of graduates fivefold. "I realized early in life," King said to Christine Reslmaier, "that education is our best enabling resource, that technical skills are important, and that my stamina for championing educational opportunity for all people is inexhaustible."

While at Metro State, King was asked by the chief executive officer of General Mills to become president and executive director of the General Mills Foundation, as well as vice president of General Mills, Inc., positions she accepted in 1988. Over the course of the next fourteen years, she increased the charitable organization's assets from under $7 million to over $50 million and oversaw the distribution of $50 million in grants, much of it earmarked for programs helping African Americans gain access to higher education. King also spearheaded a number of community programs, including the "Hawthorne Huddle," a crime-prevention initiative in Minneapolis that has put the tremendous resources of the General Mills Foundation at the disposal of disadvantaged communities since 1997.

Recognized for Diverse Achievements

"My reasons for leading," King said in *True North*, "were not centered on my needs but on the needs of my people, of women, and of my community." She explained, "The question is, what do people lead toward? I'm leading toward a cause: to get more opportunities for people. It is in my blood to remove unjust barriers and to help people appreciate themselves and be who they are."

King has received more than a dozen honorary doctorates from institutions of higher learning, including Empire State College, Marymount Manhattan College, Smith College, and the William-Mitchell College of Law. She has received the Exceptional Black Scientist Award from CIBA-GEIGY Corporation, been named one of *Ebony* magazine's Top 50 Black Executives, and received a Lifetime Achievement in Philanthropy Award from the National Center for Black Philanthropy. She was named Twin Citian of 1988 for Minneapolis–St. Paul, Minnesota.

In 1996 King was inducted into the International Adult and Continuing Education Hall of Fame. After accepting that honor, King said, "I know that the individual who pursues continuing education and lifelong learning is continually equipped to overcome social barriers to opportunity.... The best gift any person can give another is the encouragement and actual assistance that the person needs to continue his or her education."

King retired from General Mills in 2002, although she continues to serve on five nonprofit boards and three corporate boards and maintains an active schedule of writing and public speaking. King is married to N. Judge King, a chemist, with whom she has two sons, N. Judge III and Scott.

Sources

Books

George, Bill, *True North: Discover Your Authentic Leadership,* Jossey-Bass, 2007.
Notable Scientists: From 1900 to the Present, Gale Group, 2001.

Periodicals

Philanthropy Journal, June 20, 2005.
Woodrow Wilson in Focus, Fall 2005.

Online

"From the Bench to the Boardroom," *NOBCChE News Online,* Spring 2007, http://www.nobcche.org/_cms/tools/act_Download.cfm?FileID=149&/2007%20NNOL%20Spring.pdf (accessed December 27, 2007).
"Reatha Clark King," *International Adult and Continuing Education Hall of Fame,* http://www.halloffame.outreach.ou.edu/1996/kingr.html (accessed December 27, 2007).
"Reatha Clark King," *Biography Resource Center,* http:/galenet.galegroup.com/servlet/BioRC (accessed December 27, 2007).

—Roger K. Smith

Marquita Lister

1965(?)—

Opera singer

Marquita Lister is a soprano who began her career with the Houston Grand Opera in the early 1990s and since then has stunned audiences in several lead roles. Her repertoire includes title roles in the operas *Porgy and Bess* and *Salome,* but it is as the eponymous African princess in *Aida* that she garnered her first serious critical attention. *Boston Herald* critic T. J. Medrek asserted that Lister's "voice isn't beautiful," after reviewing her in a 2001 Montreal performance of *Aida,* "but it's got character and a pleasing touch of gold. It's also rock-solid and large enough to penetrate the biggest ensembles. And her technique is such that she can scale it down with great poise for the lyrical passages."

Lister grew up in Washington, D.C., and was raised in a family that emphasized academic achievement. In a joint interview with famed Hispanic-American soprano Martina Arroyo that was conducted by *Opera News* writer Ira Siff, she recounted the first inkling of her future career. "When I was in junior high school, the choir director called my mother and said, 'Your daughter has something kind of special, and I think you need to look into that and see if it's something she'd honestly like to pursue,'" Lister recalled. Subsequently, she enrolled in the local performing arts high school, Western High School, located in the Georgetown section of the city. She spent just a year there, however, before her parents deemed it not academically rigorous enough, and she returned to her regular school.

Entered Houston Training Program

As a teen, Lister began entering voice competitions sponsored by the National Association of Teachers of Singing, and then entered Boston's New England Conservatory of Music. It was there, she said in the *Opera News* interview, that one of her first mentors explained to her "that you have to develop pointy elbows to be in the opera world. What I think he meant where I was concerned was that I was the kid that loved everybody. I was the one who wanted to help everyone. And he said that there is a protectiveness that you have to have about yourself in order to pursue this career, because it's so demanding on you, of your time, your energy. Not everyone is destined to be a superstar."

Following her graduation from the New England Conservatory, Lister was invited to join a training program for opera hopefuls run by the Houston Grand Opera. In 1990 the Houston officials offered her the title role in *Aida* when they were planning the 1993 season. Nervous about accepting the demanding lead, she tracked down Arroyo and telephoned her to ask for advice. In the joint interview, Lister recalled that Arroyo posed several questions, then concluded that because the date was three years from then, Lister would probably have enough time to adequately prepare herself for the job.

Aida, Giuseppe Verdi's 1871 classic about a kidnapped Ethiopian princess brought to Egypt during the time of the pharaohs, was a choice opera for a soprano

At a Glance . . .

Born c. 1965. *Education:* Studied at the New England Conservatory of Music.

Career: Began performing career with the Houston Grand Opera, early 1990s; appeared with the Opéra de Montréal, Utah Opera, New York City Opera, Boston Lyric Opera, Connecticut Opera, Orlando Opera, Atlanta Opera, Detroit Opera Theater, and Opera Memphis.

Addresses: *Agent*—James W. Dietsch, Dietsch International, Thierschstrasse 11, 80538 Munich, Germany.

of color, and after Lister's debut in it in April of 1993, it soon became her signature role. She appeared in the title role again in October of 1994 at the Utah Opera and began to receive favorable notice in national publications. Writing in *Opera News,* Dorothy Stowe noted that Lister "displayed an ample, free soprano, never overblown or pushed out of focus," and deemed her "well suited to the Ethiopian princess physically, emotionally and vocally."

Won Accolades in Porgy and Bess

In early 1995 Lister took on another career-defining role, this one with historic resonance for the Houston Grand Opera. It restaged George Gershwin's landmark 1935 opera *Porgy and Bess,* twenty years since the venue had rescued the African-American-themed work from obscurity and mounted it in the original three-hour version that Gershwin had intended for it. Back in 1935, when *Porgy and Bess* first debuted in New York City, it created a minor firestorm of controversy, in part for its use of authentic African-American musical rhythms, but also for its depiction of life in Catfish Row, the African-American neighborhood of Charleston, South Carolina. Even leading African Americans of the day objected to some of its more realistic elements, and the opera was shortened for a more mainstream audience and then largely forgotten. The Houston Grand Opera's revival in 1975 was a stunning success, and *Porgy and Bess* went on to a successful international tour and has since become a staple in the repertoire of many U.S. opera companies.

When the Houston Grand Opera restaged *Porgy and Bess* in 1995, there was a much larger pool of professional African-American singers who could take the lead roles than there had been back in Gershwin's day, or even in 1975. Lister was part of that new generation and scored excellent reviews for her por-

trayal. Like Aida, Bess, too, is imprisoned—but by her drug habit. She escapes her pimp, Crown, for a time, finding solace with Porgy, a disabled beggar. "Lister brought a big, lush voice and alluring beauty to the role of Bess," asserted *New York Times* critic Anthony Tommasini. "The man who keeps her, the conniving drug pusher Crown, as portrayed by the dashing baritone Timothy Robert Blevins, was everything Gershwin must have envisioned: hunky, seductive and dangerous."

Another terrifically dramatic part also became part of Lister's repertoire beginning in 1999 with her debut in Richard Strauss's *Salome.* The 1905 opera is based on a play by British dramatist Oscar Wilde and recounts the biblical story of John the Baptist, the apostle who was said to have baptized Jesus. According to one of the Gospels, he caught the eye of the spoiled, bewitching stepdaughter of King Herod, the ruler of Judea placed in power during the time of the Roman conquest of the area. Salome reportedly tried to seduce John the Baptist but he rebuffed her, and she then demanded—and received—his head on a platter after complaining to Herod. As Lister told Siff in the *Opera News* interview, she was initially reluctant to take the role. "Given the Christian background I came from, the idea of asking for the head of this great saint was repulsive to me. And then, in my research, realizing it was the mother [Herodias] who coaxed her into asking for this head made it a little more palatable for me." She said she also worked with the director, and "we spent a lot of time exploring her, so that she fit into my skin. Then, once I got it, I really fell in love with her."

Stunned as Salome

For *Salome* Lister earned some of the strongest accolades of her career. Medrek, writing in the *Boston Herald,* called her appearance with the Boston Lyric Opera in their production "a stunning, revelatory performance.... With a voice unleashing torrents of burnished silver, and with every bone and sinew in her body, Lister transformed herself completely into the terrible Judean princess who demands—and gets—the severed head of John the Baptist delivered to her on a silver platter." Reviewing it for *Opera News,* Deborah Weisgall noted that "Lister commanded the stage from her entrance to her final bizarre yet gorgeous aria," and that her "energy and conviction galvanized the entire production."

In September of 2002 Lister appeared again with the New York City Opera in a production of Wolfgang Mozart's *Don Giovanni* as Donna Elvira. In 2003 she had another run as Salome, this time with the Connecticut Opera in Hartford, and took most of 2004 off. In the spring of 2005 she appeared with the Orlando Opera in the title role in *Aida* and, later that year, with the Atlanta Opera in *Porgy and Bess.* A year later she closed the Detroit Opera Theater's 2005–06 season with *Salome,* and she then began preparing for her next major role, Lady Macbeth, for Opera Memphis's production of the classic work in January of 2008.

With Verdi's *Macbeth,* Lister's character—written specifically as a Scottish noblewoman—signified her first lead role to break the color barrier in opera. Opera was changing, and directors seemed more open to color-blind casting. She noted, however, that African-American tenors and baritones faced slightly more daunting obstacles in their careers. "Many of my colleagues between the ages of thirty and forty-five believe that if they are not offered *Porgy and Bess* or *Show Boat* or *Carmen Jones,* there is no work to be had," she told Siff in *Opera News.* "I've been in the *Porgy and Bess* circle with a lot of African-American singers on varying levels, and I think the general consensus is that black men really struggle, no matter how good they are, to have the same respect as their white counterparts."

Selected discography

(Various vocal artists) *Gershwin: Sections from Porgy and Bess; Blue Monday,* conducted by Erich Kunzel, Cincinnati Pops Orchestra, Telarc, 1998.

Sources

Periodicals

Boston Herald, January 25, 2001; May 28, 2001.
New York Times, March 5, 2002; March 20, 2002; September 16, 2002.
Opera News, February 18, 1995; May, 1995; June 2001; February, 2003.
St. Petersburg Times (St. Petersburg, FL), May 4, 2005.

Online

"Marquita Lister," *Marquitalister.com,* http://www.marquitalister.com/ (accessed December 26, 2007).

—Carol Brennan

Richard Alexander Long

1927—

Scholar, writer, playwright

During his long and distinguished career, Richard Alexander Long became one of the nation's most prominent African-American scholars and published a diverse array of original and scholarly works examining culture, artistic expression, and language. As a professor at Atlanta University and later Emory University, he was one of the pioneers in developing a curriculum for African-American studies and became one of the first scholars to examine traditional dance development as an expression of culture and history. When Long retired in 2004, Associate Professor Rudolf Byrd told Emory University's Eric Rangus, "The national reputation Emory enjoys as a premier place for the study of African American literature and culture is due to Richard Long."

Richard Long was the fourth of six children born to Thaddeus B. Long and Leila Washington of Philadelphia, Pennsylvania. Though Long and his siblings were raised during the Great Depression, their father's trade as a local blacksmith allowed the family to survive without serious financial burden. However, the family suffered a major tragedy in 1932, when Leila died, leaving Thaddeus to care for the family. When Long was ready to attend high school, he was sent to live with relatives in Columbia, South Carolina, where he enrolled in the city's first African-American high school.

Studied English and Literature

Graduating from high school when he was sixteen years old, Long returned to Philadelphia to attend Temple University. He took an interest in literature and language and graduated in 1947 with a bachelor's degree in English. He remained at Temple University until 1948 to complete a master's degree in English, after which he transferred to the University of Pennsylvania for a doctoral program.

In 1949, he accepted a teaching position at West Virginia State College. He left in 1951 to accept a more intriguing offer in Baltimore, Maryland, as an instructor for Morgan State University. Long taught at Morgan State until 1954, when he left for Paris to continue his studies in literature and history. When he was awarded a Fulbright Scholarship, he decided to study literature, history, and language at the University of Paris from 1957 to 1958. After returning to Morgan State University for several years, Long decided, in 1964, to enter a doctoral program in the linguistics department at the University of Poitiers in Paris, France. During a yearlong leave from Morgan State, he completed his dissertation and worked as a lecturer in the English department.

After completing his doctorate in linguistics in 1965, Long was eventually offered a position at Hampton Institute in Virginia as a full professor teaching English and French. Besides his professorial duties, he was asked to head the university's museum. Long's first major project at the museum was to organize an exhibit of African paintings and photography for the university's centennial celebration. The following year, during the 1968 Black History Month celebration in New York City, he used the university's collections to arrange an exhibit of African and Oceanic paintings.

At a Glance . . .

Born Richard Alexander Long on February 9, 1927, in Philadelphia, PA; son of Thaddeus B. Long and Leila Washington. *Education:* Temple University, AB, 1947, MA, 1948; University of Pennsylvania, 1948–49; Oxford University, 1950; University of Paris, 1954; University of Poitiers, PhD, 1965.

Career: U.S. Army, 1944–45; West Virginia State College, instructor in English, 1949–50; Morgan State University, assistant professor, 1951–64, associate professor of English, 1964–66; Hampton Institute, professor of English and French and head of the university museum, 1966–68; Atlanta University, professor of English and African-American studies, 1968–87; Harvard University, visiting lecturer in African-American studies, 1969–71; University of North Carolina, visiting professor, 1972; Emory University, Graduate Institute of the Liberal Arts, professor, 1973–88, Atticus Haygood Professor of Interdisciplinary Studies, 1988–2004.

Memberships: American Dialect Society; American Studies Association; College Language Association (president, 1971–72); Linguistics Society of America; Modern Language Association of America; Modern Humanities Research Association; South Atlantic Modern Language Association; Southeastern Conference on Linguistics.

Awards: Fulbright Scholar, 1957–58.

During his two years with the Hampton Institute, Long developed a reputation for his expertise in African history and art. By 1968, universities across the nation were recruiting him to help develop African studies programs. Long was offered a position heading a program at Harvard University but decided to accept an alternative program at Atlanta University in Georgia. His first book, *Négritude: Essays and Studies,* written with the help of Albert H. Berrien, was completed during his time at the Hampton Institute and met with critical success when it was published in 1967.

Became a Pioneer in Black Studies

Long entered Atlanta University at a time when U.S. learning institutions were responding to pressure from African-American scholars and students to create and legitimize African-American studies as a scholarly field. One of Long's first actions at the university was to organize the first Triennial Symposium of African Art—an educational lecture and display series that celebrated and promoted African art and African-American artists. The symposium continued until the 1990s and traveled to many of the nation's major cities. In addition, Long worked with other professors at the university to establish the annual Conference on African and African-American Studies, which continued from 1968 to 1987 and became one of the premier meetings for scholars and students studying African-American studies, art, and literature.

In 1971, Long published "Black Studies, Year One" in the university's yearly report, documenting his struggles and successes in developing the African and African-American studies program. His report became an important statement of the guiding principles behind African-American studies programs and helped establish him as one of the most articulate leaders in the African-American studies movement.

Long published a number of artistic and scholarly works while he taught at Atlanta University, including several books of his original poetry. He also published a number of articles exploring African-American studies and African art. His 1985 textbook *Afro-American Writing: An Anthology of Prose and Poetry,* the first textbook of its kind, remained a seminal work in African-American studies into the twenty-first century. Among the important messages contained in Long's writing was a call for educators to increase their focus on providing intellectual grounding for the African-American studies movement so that the movement would become more than a political effort to address the inequity of the educational system and would, instead, provide a lasting contribution to the American educational culture.

Joined Emory University's Graduate Studies Program

While at Atlanta University, Long joined Emory University as a member of the faculty for the Graduate Institute of the Liberal Arts (ILA) in 1973. He divided his time between Atlanta University and the ILA, where he taught classes in African art, literature, and culture. His appointment to Emory's faculty helped establish the university as one of the nation's premier locations for African-American education. In 1988, Long became the Atticus Haygood Professor of Interdisciplinary Studies at the ILA.

In the 1950s, Long developed an interest in African dance styles. He eventually became an expert in African and other ethnic dance traditions. While working at Emory in the 1980s and 1990s, he began exploring the cultural dances of Indonesia and Oceanic cultures, and he organized some of the first national exhibitions of Indonesian dancing at Emory.

His 1989 book *Black Tradition in American Dance* became one of the first photographic works to document the history of dance among African Americans. In 1998, he helped found a new graduate course at Emory dealing with world dance styles and their relation to politics. In his unique curriculum, he related dance techniques to issues such as national identity, cultural hegemony, and internationally rivalry. "I am interested in all manifestations of dance, including concert and theatrical dance performances that involve distinctive traditional choreography," said Long in a 1999 interview with Emory University's Cathy Byrd. "Recognized as high art, dance represents a nation's culture. I explore the politics of culture: how cultural forms operate as part of cultural and political encounters."

Long's contributions to education and cultural research played a major role in defining the study of African-American culture from the 1960s to the twenty-first century. Besides becoming a pioneer in African-American studies, he was also an innovator in studying artistic traditions for their cultural and political relevance. Though generally known for his scholarly contributions, he also published a variety of original poetry and a number of theatrical plays, which appeared at university theaters from the 1960s to the 1980s. Colleagues and students often describe Long as someone whose breadth of knowledge and personable expository style set him apart from many modern scholars. In speaking about Long, Emory colleague Walter Reed told *Contemporary Black Biography,* "He is a delight to talk with on any subject under the sun."

Selected Works

Plays

Stairway to Heaven, 1964.
Reasons of State, 1966.
Black Is Many Hues, 1969.

Nonfiction

(With Albert H. Berrien, eds.) *Négritude: Essays and Studies,* Hampton Institute Press, 1967.

"The Black Studies Boondoggle," *Liberator,* September 1970, pp. 6–9.
"Scapegoat Victory: The President White House Mandate," *The Nation,* December 4, 1972, p. 555.
Ascending and Other Poems, Dusable Museum of African American History, 1975.
"Two Hundred Years of Black American Art," *Contemporary Art/Southeast,* April–May 1977, p. 42.
(With Eugenia W. Collier, eds.) *Afro-American Writing: An Anthology of Prose and Poetry,* 2nd ed., Pennsylvania State University Press, 1985.
Black Writers and the American Civil War, Blue and Grey Press, 1988.
The Black Tradition in American Dance, Rizzoli, 1989.
Black Americans: A Portrait, Crescent Books, 1993.
"Southeast Asia on the American Dance Stage, 1915–1955," *SPAFA Journal,* May–August 1993, p. 17.
(With Marcia Ann Gillespie and Rosa Johnson Butler) *Maya Angelou: A Glorious Celebration,* Doubleday, 2007.

Sources

Periodicals

Negro Digest, Vol. 17, March 1968, pp. 40–46.

Online

Byrd, Cathy, "Richard Long Studies the World of Dance since WWII," *Emory University Reports,* http://www.emory.edu/EMORY_REPORT/erar chive/1999/September/erseptember.27/9_27_99 long.html (accessed December 17, 2007).
"Historymakers Biographical Sketch: Richard A. Long," http://www.thehistorymakers.com/pro grams/dvl/files/Long_Richardf.html (accessed December 17, 2007).
Rangus, Eric, "Celebration Honors Long's Distinguished Career," *Emory University Online,* November 1, 2004, http://www.emory.edu/EMORY_RE PORT/erarchive/2004/November/er%20novem ber%201/celebration.htm (accessed December 17, 2007).
"Richard Alexander Long," *Biography Resource Center,* http://galenet.galegroup.com/servlet/BioRC (accessed December 17, 2007).

—Micah L. Issitt

Vusi Mahlasela

1965—

Musician, singer, songwriter

The captivating rhythms and powerful lyrics of Vusi Mahlasela's folk anthems both inspired and documented the antiapartheid movement in South Africa during the 1980s. After the fall of the racist government in the early 1990s, Mahlasela's music became a compelling call for peace, deliberation, and forgiveness in the newly liberated state. Often called simply, "The Voice," because of his wide range and vocal versatility, Mahlasela has become a well-known musical ambassador of the South African struggle for freedom and equality. His poetic lyrics and afro-fusion cadences embody the healing role that music has often played in African culture, a complex soundtrack that captures the pain of the past and the hope for the future.

Mahlasela, Vusi, photograph. © John Kershaw/Alamy.

Vusi Sidney Mahlasela Ka Zwane was born in 1965 in Lady Selborne, a township near the South African administrative capitol city of Pretoria. Under the racist apartheid system that existed in South Africa before the 1990s, townships were impoverished areas outside of cities where people of color were segregated. Mahlasela never knew his father, and his mother frequently had to work far from home, so he was raised by his grandmother, who operated a *shebeen,* or informal community nightclub, in the nearby township of Mamelodi.

Mamelodi township has long been a center of African culture and art, and Mahlasela grew up surrounded by artists, poets, and musicians. The vibrant rhythms that poured from his grandmother's shebeen became his first lullabies, and he was quoted by Music.org.za as saying, "I'm sure I learned to sing before I could talk." With no money for instruments, he made his first guitar himself, out of an empty cooking oil can and fishing line, and taught himself to play. By the age of nine, he and some friends had formed a band to entertain the neighborhood with songs ranging from traditional African folk to American rock and soul.

Joined Struggle Against Apartheid

In spite of the poverty and racial discrimination that defined life for most South African blacks, Mahlasela had a happy childhood and remained relatively unaware of the political situation surrounding him until he was eleven years old. On June 16, 1976, students in

At a Glance . . .

Born Vusi Sidney Mahlasela Ka Zwane in 1965 in Lady Selborne, South Africa.

Career: Singer-songwriter, 1979—.

Memberships: African National Congress Youth League; Ancestors of Africa; Congress of South African Writers.

Awards: South African Music Awards, Best Male Vocalist, Best Album (for *Silang Mabele*), 1998; Public Radio International, Afropop Worldwide, Afropop Hall of Fame, 2006; South African Music Awards, Best Male Artist, 2007.

Addresses: *E-mail*—Vusi@RedLightManagement.com.

the township of Soweto walked out of classes to protest a law requiring that half their classes be taught in Afrikaans, a Dutch-based language spoken by many white South Africans. The students' rally was met by police, who fired into the crowd, killing several young protesters. This event prompted many black South Africans to join the liberation struggle, including Mahlasela, who joined the African National Congress Youth League and began working to end the domination of the country by racist whites.

From its very beginnings in the 1940s, the political struggle to end apartheid had grown alongside a strong cultural movement in literature, art, and, especially, music. Mahlasela began to add his voice to the chorus of musicians singing for freedom. In the early 1980s he joined a group of political poets called Ancestors of Africa and began writing poems and songs that he performed at antiapartheid rallies and demonstrations. The police frequently confiscated written political material, so Mahlasela memorized his work in order not to be silenced.

Indeed, police harassment became a regular feature of Mahlasela's life. Like many activists, he was required to obtain special permission at the police station to attend church and other community events. Members of the antiapartheid movement were frequently arrested if police even suspected that they planned a protest, and Mahlasela spent many nights in jail after such arrests. However, he did not let fear of punishment stop him from working for justice.

In the late 1980s Mahlasela experienced another personal loss when his mother collapsed during a church service and died. He would later write a memorial to her in the song "River Jordan." In 1988 he joined the Congress of South African Writers, where he met other political writers and, through his work with them, gained confidence as a poet. He was especially influenced by the work of other radical songwriters, such as Miriam Makeba, a singer from South Africa, and Victor Jara, a leftist poet from Chile who had been killed in 1973. Through his work with the Congress of South African Writers, Mahlasela also met the South African novelist Nadine Gordimer, who became both a friend and mentor, paying for his first professional guitar lessons. Mahlasela continued to develop his unique musical style, combining influences from all the music he loved, including African folk, jazz, and pop, rhythmic a cappella music called *mbube,* and African-American blues, jazz, and scat.

By the early 1990s the racist regime of apartheid had fallen in South Africa, and, for the first time, the nation held open elections, making Nelson Mandela its first black president. In 1992 Mahlasela released his first album, *When You Come Back,* and dedicated it to those who had been forced into political exile by the white racist regime. In 1994 he performed at Mandela's inauguration ceremony, an occasion of joyous celebration throughout South Africa's antiapartheid community.

Those who had worked to end apartheid were determined that the extreme unfairness and violence of that system should not be replaced with an atmosphere of bitterness and revenge. The new government called for peace and forgiveness, and Mahlasela echoed this call in his music, changing from a call to action to a call for mercy and understanding. His second album, released in 1994, was *Wisdom of Forgiveness* and offered a message of hope for the new nation.

In 1997 Mahlasela followed *Wisdom of Forgiveness* with a third album, *Silang Mabele,* which means "crush the corn" in Tswana, one of South Africa's many languages. In South African culture the phrase means "let's get to work," and Mahlasela intended the album as a call to action. He explained the progression of his works to Music.org.za: "We celebrated when our leaders and culture returned from exile. When conflict was expected we applied the wisdom of forgiveness. After celebration and forgiveness, the time has come to produce. *Silang Mabele* is a call for unity to fight poverty." Mahlasela's third album earned him awards for Best Male Vocalist and Best Album at the 1998 South African Music Awards.

Gained International Audience

During the 1990s Mahlasela's music began gaining popularity around the world. After touring throughout Africa, he performed at a number of international festivals, including the Zabalaza Festival in London in

1990, and the Dranouter Festival in Belgium in 1996. He also performed in North America for the first time in 1996, a concert with the famous reggae band the Wailers at the House of Blues in Los Angeles. A 2002 documentary film increased Mahlasela's international reputation still further. *Amandla! A Revolution in Four-Part Harmony* explored the important role of music in the South African defeat of apartheid, and, among many other artists, the film highlighted the work of Mahlasela. European and American listeners wanted more, so in 2003 Mahlasela released an album for distribution to those audiences. *The Voice* was a compilation of his best work and included songs in six different South African languages, including English.

As part of the rapidly growing genre of world music, Mahlasela has become an international star, touring to perform regularly in Africa, Europe, and the United States. Music fans around the world have continued to love his pure tenor voice and his fusion of a variety of African styles with elements of New World reggae, jazz, and blues. His 2007 album, *Guiding Light,* contains duets with diverse musical performers, from fellow South African Dave Matthews to Welsh singer-songwriter Jem.

In spite of his increasing fame and stardom, Mahlasela has continued to create music that celebrates peace, justice, and a simple joy in living. He frequently dedicates his songs to those who have influenced him the most, such as "Thula Mama," which he dedicates to the many courageous women of South Africa, especially his grandmother. In an interview with National Public Radio's *Weekend Edition,* he explained his personal artistic vision, "I want my music to be accessible to every listener because I know that I really have something to say in terms of ... removing thorns from people, thorns that really make us unaware that we are bleeding with these thorns, like pain, grief, jealousy and so on."

Selected discography

When You Come Back, BMG Africa, 1992.
Wisdom of Forgiveness, BMG Africa, 1994.
Silang Mabele, BMG Africa, 1997.
(With Louis Mhlanga) *Vusi and Louis Live at the Bassline,* BMG Africa, 1999.
Miyela Africa, BMG Africa, 2000.
(With the Proud Peoples Band) *Jungle of Questions,* BMG Africa, 2002.
The Voice, ATO Records/BMG, 2003.
Guiding Light, ATO Records, 2007.

Sources

Periodicals

Billboard, November 18, 2000, p. 20; September 6, 2003, p. 39.
Sing Out!, Spring 2007, p. 11.

Online

"Music and History with Vusi Mahlasela," *NPR Music,* http://www.npr.org/templates/story/story.php?storyId=9794115 (accessed December 28, 2007).
"The Voice of Liberation," *The Age,* http://www.theage.com.au/news/Music/The-voice-of-liberation/2004/12/23/1103391880963.html (accessed December 28, 2007).
Vusi Mahlasela, http://www.vusimahlasela.com/?sid=2 (accessed December 28, 2007).
"Vusi Mahlasela's Musical Journey," *National Public Radio,* http://www.npr.org/templates/story/story.php?storyId=1436672 (accessed December 28, 2007).
"Vusi Mahlasela, South Africa," *Music.org.za,* http://www.music.org.za/artist.asp?id=102 (accessed December 28, 2007).

—Tina Gianoulis

Haile Mariam Mengistu

1937—

Dictator

Haile Mariam Mengistu was a popular army officer who was installed as ruler of Ethiopia following the country's 1974 revolution. He remained in power for the next seventeen years, and his attempt to mold the country into a Soviet-style socialist paradise plunged it into a brutal reign of terror instead. Ethiopia's government-sanctioned campaign of political repression resulted in an estimated 150,000 deaths, and Mengistu became known as "the Butcher of Addis Ababa" for it. Fifteen years after his 1991 flight into exile, he was tried in absentia and found guilty of genocide. He remains in Zimbabwe, in a walled compound, but the legacy of his long and bloody rule was to destabilize the Horn of Africa and reshape the borders of its countries through the armed rebel groups that worked to unseat him.

Mengistu's background and childhood have been the topic of rumor and even myths connecting him to Ethiopia's royal bloodline, but actual information on his family and upbringing is scarce. Darker-skinned blacks like himself, however, had long been discriminated against by Ethiopia's elite, and this prejudice may have been the basis for some of his later punitive acts as leader. He was born in 1937 in Walayta, a district in the southern part of Ethiopia, and his father was a soldier in the Ethiopian army. His mother, a domestic, may have brought him to live with her in a well-connected household in Addis Ababa, the capital, where she had taken a job. As a young man, Mengistu enlisted in the Ethiopian army, then trained at the Holeta Military Academy. He graduated in 1966 with the rank of second lieutenant, and in the late 1960s he was one of four thousand Ethiopia military personnel sent to the United States for advanced military training.

After returning to Ethiopia, Mengistu rose quickly through the army's ranks, becoming a major by 1974. During the summer of that year, however, growing internal dissatisfaction began to destabilize Ethiopia. Since 1916 the country had been under the control of Emperor Haile Selassie, who styled himself as a god on earth and doled out favors and resources to a select group of nobles. For generations before Selassie, however, Ethiopia had been plagued by periodic draughts, and its arable land was a lone, precious resource. By the time of Mengistu's childhood, nearly all the land in Ethiopia was owned by nobles, while peasants toiled on these estates in conditions approximating slavery.

Famine Hastened Rise to Power

Unlike nearly every nation on the African continent, Ethiopia was unusual in that it was colonized only briefly, in the late 1930s, and by Italy—a somewhat lax overseer compared to Britain or France. Furthermore, Ethiopia's formidable mountains had protected it from invasions for centuries, and it boasted one of the oldest national identities in the world. These factors converged to keep the country in near-feudal conditions until the early 1970s, when word of the achievements in the newly democratic nations of Africa began to filter in. Then, in 1972 draught and famine struck once again, this time in the Wollo province, and an estimated 150,000 people died from it. The catastrophe was covered up by the Selassie government, who was also

At a Glance . . .

Born in 1937 in Walayta, Ethiopia; son of a soldier and a domestic; married Ubanchi Bishaw; five children. *Education:* Graduated from Holeta Military Academy, 1966; received advanced military training in the United States, late 1960s.

Career: Officer with the Ethiopian army, after 1966; head of Ethiopian government, 1974–91; Armed Forces Coordinating Committee (Derg), member, 1974–91, and chair, after July 1974; Provisional Military Administrative Council, first vice chair, 1974–77, and chair, 1977–92; commander in chief of the Ethiopian armed forces, February 1977–May 1991; Workers' Party of Ethiopia, secretary general, 1984–91.

Addresses: *Agent*—Embassy of Zimbabwe, 1608 New Hampshire Ave., Washington, DC 20009.

suspected of withholding emergency food supplies to Wollo in efforts to squelch antigovernment rebels in the region. In light of these events, the political outlook of many young Ethiopians began to take a dangerous shift to the left, and Mengistu was among that group.

An impressive number of Mengistu's colleagues in the army were also eager to see change and began taking action. In June of 1974 a Coordinating Committee of the Armed Forces, Police, and Territorial Army was established, and it became known by its shortened version in the Ge'ez language as the Derg. It was originally established as an internal-investigations unit to root out corruption but soon took on characteristics of a military junta. Its membership roster of roughly 126 officers was then closed to new members, and Mengistu was elected to chair it in July. The Derg began to seize foreign-held properties under a new nationalization policy called *Ethiopia Tikdem* ("Ethiopia First"), and it also moved to isolate Selassie and his government at the royal palace. The emperor agreed to sweeping concessions demanded by the Derg, but the end of the monarchy was near. In September Selassie was formally deposed. Less than a year later, it was announced that the former emperor had died during prostate surgery.

The overthrow of the Selassie government was a popular uprising until November of 1974, when sixty members of the imperial government were executed. From that point forward, Mengistu and the Derg controlled Ethiopia, and antigovernment sentiment was deemed counterrevolutionary and punishable by prison or death. Newly allied with the Soviet Union, the

Derg began implementing a sweeping reform program carried out under Marxist-Leninist principles. The estates of the landowning class were seized, and the land was redistributed to peasants. All major industries were nationalized, and the country's college- or foreign-educated management class were stripped of their perks and property and, in some cases, were jailed or died in custody; others fled the country permanently. "That left nobody who could run anything," a report in the *Economist* explained years later. "Soviet ministries were ordered to fill the gaps, and sent their discards. Ethiopia became a punishment station for rejects from one the world's most incompetent bureaucracies."

Red Terror Launched

Mengistu remained in charge as head of the Derg, but he seized power more firmly in February of 1977, when he became commander in chief of the Ethiopian armed forces. Two months later, he spoke at a rally and promised that all enemies of Ethiopia's historic revolution would be brought to justice, and he smashed bottles that he claimed were filled with blood to emphasize his point. The Ethiopian Red Terror of 1977–78 began with that speech, and hundreds of suspected enemies of the regime were arrested, detained without trial, tortured, and even killed. The victims were primarily university students and bureaucrats who had voiced dissatisfaction with the pace or tenor of Mengistu's Soviet-style revolution. Some elements of the Red Terror were borrowed from Mao Tse-tung's Cultural Revolution in China that began a decade earlier, following a well-defined plan of action to find, punish, and reverse what was deemed bourgeois—and therefore counterrevolutionary—thought.

Some estimates place the number of Red Terror deaths as high as half a million. Scores more fled the country, some settling in other Horn of Africa nations and others establishing the first serious communities of Ethiopians in the United States, Canada, and Europe. Inside Ethiopia, as well as in Somalia, Sudan, and other neighboring countries, Mengistu's opponents joined various armed groups established to fight the Derg and its harsh rule, but these groups had competing ideologies and goals that ranged from continuing the socialist revolution to restoring the monarchy. A secessionist movement in Ethiopia's region of Eritrea, which had begun long before Mengistu came to power, was also problematic. Eventually, there were serious insurgency movements in all the provinces of Ethiopia, and the country descended into outright civil war.

In 1980 Mengistu announced the formation of the Committee to Form the Party of the Workers of Ethiopia, with himself as chair. Four years later a full-fledged Party of the Workers of Ethiopia was established, modeled on the Communist Party of the Soviet Union, and again Mengistu was its chief. The political killings continued. "In the mid-1980s it was not uncommon to see students, suspected government critics or rebel sympathisers hanging from lampposts each morning," wrote Jonathan Clayton in the *Times* of London. "Ordinary people were too terrified to talk to Western reporters. Other people were executed in the notorious state prison on the edge of the capital, Addis Ababa. Families had to pay a tax known as 'the wasted bullet' to obtain the bodies of their loved ones. At the height of his power, Mengistu himself frequently garrotted or shot dead opponents, saying that he was leading by example."

Ouster Triggered by Famine

Once again, mass famine altered the political landscape of Ethiopia, though it took several more years for Mengistu to finally resign from office. In 1983 draught hit areas of Wollo, Tigray, and Eritrea, and the Derg government's policy of agricultural collectivization had exacerbated, not eradicated, the cycle of draught and starvation the 1974 revolution had once promised to end. This time the famine was well-publicized thanks to a British Broadcasting Corporation documentary, which resulted in a massive outpouring of media attention and sympathy in the West, and Mengistu was forced to accept relief aid from other nations. Despite the help, an estimated one million Ethiopians died between 1983 and 1985.

Mengistu even began to grant some interviews with Western media, sitting down with two journalists from *Time* magazine in 1986 to defend Ethiopia's forced resettlement program, known as villagization and criticized for its widespread human-rights violations. "It is only when you have peasants together in villages that they can benefit from science and technology to combat difficult conditions," he told the magazine's Henry Muller and James Wilde. "Why is this well-intentioned strategy viewed with prejudice in some quarters in Western countries?" he wondered. The *Time* article noted that Mengistu "spoke softly, [but] his words carried a tone of icy, uncompromising certitude. Not once did his *eyes* focus on his guests; at times he appeared to be speaking to an unseen audience, or to the portraits on the wall."

The fall of the Berlin Wall in 1989 hastened the inevitable collapse of Mengistu's regime. Less than two years later, Soviet-backed regimes elsewhere had collapsed, and then the Soviet Union itself, and the flow of rubles that had kept the Derg in power dried up for good. Anti-Derg rebel militias began winning significant victories, and finally in 1991 the United States brokered an agreement between Mengistu and rebels: he was to resign from office and leave the country, and in exchange the capital city of Addis Ababa would not be targeted and widespread bloodshed there could be averted. Mengistu fled on May 21, 1991, and was given refuge by President Robert Mugabe of Zimbabwe. Mengistu and his family, which included five children, settled into a villa near Harare, Zimbabwe's

capital. He has been seen in public only twice since 1992—once in a restaurant and another time in a bookstore. In 1999 he went to South Africa for medical treatment but was forced to flee back into his protected exile in Zimbabwe when an extradition order was issued.

Convicted in Absentia

That order came from the post-Derg Ethiopian government, which launched an inquiry into the Red Terror era soon after taking power in 1991. Mengistu was tried in absentia for genocide, along with seventy-three other members of the Derg. Only then were the actual details—which many had already suspected—of Selassie's death finally revealed: Mengistu had ordered the emperor's death, and the eighty-three-year-old monarch was smothered by a pillow and then buried under a bathroom floor in one of his palaces. Mengistu's trial began in 1994 and included eight thousand pages of charges and evidence linking him to two thousand specific deaths. The Ethiopian High Court found him guilty on December 12, 2006, but because Zimbabwe refuses to comply with the extradition order, Mengistu remains at his Harare home. There are rumors that he is a heavy drinker and abusive to the remaining family and associates who are close to him.

The rebel groups that sprang up to combat the Derg would later play a significant role in shaping the political landscape of the Horn of Africa. Eritrea finally gained its independence in 1991, but factions that took root in Somalia, Sudan, and other neighboring countries grew in strength or split off, and these groups continued to exert their influence via force. Few countries in the area have enjoyed stable, democratic governments in the years since.

Sources

Books

Encyclopedia of World Biography, 2nd edition, Gale, 1998.

Periodicals

Economist, May 25, 1991.
New York Times, December 13, 2006.
New York Times Magazine, June 4, 2006.
Time, August 4, 1986.
Times (London, England), April 20, 1991; December 13, 2006.

Online

"Profile: Mengistu Haile Mariam," *BBC News,* http://news.bbc.co.uk/1/hi/world/africa/6171927.stm (accessed December 26, 2007).

—Carol Brennan

Irene Morgan

1917–2007

Civil rights activist

Irene Morgan made history in 1944, when her act of civil disobedience—refusing to relinquish her seat on an interstate bus to a white passenger—became a crucial legal battle in the struggle to end institutionalized segregation. Morgan's case was brought before the U.S. Supreme Court and set a legal precedent that was used in later years to fight against other forms of segregation. Despite the wide-reaching consequences of Morgan's actions, by the 1960s Morgan's case had largely been forgotten. In the twenty-first century, interest in Morgan's story resurfaced, and she was honored by civil rights organizations and the federal government for her role as a pioneer of the civil rights movement.

Irene Morgan was born on April 9, 1917, in Baltimore, Maryland. She was the sixth of nine children born to parents who were the children of former slaves. Morgan later described her father as having worked various jobs during the Great Depression era to keep the family together, while she and her siblings also worked to contribute to the family's income. After high school, she married Sherwood Morgan with whom she had two children: Sherwood Jr. and Brenda Morgan (later Brenda Morgan Bacquie). Morgan's mother relocated to Gloucester, Virginia, while Morgan remained in Baltimore with her husband and children.

Defied Federal Laws as Unjust

In 1944, Morgan visited her mother in Gloucester after suffering a miscarriage. Morgan had been feeling ill and decided to return to Baltimore for a doctor's visit. At the time, segregation laws in Virginia required African-American passengers to sit in the rear of public busses and relinquish their seats, if needed, to white passengers. Morgan had ridden the segregated busses on numerous occasions and, when boarding the Greyhound Bus, she took a seat in the section designated for African Americans.

Less than an hour into the five-hour bus ride from Gloucester to Baltimore, a white couple boarded the bus and the bus driver asked Morgan and a young African-American woman with an infant in tow to vacate their seats. Morgan refused to move and attempted to prevent her seatmate from obeying the driver. According to Morgan's recollections in a 2000 interview with Carol Morello of the *Washington Post,* she asked the young mother sitting next to her, "Where do you think you're going with that baby in your arms?" In justification for her actions, Morgan said to Morello, "I didn't do anything wrong. I'd paid for my seat. I was sitting where I was supposed to." She added, "I can't see how anybody in the same circumstances could do otherwise."

When it became clear that Morgan would not relinquish her seat, the bus driver threatened to have her arrested, and Morgan challenged him to follow through on his threat. The Greyhound bus driver drove the bus to a county jail in Saluda, Middlesex County, Virginia, where a sheriff's deputy boarded the bus with a warrant for Morgan's arrest. Refusing to leave the bus, Morgan took the deputy's warrant, tore it to pieces, and threw them out the window of the bus. When the deputy attempted to physically remove Morgan from her seat, she struggled. "He touched me. That's when I kicked him in a very bad place."

A second deputy then entered to bus to assist in removing Morgan. When the second deputy attempted to gain control of her, Morgan clawed him and ripped his uniform. "I was going to bite him," she recalled to Morello, "but he was dirty, so I clawed him instead." When the deputy threatened to use his nightstick, Morgan replied, "We'll whip each other." Morgan was eventually dragged from the bus and jailed in Saluda. She recalls yelling to African Americans passing outside the window to contact her minister and notify her family of her situation. Morgan's mother arrived on the same day and posted the $500 bail for her daughter's release.

Morgan was ordered to return to Middlesex County to stand for trial, where she plead guilty to resisting arrest and was fined $100, but she refused to plead guilty to violating the state's segregation laws. Morgan's lawyer, Spottswood Robinson III, utilized a unique legal strategy by arguing that enforcing segregation on busses traveling between states violated federal laws regarding interstate commerce. Though Robinson would have preferred to challenge state segregation laws, by restricting his arguments to federal commerce Robinson was able to argue that the case fell under federal jurisdiction. The Middlesex County courts disagreed with Robinson's argument and ordered Morgan to pay $10 for violating state laws.

Took Case to the U.S. Supreme Court

Robinson appealed Morgan's case to the Virginia Supreme Court, where the court ruled against Morgan a second time. It was during this time that the case drew the attention of the National Association for the Advancement of Colored People, who sent Thurgood

Marshall (later the first African American to sit on the U.S. Supreme Court) and William Hastie, the dean of Howard University's Law School, to assist Robinson in preparing the case for the U.S. Supreme Court.

The Supreme Court case of *Irene Morgan v. Commonwealth of Virginia* began on March 27, 1946, almost two years after the incident occurred. Marshal and Hastie continued to argue that Virginia state laws were in violation of interstate commerce, essentially asserting that federally regulated commercial transactions, such as those governing interstate travel, could not be subordinate to state laws. On June 3, the Court ruled 6–1 in favor of Marshall and Hastie's arguments. The majority opinion held that state laws could not supersede congressional mandates but did not address the legality of state segregation.

Greyhound Bus and other interstate travel companies were ordered to institute a desegregated policy; however, drivers and bus companies in some states refused to acknowledge the Court's decision. In 1947, Bayard Rustin, who later gained fame within the civil rights movement for organizing a major march in Washington D.C., led an interracial group of eight whites and eight African Americans on a mission to travel on interstate busses through four southern states to promote and test compliance to the newly imposed federal regulations. Along the ride, called the "Journey of Reconciliation," the activists sung the protest song "You Don't Have to Ride Jim Crow," which contained the lyric "Get on the bus, sit anyplace, 'cause Irene Morgan won her case." Twelve of the sixteen bus riders were arrested for refusing to move to segregated seating.

Became a Forgotten Icon

Within a few years of her case, Morgan's role in the civil rights movement was largely forgotten, though the legal precedent set by her case became a lynch pin in later legal battles to attack the foundations of segregation. Morgan continued to take an active role in the civil rights movement by distributing flyers for desegregation in Baltimore and visiting various civil rights committees, but she did so often without revealing her own role in the Virginia court case, preferring to remain among the nameless hundreds of everyday citizens who were joining in the struggle against institutionalized racism.

Morgan's first husband died in 1948, after which she met and married Stanley Kirkaldy, the owner of a dry-cleaning business. After their marriage, the couple moved to New York City, where Morgan started a business that provided domestic cleaning coupled with childcare services. By the time of Rosa Parks's historic struggle, which began in 1955 and resulted in the desegregation of all public transportation, Morgan was only passively involved in the civil rights movement.

In the 1980s, Morgan entered and won a radio contest offering a scholarship to study at St. John's University. She received a bachelor's degree in communications at age sixty-eight and continued at Queen's University, where, in 1990, at age seventy-three, she earned a master's degree in urban studies. Morgan remained involved in combating injustice within her own community—as when she wrote letters to the pope protesting a situation in which a Haitian family had been denied entrance into a parochial school in New York.

Honored as a Pioneer for Civil Rights

In 2000, researchers preparing for Gloucester's 350th anniversary celebration uncovered information about Morgan's connection to the county. Representatives of the Virginia state government invited Morgan to return to Gloucester as part of the celebration, in a day called "A Homecoming for Irene Morgan." Morgan accepted and was honored by state officials at the celebration, where it was announced that four scholarships had been established in Morgan's honor. Morgan was modest about her personal accomplishments by declaring in numerous interviews that her acts were not extraordinary. When offered an honorary doctorate from the prestigious Howard University in Washington D.C., Morgan refused on the basis that she had not earned the degree.

In 2001, acknowledgement of Morgan's role came again from Washington, D.C., when she was chosen by the Clinton administration to receive the Presidential Citizens Medal, which is considered the second highest presidential honor after the Presidential Medal of Freedom. The government citation read in part, "When Irene Morgan boarded a bus for Baltimore in the summer of 1944, she took the first step on a journey that would change America forever."

Though the twenty-first century saw Morgan's return to the spotlight, she continued to live an unassuming life, eventually moving from New York to Gloucester, after an illness left her husband a quadriplegic. Stanley Kirkaldy died in 2006, and Morgan was soon diagnosed with Alzheimer's disease. She died on August 10, 2007, while living at her granddaughter's home in Virginia. In the wake of her death, numerous newspapers ran stories detailing Morgan's trial and her effect on the civil rights movement.

Morgan's family recalled her life as dignified, moral, and honorable, both as a civil rights leader and as a citizen. "She always taught us that if you know you're right, it doesn't matter what anyone else thinks," said her daughter, Brenda Bacquie, to Morello. "It's a moral thing. It's something you have to do. She doesn't see herself as a hero. She saw something that had to be done, and she rushed in, like all heroes."

Sources

Periodicals

Daily Press (Newport, VA), August 19, 2007.
New York Times, August 13, 2007.
Washington Post, July 30, 2000.

Online

"Civil Rights Pioneer, Irene Morgan Kirkaldy, Dies in 90," *Gloucester Institute,* http://www.gloucesterinstitute.org/index.asp?bid=166 (December 12, 2007).
"Irene Morgan, 1917–2007: Articles on Irene Morgan," *Robin Washington Online,* http://www.robinwashington.com/jimcrow/2_journey.html (December 12, 2007).
Wormser, Richard, "The Rise and Fall of Jim Crow," *PBS Online,* http://www.pbs.org/wnet/jimcrow/stories_events_morgan.html (December 12, 2007).

Other

National Public Radio Special, "Fighting Jim Crow Before Rosa Parks," recorded, August 15, 2007.

—Micah L. Issitt

Ne-Yo

1982—

Singer, songwriter

Ne-Yo, photograph. Francis Specker/Landov.

Singer-songwriter Ne-Yo began his musical career while he was still a teenager, performing in his own amateur band and writing songs for professional musicians. By the time he was twenty-three, he had become coauthor of a hit song and had his own recording contract. His career has continued to develop rapidly, as Ne-Yo has become a sought-after songwriter for other recording artists and an award-winning performer in his own right. However, in an industry known for instant fame followed by instant obscurity, Ne-Yo is determined to become more than an overnight wonder. Captivated since childhood by the power of great songs to resonate across miles and generations, Ne-Yo draws on his own emotional experience in hopes of creating classic songs that will have an enduring power to move those who sing them or hear them.

Ne-Yo is the stage name of Shaffer Chimere Smith, who was born on October 18, 1982, in the southern Arkansas town of Camden. A member of a musical family of African-American and Chinese heritage, he developed a love of music at an early age. His father was absent through much of his childhood, and Ne-Yo's mother raised her children alone. Seeking better employment opportunities, she moved her family to Las Vegas, Nevada. There, growing up near the glamour and flash of the Las Vegas strip, young Ne-Yo began to dream of show business.

Found Success as a Songwriter

While in high school, he began performing with a group of friends in a rhythm and blues (R&B) band called Envy. While singing with Envy, Ne-Yo used the stage name Gogo. After graduation, the group went to Los Angeles, California, with a bold and theatrical plan: to sing outside the offices of Capitol Records until someone offered them a recording contract. They did attract the attention of Capitol executives, who threatened to call the police if they did not leave. However, Ne-Yo used his time in the music industry capital to make contact with other musicians in hopes of gaining work as a songwriter. His first success came with the sale of several songs to a boy group from Ohio called Youngstown. Youngstown included a number of Ne-Yo songs, such as "Don't Worry," "Lose My Cool," and "Float Away" on their albums *Let's Roll* and *Down for the Get Down*.

At a Glance . . .

Born Shaffer Chimere Smith on October 18, 1982, in Camden, AR; divorced; one son: Chimere.

Career: Singer and songwriter, 2000—.

Awards: Music of Black Origin Awards, Best Song for "Because of You," 2007; Best R&B, 2007; Soul Train Music Awards, Best R&B/Soul or Rap New Artist for "Sexy Love," 2007; Black Entertainment Television Awards, Best R&B Male Artist, 2007.

Addresses: *Office*—Compound Entertainment, PO Box 93303, Atlanta, GA 30377.

Even though Envy broke up in 2000, Ne-Yo remained in Los Angeles working to develop his music career. He began using the stage name Ne-Yo after a friend commented that he seemed to be able to "see" music, like the protagonist Neo in the 1999 science-fiction film *The Matrix*. A fan of the film, Ne-Yo enjoyed the comparison and adopted the name, changing the spelling to incorporate the hip-hop salute, "Yo!" Interestingly, the performer Ne-Yo is three years younger than his alter ego, Shaffer Smith.

Ne-Yo continued to write songs, frequently making demonstration tapes to show other singers how his music would sound. Before long, record company executives noticed the clear, expressive voice of the songwriter, and Ne-Yo finally won the recording contract he had sought. However, even though he recorded an album with Columbia Records, the company did not release it, believing that it did not contain the big radio hit necessary to ensure album sales. The company dropped his contract in 2003, and Ne-Yo decided to devote his energies to writing rather than performing.

After writing songs for a number of popular singers, including Marques Houston and Christina Milian, his breakthrough hit came in 2004, when Mario, a teenage R&B star, recorded "Let Me Love You," a poignant and complex love song, cowritten by Ne-Yo, Scott Storch, and Kam Houf. "Let Me Love You" reached number one on *Billboard*'s R&B list and Hot 100 Singles chart and became one of the most-played records of the year on U.S. radio stations. Soon, Ne-Yo had another recording contract, this time with Def Jam Records, a hip-hop label that he felt would understand his music more completely.

Gained Fame as a Performer

In 2006 Def Jam released Ne-Yo's first album, *In My Own Words,* because he had written or cowritten each of its songs. The album sold over one million copies, with a hit single, "Stay," that reached *Billboard*'s R&B Top 40 list. Another single, "Sexy Love," earned Ne-Yo a 2007 Soul Train award for Best R&B/Soul or Rap New Artist. One of the album's major hits, "So Sick," crossed over to reach the number-one position on *Billboard*'s Pop Top 40 list. *In My Own Words* was followed in 2007 by Ne-Yo's second album, *Because of You,* a tribute to his pop music hero, Michael Jackson. The album's title cut won the Music of Black Origin award for best song of 2007.

As Ne-Yo's reputation as a songwriter continued to spread, a number of major music stars sought him out, not only R&B and hip-hop artists, such as Mary J. Blige, Beyoncé, and Rhianna, but also world famous pop stars, such as Celine Dion and Whitney Houston. Ne-Yo continued to draw on his personal experience to help him write meaningful lyrics. "Let Me Love You" had been inspired by an evening spent comforting a heartbroken friend, while songs for female stars, such as "Irreplaceable," which had been a top-ten hit for Beyoncé, were born out of conversations with his mother, sisters, and aunts about a woman's view of life and love.

Though Ne-Yo's music has a twenty-first century style and flavor, he has also been inspired by his predecessors, including Michael Jackson, Frank Sinatra, and Sammy Davis Jr. As a child, he developed his voice by listening to his mother's albums, especially pop classics such as Jackson's *Off the Wall* and Stevie Wonder's *Hotter Than July.* As he began writing his own songs, his goal became to create songs that would become classics themselves.

A well-rounded artist, who values originality and innovation over repeating a successful formula, Ne-Yo has taken risks to expand his career. In 2004, along with Reynell Hay, he helped found Compound Entertainment, an Atlanta, Georgia, based music production company where, besides writing and performing, he has begun learning the technical skills of record production. Along with writing songs and performing on his own albums, Ne-Yo has also made guest appearances on a number of albums, including Ghostface Killah's 2006 *Fishscale* album. He made his film debut as Mixx in the 2006 David Petrarca movie *Save the Last Dance 2,* followed in 2007 by a role in *Stomp the Yard,* directed by Sylvain White.

Ne-Yo's dual career of singer and songwriter has exposed him to two different sides of show business. As a songwriter, he has worked behind the scenes, earning success and critical praise, but remaining relatively anonymous. As a performing artist, he has gained fame and recognition but lost much of his privacy. His determination to avoid the superficial values of stardom has made him especially appreciate his behind-the-scenes work as part of the Compound Foundation, a branch of Compound Entertainment that helps foster education and entrepreneurship to group homes and schools for at-risk teenagers in Georgia and New Jersey. Besides his show business career, Ne-Yo is a visual artist, a martial arts devotee, and a dedicated father to his young son, Chimere.

Selected works

Albums

In My Own Words, Def Jam Universal, 2006.
Because of You, Def Jam Mercury, 2007.

Films

Save the Last Dance 2, 2006.
Stomp the Yard, 2007.

Sources

Periodicals

Billboard, April 14, 2007, p. 49; June 2, 2007, pp. 44, 65.
Entertainment Weekly, April 27, 2007, p. 139.
Essence, July 2007, p. 64.
Jet, June 4, 2007, pp. 58–62.

Online

Adaso, Henry, "Quality R&B," *SoundSlam,* http://www.soundslam.com/articles/interviews/interviews.php?interviews=in060130neyo (accessed December 28, 2007).

Davenport, Leigh, "Almost Famous," *Chocolate Magazine,* http://www.chocolatemagazine.co.uk/features.php?article=32 (accessed December 28, 2007).

"Exclusive Interview with Ne-Yo," *Concrete Loop,* http://concreteloop.com/2007/02/exclusive-interview-with-ne-yo-now-up (accessed December 28, 2007).

"Ne-Yo," *Def Jam Recordings,* http://www.defjam.com/site/artist_bio.php?artist_id=593 (accessed December 28, 2007).

"Ne-Yo," *MusicSnippet,* http://www.musicsnippet.com/RBArtistView.php?Name=Ne%20-%20Yo (accessed December 28, 2007).

"Ne-Yo Biography," *AOL Music,* http://music.aol.com/artist/ne-yo/737022/biography (accessed December 28, 2007).

Official Ne-Yo Fan Club, http://ne-yofan.com/ne-yo/ (accessed December 28, 2007).

—Tina Gianoulis

Joshua Nkomo

1917–1999

Political leader

Nkomo, Joshua, photograph. © Peter Jordan/Alamy.

Joshua Nkomo, who was called the "father of Zimbabwean nationalism" for his role in ensuring black majority rule in the African nation of Zimbabwe (formerly Southern Rhodesia), later served as one of two vice presidents in a one-party government headed by Robert Mugabe. *New Leader* correspondent Kurt M. Campbell wrote of Nkomo: "The man who founded the nationalist resistance to white rule and spent a decade in a Rhodesian prison ... has now assumed the mantle of elder statesman in the government." Nkomo's acceptance of the position in 1988 brought a lasting partnership of the country's two leading political parties, thus effectively ending a half-decade of bloody civil war.

Nkomo told the *New Leader,* "The unity between our [Zimbabwean] peoples is something we had to bring about. We could look around the region and see how South Africa has played on our weaknesses. Now we are together.... Zimbabwe is situated in a volatile, violent region, and we need to face the future united." The unity that Nkomo sought as Zimbabwe's vice president was no longer challenged by deadly tribal warfare, but by persistent calls for a multiparty democ-

racy in future national elections.

The history of European settlement in the territory now known as Zimbabwe began on September 13, 1890, when the flag of Great Britain was raised at Fort Salisbury. The British colonists called the area Southern Rhodesia, in honor of millionaire industrialist Cecil Rhodes. Rhodes had plans for the landlocked region, and he paid armed soldiers to subdue the native African tribes, especially the Shona and Ndebele, who had united against the invaders. By 1901 white settlers were pouring into Southern Rhodesia, forcibly seizing the best farmland and overseeing the mining of gold, chrome ore, and platinum.

Was Born into Colonialism

Joshua Nkomo was born in 1917 in the part of Southern Rhodesia that became known as Matabeleland. He was a member of the Ndebele tribe, a minority group next to the larger, more powerful Shona tribe. Despite the imposition of white rule, Nkomo's father was able to hold onto some prime grazing land. The family owned a thousand head of cattle and was prosperous enough to seek formal education for the children. The young Nkomo attended a Catholic mission school, where he completed the equivalent of an elementary school education.

As a teen, Nkomo moved to the regional capital, Bulawayo, where he made money for secondary school by working as a carpenter and truck driver. He was able to earn enough to move to South Africa, where he completed his secondary education at the Government School of Adams College. He then attended the Jan Hofmeyer School of Social Work in Johannesburg, before returning to his homeland in 1947 to take a job as a social welfare worker with the Rhodesian Railways. He was the first black man to hold such an important job on the nation's rail lines.

The country Nkomo called home was prosperous enough—though mainly for white settlers only. By 1930, the colonists from Great Britain had taken control of the government and forcibly relocated black farmers and businessmen to give more economic opportunity to the whites. Native Africans were moved to the poorest and most inaccessible land and were forbidden to compete with whites in growing cash crops such as tobacco and cotton. Blacks were relegated to positions of servitude within commercial farming or industry, and few of them were able to earn a college degree.

Shifted from Welfare Work to Politics

As one black man who did graduate from college—earning a bachelor's degree from the University of

South Africa—Nkomo was appalled by the state of affairs in his country. Even though he had a good job with the Rhodesian Railways, the inequity visited upon his fellow Zimbabweans moved him to exert himself politically. He became general-secretary of the Rhodesian Railways African Employees' Association and built that group into a powerful organization with twenty-two branches and more than twenty-five hundred members. His activities with the organization met with white approval because he seemed willing to cooperate with the ruling regime. In fact, he was perceived as such a moderate that he was invited to London in 1952 to represent black opinion at a planning conference for three British colonies, including Southern Rhodesia.

That conference represented the turning point in Nkomo's career. He rejected all proposals that left the government of Southern Rhodesia in white hands, and he returned home in protest. Within the year, he was elected president of Southern Rhodesia's African National Congress (ANC), a nationalist organization devoted to ending white minority rule. Nkomo served as president of the ANC from 1953 until the party was banned in 1959. His duties included travel abroad to speaking engagements on the party's behalf, and thus he was outside of Southern Rhodesia when the white government cracked down on the ANC and jailed some of its leaders.

The 1960s brought heightened tensions to many African nations caught in the yoke of colonial rule. In Southern Rhodesia a series of white prime ministers adopted harsher and harsher tactics against black nationalists. In turn, the blacks learned guerilla warfare techniques from sympathizers in the Soviet Union and China. Even though they were constantly under the threat of drought and poor farm yields, Southern Rhodesia continued to prosper economically, which in turn drew more whites into the country.

Founded the Zimbabwe African Peoples' Union

In July of 1961 Southern Rhodesia adopted a new constitution that allowed a small number of native Africans to enter Parliament. Nkomo supported the new constitution at first, but then changed his mind. Still perceived as a moderate, he watched his popularity erode while more militant Africans demanded black majority rule immediately. In response, he formed a political party, the Zimbabwe African Peoples' Union (ZAPU), and appealed to the United Nations for economic sanctions against Southern Rhodesia. His passionate speech in New York City in 1962 brought results. Many nations agreed to the sanctions, but some—including England and the United States—continued to offer covert support to Southern Rhodesia.

In the meantime, ZAPU was gaining popularity—and making military in-roads—in Southern Rhodesia. During 1963, Nkomo was arrested and brought to court four times for leading demonstrations and making subversive statements. Even so, he was perceived as too moderate by a wing of ZAPU, and the more radical elements formed a new party, the Zimbabwe African National Union (ZANU). The methods proposed by ZAPU and ZANU were slightly different, but the aim remained the same: to oust white minority rule in favor of a government run by black Africans.

In April of 1964 Ian Smith was named prime minister of Southern Rhodesia. A white conservative determined to make the country safe and even more prosperous for its white inhabitants, Smith began a ruthless crusade against the black nationalists. One of Smith's first acts was to banish Nkomo to a detention center in a remote region. Violent riots broke out all over the nation, but they were suppressed. All told, Smith kept Nkomo in a series of isolated "camps" for ten years. Just as in the case of South African activist Nelson Mandela, this incarceration without trial only served to heighten Nkomo's popularity, and both ZAPU and ZANU attracted recruits for the struggle against the Smith administration.

The end of Portuguese rule in the African nations of Angola and Mozambique in 1974 gave impetus to the nationalist movement in Southern Rhodesia, and Smith was finally forced to free Nkomo. As leader of ZAPU, Nkomo moved to Zambia, using that African country as a staging area for guerilla attacks on whites in Southern Rhodesia. Smith called for peace talks, but the violence continued because Nkomo refused to halt the warfare while the white government negotiated a new constitution. Smith found himself besieged by the forces of ZAPU—drawn mostly from the Ndebele peoples—and ZANU—a larger group of primarily Shona tribespeople led by Mugabe. The white prime minister opened formal negotiations with Nkomo, perceiving him as the more moderate individual, only to be told that any new constitution would have to mandate black majority rule immediately.

Helped Establish the Republic of Zimbabwe

The final blow for Smith came in 1979, when Nkomo and Mugabe put aside their differences and united ZAPU and ZANU for an all-out attack on Southern Rhodesia. The unity of rebel leaders forced Smith to the bargaining table in London, and the Republic of Zimbabwe was born. Black majority rule was restored to the nation, with elections set for 1980. Voting in the first Zimbabwean election reflected party strengths. Mugabe, the leader of ZANU and a member of the more numerous Shona tribe, was elected prime minister. He immediately appointed Nkomo as one of his top deputies, thus giving ZAPU supporters a role in the new government.

The alliance was a fragile one, however. Within two years, Mugabe fired Nkomo and accused him of plotting a coup with ZAPU soldiers. Nkomo denied any plot, but many of his followers resorted to violence in protest of Mugabe's actions. In the spring of 1983 the situation became so precarious for Nkomo that he fled Zimbabwe in secret. His home was ransacked and his servant murdered by Mugabe's government troops. "I ran away from my grave," Nkomo told *Newsweek*. By August, he was back in Zimbabwe, but the fighting between ZAPU and ZANU supporters continued. The warfare split Zimbabwe along tribal lines, and even though atrocities were committed by both sides, the smaller Ndebele tribe—Nkomo's people—reportedly suffered the most. Fighting was concentrated in Matabeleland, the province where Nkomo was born.

In 1987 ZAPU was forbidden to hold rallies, and its offices were closed by the government. Nkomo had lived through the years of white repression only to see his political party repressed by yet another regime. The violence continued, and even though Nkomo told the *New Leader* that the dissidents "acted alone, without external support or higher command," it seemed increasingly likely that arms were being supplied to ZAPU by South Africa to continue the civil war in Zimbabwe.

This knowledge—and the continuing atrocities—led Mugabe to seek an accord with Nkomo. During the Christmas holidays in 1987, the two former rebels joined hands, symbolically fusing their political parties, and called for an end to the fighting. *Africa Report* contributor Andrew Meldrum wrote that throughout the spring of 1988, "Nkomo was featured making impassioned appeals for his followers to support the … government and to end all cooperation with the dissident rebels. At his side were top ZANU ministers, who just a year earlier had described Nkomo himself as a dissident."

Became the Vice President of Zimbabwe

Nkomo became vice president of Zimbabwe, with duties that included the development of rural areas such as Matabeleland. The combination of ZANU and ZAPU (which became known as ZANU-PF) effectively brought one-party rule to Zimbabwe. In 1990 Mugabe was reelected as executive president under a new constitution, Nkomo was retained as one of two vice presidents, and ZANU-PF won 116 of 120 seats in Parliament.

A diplomatic and political victory of such massive proportions seemed to indicate strong electoral support for a one-party state. Unfortunately for the Mugabe administration, Zimbabwe has been beset by problems, from unemployment running as high as 50 percent to soaring inflation and industrial decay. The whites who once ran the industries and commercial farms left the country without training blacks to assume professional roles. Although the government controls the principal newspaper and the only television and radio stations in the country, reports of high-level corruption have repeatedly surfaced.

Nkomo served as vice president from 1988 until his death in 1999. In the final years of his tenure, his deteriorating health and failure to address political challenges led to a decline in his influence. While Nkomo disagreed with Mugabe's tendency toward autocracy, he was unable to mount a successful political resistance. Nkomo withdrew from the public during the last years of his life and died in July of 1999 of complications from prostate cancer. He left a lasting impression on the Zimbabwean populace. Though many feared that a civil war might erupt in the wake of his death, government leaders praised Nkomo for his leadership and pledged to work toward conciliatory policies in his honor. Nkomo was buried in the National Heroes Acre in Harare, at a funeral attended by thousands of mourners including a number of international dignitaries. In his speech, President Mugabe spoke with admiration about Nkomo's role in history and described him as the "founder of the nation."

Sources

Books

Charlton, Michael, *The Last Colony in Africa: Diplomacy and the Independence of Rhodesia,* Basil Blackwell, 1990.

Periodicals

Africa Report, March–April 1988; March–April 1990; July–August 1990; January–February 1991; March–April 1992; July–August 1992.
Al-Ahram Weekly, July 21, 1999.
Christian Science Monitor, June 28, 1963.
New Leader, April 18, 1983; December 12, 1988.
Newsweek, March 21, 1983; August 29, 1983.
New York Times, July 2, 1999.
Time, March 18, 1985; January 4, 1988.

Online

"World: Africa Mandela Leads Tributes to Joshua Nkomo," *BBC Online,* http://news.bbc.co.uk/2/hi/africa/382604.stm (accessed December 19, 2007).

Other

Additional information supplied by the Zimbabwe embassy, Washington, D.C.

—Anne Janette Johnson and Micah L. Issit

Bisola Ojikutu

1974—

Medical researcher, educator

As a specialist in infectious diseases with a background in political science, Bisola Ojikutu has become a global leader in the fight to prevent the spread of the human immune deficiency virus (HIV)/acquired immune deficiency syndrome (AIDS) in South Africa. Ojikutu has worked with the U.S. and South African governments to develop community education programs and to promote health and safety practices to underserved communities. As the HIV epidemic continues to be one of the chief medical issues of the twenty-first century, Ojikutu's training and experience places her at the head of the global efforts to combat the disease.

Bisola Ojikutu was born on June 5, 1974, in the south side of Chicago, Illinois. Her father emigrated from Nigeria to the United States in 1964, where he met and married Ojikutu's mother in 1970. Her father attended classes to become a podiatrist, while her mother worked at a local bank. After finishing his training, Ojikutu's father obtained work in the Chicago Heights suburb.

Ojikutu attended Bloom Township High School, where she became an academic and student body leader and participated in a number of extracurricular activities, including sports clubs, mathematics competitions, and the school newspaper. Ojikutu credits her involvement in extracurricular activities as an important lesson in leadership that she carried with her into her professional career. Ojikutu gradated as valedictorian of her high school class.

From Political Science to Medical School

Ojikutu enrolled in Washington University in St. Louis, Missouri, where she worked toward a degree in political science. The decision to attend Washington University was made partially to comply with her father's wishes. "I actually wanted to go to Stanford," Ojikutu recalled in an interview with Karen Hopkin of the Howard Hughes Medical Institute, but because her father did not want her to travel as far away as California, she was urged toward a closer choice.

Ojikutu became involved in a number of community activities during her time in St. Louis, such as working with a nonprofit organization to create after-school programs for inner city children and working with teenage mothers at the St. Louis Regional Hospital. During her community activities, Ojikutu became disillusioned with the idea of entering politics to positively affect underserved communities. "I loved the work, and I thought it was great to try to get people mobilized to take action for themselves. But I also saw that I couldn't make a practical contribution," Ojikutu told Hopkin.

Ojikutu became intrigued watching friends and colleagues struggle with Washington University's medical school preparatory program. Driven by the need for a challenge and looking for a way to make a direct impact in the community, Ojikutu altered her focus and entered the premed program. The decision to enter medical school was unexpected for Ojikutu, who had never envisioned herself pursuing a career in science.

At a Glance . . .

Born Bisola Ojikutu on June 5, 1974, in Chicago, IL. *Education:* Washington University in St. Louis, BA, 1995; Johns Hopkins University School of Medicine, MD, 1999; Harvard School of Public Health, MPH, 2003.

Career: New York Presbyterian Hospital (Cornell University), intern, 1999–2000; New York Presbyterian Hospital, resident, 2000–02; Harvard University Fellowship in Minority Health Policy, fellow, 2002–03; Massachusetts General Hospital/Brigham and Women's Hospital, infectious disease fellow, 2003–05; William J. Clinton Foundation's HIV/AIDS Initiative, South Africa, consulting team member, 2003–04; ARV Task Team, South Africa, consultant, 2003–04; Harvard Medical School, South Africa HIV/AIDS Programs, 2005–06, director; World Health Organization, Treat, Train, and Retain Campaign, consultant, 2006; Harvard Medical School, Office of International Programs, director, 2007—.

Memberships: Infectious Disease Society of America; International AIDS Society; National Medical Association.

Awards: Harriet S. Kluver Scholar Award, 1993; Howard Hughes Research Fellowship, 1994; Ralph Bunche Scholar Award for Academic Excellence, 1995; Charles Uribe Award for Outstanding Service to Underserved Communities, 2002; Massachusetts General Hospital, Clinician-Teacher Award, 2006.

Addresses: *Office*—401 Park Drive, Second Floor East, Boston, MA 02125.

"To be absolutely honest, I really didn't like science. The way it was taught in school was uninspiring," Ojikutu told *Contemporary Black Biography* (*CBB*). However, Ojikutu thrived on the challenge and displayed an aptitude for her premed classes.

Became Interested in the AIDS Epidemic

Ojikutu had her choice among a number of prominent medical school programs and eventually chose to attend Johns Hopkins University in Baltimore, Maryland.

Among her reasons for choosing Johns Hopkins was the school's history of promoting a number of prominent and "outspoken" African-American physicians, including pediatric neurosurgeon Ben Carson, renowned cardiac surgeon Levi Watkins, and Claudia Lynn Thomas, who was the first African-American woman to become an orthopedist. In addition, Ojikutu felt that the Baltimore area was a city with a wide host of social issues, including rampant unemployment, poverty, and drug use. Ojikutu felt that, besides obtaining an excellent medical education, she could potentially help take part in the revitalization of the Baltimore community. "It was an environment I thought I could immerse myself in and learn from and maybe even make an impact on," she told *CBB*.

After receiving her MD from Johns Hopkins in 1999, Ojikutu was placed in an internal medicine residency program at Cornell University's New York Presbyterian Hospital. It was during her residency that Ojikutu first became involved in working with AIDS patients. She worked from 2000 to 2002 at the university's Harlem United Health Care Clinic, where she helped create a curriculum for training staff on how to care for HIV/AIDS patients in the community. In working with AIDS patients, Ojikutu found a way to combine her medical training with her desire to fill a leadership role and to have a political social impact.

In 2002, Ojikutu was accepted into the Harvard School of Public Health, where she earned a master of public health. Ojikutu continued working on HIV/AIDS issues and became a consultant for the MassHealth Expansion Program, helping to evaluate the success of the program in providing treatment and care to uninsured Massachusetts residents. During this time, Ojikutu began networking to find out about opportunities to work with patients in Africa, where the AIDS epidemic spread rapidly during the 1990s and where treatment and outreach facilities are relatively scarce in comparison to the United States. It was Bruce Walker of the Howard Hughes Medical Institute in Maryland who first informed Ojikutu about the possibility of becoming involved in AIDS programs in South Africa. In the interview with Hopkin, Ojikutu remembered Walker's message, "He said, 'Go there and help. I believe you have the energy. I believe you have the potential. Just do it.'"

Fought the AIDS Epidemic in South Africa

In 2003, Ojikutu traveled to Pretoria, South Africa, where she conducted research and worked as a consultant for the newly established William J. Clinton Foundation's HIV/AIDS Initiative. Ojikutu helped to prepare a nationwide training program for HIV/AIDS workers and health-care professionals and to accredit hospitals preparing to initiate an antiretroviral (ARV) treatment program in South Africa.

Ojikutu then traveled to KwaZulu-Natal, South Africa, the province with the highest prevalence of HIV cases in the country, where she prepared South African medical workers for the transition to the ARV program. She designed the KwaZulu-Natal Provincial HIV Training Curriculum, which was established as the standard teaching system for specialists and volunteers treating patients in the region. Ojikutu also evaluated the effectiveness of the provincial treatment facilities and worked with local specialists to improve and enhance treatment guidelines. At McCord Hospital, in Durban, South Africa, Ojikutu saw patients directly and educated local physicians, nurses, and students in how to administer medications and track patient progress.

After a year, Ojikutu returned to the United States to finish her research, but was determined to return and continue working to improve patient care and treatment access in South Africa. "When I arrived in 2003, fewer than two thousand people were on antiretroviral therapy," she said to *CBB,* adding that over one million were in need of treatment in 2004. "It's a tragedy, but it makes you want to keep coming back, want to keep helping."

Directed Harvard's South Africa HIV/AIDS Programs

In 2004, Ojikutu enrolled in a second fellowship at Massachusetts General Hospital and Brigham and Women's Hospital, specializing in infectious diseases. When she finished the fellowship in 2005, she was asked to direct Harvard University Medical School's South Africa HIV/AIDS Programs.

From 2005 to 2006, Ojikutu traveled between Boston and South Africa, where she initiated a mobile training program for health-care workers operating in rural regions in South Africa. Ojikutu also sponsored Harvard University's undergraduate and medical student program, which sent students and residents to South Africa to perform volunteer work with regional hospitals. She directed the BroadReach Healthcare/Harvard University President's Emergency Plan for AIDS Relief Initiative, which expanded primary ARV access and care in South Africa and worked with five important clinics and hospitals to improve patient care. Ojikutu was the founder and director of the Umndeni Family Care Program in South Africa, which was formed in collaboration with Habitat for Humanity and specializes in providing care for women and orphans in KwaZulu-Natal.

Ojikutu not only remained active in South Africa but also worked with patients and health-care administrators in Boston. She was the chairperson of the Third International HIV/AIDS Conference, which addressed the problems and potential solutions to administering ARV treatment both in impoverished international communities and in domestic communities. She also

served as the editor-in-chief for a supplementary issue of the *Journal of Infectious Diseases,* which focused on the ARV program in South Africa to educate the U.S. health-care community on the progress of the African AIDS epidemic.

In 2006, Ojikutu served as a consultant for the World Health Organization's Treat, Train, and Retain Campaign, which aims to improve health care in areas with limited access to medical supplies. Shortly after becoming an instructor in medicine for Harvard Medical School, she received the 2006 Clinician-Teacher Award from Massachusetts General Hospital, in recognition of both her pioneering work and her success and capability as an educator. In 2007, Ojikutu was selected to be the director of Harvard Medical School's Office of International Programs.

In October of 2007, Ojikutu continued functioning in both the United States and in South African communities as a chief researcher in the ongoing struggle to combat the spread of HIV/AIDS. Even though Ojikutu never imagined during her childhood that she would be immersed in science, she has come to view medicine as the perfect complement to her interests in social service. As she told Hopkin, "I like the science now that I can translate it into patient care. That makes it real to me [and] motivates me to stay in this world."

Selected writings

Nonfiction

(With Beth S. Lee and L. Shannon Holliday) "Osteoclasts Express the B2 Isoform of Vacuolar H+-ATPase Intracellularly and on Their Plasma Membranes," *American Journal of Physiology: Cell Physiology,* Vol. 270, 1996, pp. C382–388.

(With Valerie E. Stone) "Women, Inequality, and the Burden of HIV," *New England Journal of Medicine,* Vol. 352, 2005, pp. 649–652.

"The Realities of Antiretroviral Therapy Roll-Out," *Journal of Infectious Diseases,* Vol. 196, 2007, pp. S445–448.

(With Lisa R. Hirschhorn and William Rodriguez) "Research for Change: Using Implementation Research to Strengthen HIV Care and Treatment Scale-up in Resource-Limited Settings," *Journal of Infectious Diseases,* Vol. 196, 2007, pp. S516–522.

(With Chris Jack and Gita Ramjee) "Provision of Antiretroviral Therapy in South Africa: Unique Challenges and Remaining Obstacles," *Journal of Infectious Diseases,* Vol. 196, 2007. pp. S523–527.

(With Hui Zheng, Rochelle Walensky, Elena Losina, Kenneth Freedberg, Zhigang Lu, and Janet Giddy) "Predictors of Mortality in Patients Initiating Antiretroviral Therapy," Twenty-sixth International AIDS Conference, Toronto, Canada, August 18, 2006.

Sources

Online

"Fellows Bios, 2002–2003," *Commonwealth Fund/ Harvard University Fellowship,* http://www.mfdp. med.harvard.edu/fellows_faculty/cfhuf/fellows/ bios/2002/bisola.htm (December 12, 2007).

Hopkin, Karen, "Serving the Community," *Howard Hughes Medical Institute,* http://www.hhmi.org/ biointeractive/disease/ojikutu.html (December 12, 2007).

Ledger, Kate, "In a Sea of White Faces," *Hopkins Medical News,* http://www.hopkinsmedicine.org/ hmn/W98/sea.html (December 12, 2007).

Other

Additional information for this profile was obtained through interviews with Bisola Ojikutu on October 21 and October 23, 2007.

—Micah L. Issitt

Rissi Palmer

1981—

Singer, songwriter

In 2007, singer/songwriter Rissi Palmer became the first African-American woman to reach *Billboard* Country Singles Chart in twenty years. From her debut as a professional singer in 1997 to the release of her first solo album in 2007, Palmer has been hailed by some industry analysts as a leader in the evolution of the country music genre.

Palmer was born on August 19, 1981, in Sewickley, Pennsylvania; a small town located less than an hour from Pittsburgh. Palmer's father, Johnny Palmer, a manager for retail shopping chains, and mother, Donzella Palmer, an airline attendant for Delta Airlines, met and married in their mutual home state of Georgia before moving to Pennsylvania. Palmer told *Contemporary Black Biography* (*CBB*) that her parents were "extremely instrumental" in her love of music. Palmer remembers her mother listening to a variety of country and gospel, including Patsy Cline, who was one of her mother's favorites. Her father also enjoyed a diverse interest in music, and Palmer remembers that her childhood home was filled with diverse array of music.

Palmer, Rissi, photograph. Sarah J. Glover/MCT/Landov.

Palmer's mother was diagnosed with colon cancer in the early 1980s and died in 1988, leaving Palmer's father as her sole caretaker. "My mother's death had a very profound affect on me," Palmer told *CBB*. "It was at this time that I started to write poems that would later turn into songs. She has remained one of my biggest inspirations." Palmer also remembers the years that her father struggled to provide her with a healthy, happy lifestyle while suffering from the loss of his wife and maintaining a demanding work schedule. "My dad is my hero," Palmer told *CBB*. Palmer's father remarried in 1990 to Darlene Carpenter, a native of Sewickley who worked as an elementary school teacher, and the following year the couple had a son, John Loran Palmer.

Palmer's family remained in Pennsylvania through 1993, where she attended parochial schools. "It was very clear as a child, to everyone, that I wanted to be a singer and entertainer," Palmer told *CBB*. In 1984, when Palmer was three, her parents enrolled her in dance, choir, and voice and piano lessons. In 1985, Palmer got her first public performance at Antioch Baptist Church in Sewickley, singing "Jesus Loves

Me," while standing on the milk crate to reach the microphone. "I was hooked after that." she added. In 1994, Palmer's family moved to Grover, Missouri, a town located near St. Louis.

Began Touring as an Entertainer

In 1995, while involved with a youth group at the First Baptist Church of Chesterfield, Missouri, Palmer was asked to compete in the Miss Missouri Hal Jackson's Talented Teen competition. Palmer competed in the talent show in both 1996 and 1997, where her performance was noticed by Ray Parks, a choreographer and producer for Team 11, a singing and dance troupe composed of youth between fourteen and twenty-one that performed for corporate functions, school presentations, and as part of St. Louis's Channel 11 programming. Team 11 was Palmer's first employment opportunity, and she told *CBB* that she felt "rich and famous at sixteen," given the small stipend the troupe paid to its performers.

In October of 1998, Palmer accompanied Team 11 to the Arkansas State Fair, where she decided to perform a version of Shania Twain's "Any Man of Mine." Palmer vividly remembers that performance, which was given to a crowd composed primarily of farmers, as a key moment in her career. "When it was time for us to perform, the stage was covered in feathers and bird poop," she told *CBB*. After the show, she said that "a man came over to me and said "Girl, I wasn't sure what you were about to do, but you're pretty good at that. You might want to think about doing that for a living."" Palmer added, "I guess you can say that was the beginning of my official career!"

While performing with Team 11, Palmer met Dana Lyons and Leslie Leland of Us Girlz Entertainment, a Georgia-based promotions and artist-management company. Palmer left Team 11 in 1999 and traveled to Chicago, Illinois, where she enrolled in DePaul University. But after her first semester, she left school to pursue her music career full time. In early 2000, she relocated to Atlanta to work with Lyons and Leland.

Though Palmer was drawn to country music, she felt that she would not be accepted by mainstream country audiences because, as she told *CBB*, "There are no black women country singers." Regardless, Lyons and Leland encouraged Palmer to pursue country music and brought country artist Deborah Allen to the studio to work with Palmer on a professional demo album, which she began shopping to country labels after 2000.

Though mainstream country labels were reluctant to accept her, Palmer was offered a recording contract by Jimmy Jam and Terry Lewis of Flyte Time Records, who were the producers of successful rhythm and blues (R&B) artists Janet Jackson and Mariah Carey. Jam and Lewis wanted Palmer to alter her style to conform to a more urban, pop appeal. "While I love pop and R&B, that's not what I want to sing," Palmer told *CBB*. "I couldn't imagine having to sing or write about something I didn't believe in." After contemplation, Palmer decided to reject the offer and continue to pursue a country music contract. "My genuine love for country music is what motivated my decision."

Obtained a Publishing Deal

Palmer stayed in Atlanta until 2001 and then moved to New Jersey, where she worked at various jobs to supplement her income. In 2001, Palmer was approached by representatives of the Nashville-based Song Planet music publishing company, which offered her a publishing deal helping to write songs for country artists. Palmer remembers her time with Song Planet, from 2001 to 2003, as a "pivotal" moment in her career, because she was able to develop her skills as a lyricist while having the opportunity to work with a number of established country music writers. "In many ways I feel like this was my version of college," Palmer told *CBB*.

In February of 2002, Palmer traveled to New York to perform at the Sugar Bar, after being told by Lyons that scouts for the reality television series *Star Search* were recruiting at the venue. Palmer was selected by scouts for the show and within a few months she was in Los Angeles preparing for the competition. Palmer told *CBB* that she remembers *Star Search* as "the most trying experience of my career, thus far." Palmer lost her voice due to vocal fatigue during the semifinals and eventually lost in the final round. Though she was disappointed with having lost the competition, she believes the experience and exposure were extremely positive for her career. Bob Doerschuk of Great American Country stated that the show's judges were supportive of Palmer's performances, especially country music star Naomi Judd, who said, "There are only two kinds of music, good and bad—and Rissi is good."

After the competition, Palmer was asked to record songs for the ABC television special *Dance Fever,* and shortly thereafter she was one of several artists featured in Country Music Television's special *Waiting in the Wings: African Americans Journey in Country Music.* Despite her increasing exposure, Palmer was still lacking in a record deal and, somewhat discouraged by her progress, was considering pursuing a career as a songwriter.

Signed with a Major Label

While visiting Los Angeles in 2005, Palmer met Bernard Alexander, general manager of 1720 Entertainment, who, after a conversation with Palmer, took her demo album to label president Terry Johnson. Johnson decided to offer Palmer a recording deal, and two months later she was in the studio recording material for her debut album. "1720 has done so much for my career," Palmer told *CBB.* "Terry's philosophy is the artist comes first, and he helps to manifest major career and financial opportunities for us. I am allowed and encouraged to be hands on in my career."

Palmer's first single, "Country Girl," was released on a four-song collection produced by Starbucks Entertainment and available exclusively through iTunes. In 2007, the song debuted on the *Billboard* Country Singles Chart at number 58, a historic moment as Palmer became the first African-American woman to reach the *Billboard* rankings since Dona Mason's song "Green Eyes" reached number 62 in 1987. By August of 2007, Palmer's album was one of the five best-selling country albums on iTunes. Palmer's self-titled debut album was released in October of 2007 and included twelve songs, of which nine were originals composed by Palmer.

In June of 2007, Palmer achieved a long sought after goal when she was asked to perform at the Grand Old Opry theater in Nashville, which is arguably the most famous and important venue for country music in the United States. In an interview for *Newsweek*'s Jamie Reno, Palmer said of her appearance, "That was truly one of the most amazing moments of my life…. It was extremely emotional. I cried several times that night. I feel like it was a milestone in my career, it was validating."

"Being 'country' is more about a state of mind and how you live your life—not so much where you're from or the color of your skin," Palmer said in an interview with Margena A. Christian of *Jet* magazine. In Palmer's estimation, being an African-American country singer has been both a blessing and a challenge. "It definitely causes people to sit up straight and pay attention, which has been very beneficial in getting people to listen to my music," she told *CBB.* "However, it puts a huge amount of scrutiny on me. I find that my sincerity and authenticity are questioned a lot." Palmer thinks that many feel her decision to sing country music is a "gimmick," but she fervently believes that once people experience her music they will know that it is genuine. "I've been blessed in that I'm judged primarily on my talent more than anything, that's all you can really ask." When asked her hopes for the impact her music and story will have on her listeners, Palmer said to *CBB,* "I hope that in pursuing this unconventional career path, I show that staying true to who you are and what your heart desires can pay off and also that people of color, especially young women, don't have to fit in the boxes that society has picked out for us. The possibilities are truly limitless."

Selected Works

Albums

Rissi Palmer, 1720 Entertainment, 2007.

Sources

Periodicals

Jet, September 10, 2007.
Newsweek, August 24, 2007.
Tennessean, August 26, 2007.
Wall Street Journal, September 28, 2007.

Online

"As a Black Woman, Rissi Palmer Is Country Rarity," *MSNBC Online,* http://www.msnbc.msn.com/id/21307946/ (accessed December 16, 2007).
Doerschuk, Bob, "New Artist Spotlight: Rissi Palmer," *Great American Country,* http://www.gactv.com/gac/nw_cma_close_up/article/0,3034,GAC_26068_5761155_,00.html (accessed December 16, 2007).

Other

Additional information for this interview was obtained through an interview with Rissi Palmer on October 23, 2007.

—Micah L. Issitt

Sydney Tamiia Poitier

1973—

Actor

Sydney Tamiia Poitier shares most of her name with her famous father, Academy Award–winner Sidney Poitier. She admits that her name has sometimes helped open doors for her, but it has also been a mixed blessing. "I think I got a lot more auditions that way," she told *Jet*. "There were certainly higher expectations placed on me. And people have pre-conceived notions of me before I walk into a room because they're so familiar with my father. So, that actually works against you a little bit."

Poitier, Sydney Tamiia, photgraph. UPN/Landov.

Rohmer, and Jean-Luc Godard. She and Sidney Poitier appeared together in a 1969 film called *The Lost Man,* about a group of black militants planning a heist to fund their revolution. Shimkus's last film appearance was in the 1971 marital farce *The Marriage of a Young Stockbroker* alongside Richard Benjamin, and she gave birth to Sydney Tamiia Poitier's older sister, Anika, in early 1972.

Poitier was born in November of the following year, and her parents did not wed until 1976. This was a period of transition for her father, who was moving from acting to directing. "By the time I came along, my dad wasn't working as much, so he was home a lot," she told Champ Clark in *People*. That changed after *Stir Crazy,* which in 1980 became the highest-grossing film by an African-American director and remained in that spot until *Scary Movie* from Keenan Ivory Wayans twenty years later. Poitier grew up in the Los Angeles area with Anika and four stepsisters from her father's previous marriage, and she pursued a drama degree at the Tisch School of the Arts of New York University. It was at this point in her life that her parents voiced concern about the uneven job prospects and uncertain financial future for actors. "I

Poitier was born in 1973, exactly a decade after her father became the first African-American male to win an Oscar for a lead role, which he earned for his performance in the movie *Lilies of the Field*. The first African American to win an Academy Award was Butterfly McQueen in 1939 for her supporting role in *Gone with the Wind*. After Poitier's 1963 win, another twenty-eight years would pass before another black actor—Denzel Washington—would earn an Oscar for a lead role. Sydney Tamiia Poitier's mother, Joanna Shimkus, was an actor, too, and had appeared in the 1965 cult classic *Paris vu par ...,* which featured vignettes of Paris made by several living legends of French cinema, among them Claude Chabrol, Eric

At a Glance . . .

Born November 15, 1973, in Los Angeles, CA; daughter of Sidney Poitier and Joanna Shimkus. *Education:* Earned degree from the Tisch School of the Arts, New York University; studied acting at the Stella Adler Conservatory.

Career: Made film debut in *Park City,* 1998; cast in the television series *First Years,* 2001, and *Abby,* 2003.

Addresses: *Agent*—International Creative Management, 8942 Wilshire Blvd., Beverly Hills, CA 90211.

was encouraged to have some sort of backup plan," she told Diane Baroni in *Interview* magazine. "They wanted me to be cautious and to know just how difficult it is to have an acting career. So while they were supportive, they were also smart and tried to get me to think things through."

Poitier also trained at the prestigious Stella Adler Conservatory and won her first film role in a small, little-seen 1998 film called *Park Day,* about African-American teens in Missouri. She followed that with a role in the Clint Eastwood blockbuster *True Crime* a year later, and she also made her first appearance alongside her father in *Free of Eden,* which aired on the Showtime cable channel. Based on a novel by Leon Ichaso, *Free of Eden* centered on the elder Poitier as a successful business mogul who reluctantly agrees to tutor a young woman from the projects, played by the younger Poitier. "It was weird the first week we had rehearsals," she said in an interview with *Jet,* when asked what it had been like to work with a parent. "I just kept cracking up. It was so hard for me to look him in the face and treat him as this character and not my dad. I just kept seeing Dad. After a couple of days, it was fine, but in the beginning I was giggling uncontrollably."

As her parents had feared, Poitier struggled to find meaningful roles and maintain a steady income. In 2001 she appeared in *MacArthur Park,* a gritty fictional look at drug addicts in the famous Los Angeles landmark park, and in 2003 she was surprised to win a starring role in a television sitcom. The series was called *Abby* and ran for just four episodes on UPN. She played a San Francisco sports producer, Abigail "Abby" Walker, who is forced to remain roommates with her ex-boyfriend, played by Kadeem Hardison. Following the series' abrupt cancellation, Poitier appeared in eight episodes of *Joan of Arcadia* in 2003 and 2004, followed by a seven-episode run on *Veronica Mars.*

In 2004 Poitier and her sister Anika teamed to make *The Devil Cats,* a faux documentary about a fictional all-female rock band. Anika wrote and directed the comedy, and Poitier produced it and appeared as one of the musicians. A year later, Poitier appeared in the large, all-star ensemble cast for the film *Nine Lives,* featuring a series of interconnected stories about nine women in Los Angeles. In 2006 she was cast in the Snoop Dogg cautionary moral tale/horror film *Hood of Horror,* but earned more attention in early 2007 for her part in *Grindhouse.* The dual-story movie from directors Quentin Tarantino and Robert Rodriguez was designed to be a send-up of racy horror movies of an earlier era, and in Tarantino's "Death Proof" segment she appeared as Jungle Julia, one of the actresses terrorized by a psychotic stuntman played by Kurt Russell. Later in 2007, the two halves of the movie were released separately, under their respective segment titles.

Poitier is grateful to her parents for their advice, and in retrospect she admits they may have been right to want her to have a backup plan. "I have a very romantic view of the business because of the movies my dad made and that I watched growing up," she told *Detroit Free Press* writer Mike Duffy. Two of Sidney Poitier's most memorable roles were in the interracial dating comedy *Guess Who's Coming to Dinner?* and the civil rights drama *In the Heat of the Night,* both critically acclaimed films from 1967. "They don't make movies like that anymore," she noted. In spite of knowing the pitfalls of following in her father's footsteps, she is thankful for her father's generous store of wisdom. "I have someone to go to at all times for advice in this crazy business," she told Duffy. "And this is a hard, weird business."

Selected works

Films

Park Day, 1998.
True Crime, 1999.
MacArthur Park, 2001.
Happy Birthday, 2001.
(Also producer) *The Devil Cats,* 2004.
Nine Lives, 2005.
The List, 2006.
Hood of Horror, 2006.
Grindhouse, 2007.
Death Proof, 2007.

Television

Abby, 2003.
Joan of Arcadia, 2003–04.
Veronica Mars, 2004.

Sources

Periodicals

Detroit Free Press, February 11, 2003.
Film Journal International, November 2005.

Interview, March 2003.
Jet, February 22, 1999; January 27, 2003.
New York Times, September 9, 2007.
People, April 16, 2007.

—Carol Brennan

Prince

1958—

Musician, singer

Prince, photograph. Chris Pizzello/Reuters/Landov.

"Everybody knows what song is going to be played on New Year's Eve 1999," filmmaker Spike Lee remarked to the Prince during a feature in *Interview* magazine. He was referring to Prince's apocalyptic anthem, "1999," from his 1982 album of the same name, one of the earliest and brightest hits in a career that has spanned four decades. In that time, Prince became one of the most prolific and successful pop musicians of all time. A performer whose music synthesizes elements of funk, soul, jazz, hip-hop, and rock, Prince is regarded as an innovator whose influences are felt not only through the many imitators of his musical style but also in the way that music is produced, the relationship between artists and music labels, and the methods by which songs are distributed.

He was born Prince Rogers Nelson in Minneapolis on June 7, 1958. His parents were both musical, and he was named after his father's jazz combo, the Prince Rogers Trio. After his parents' divorce, Nelson's home life became difficult; he lived sometimes with his mother and stepfather, sometimes with his father, and sometimes with family friends. By the time he was a teenager, the years of being passed (or running) from home to home had taken an emotional toll. He withdrew into music, mastering by some accounts a dozen instruments by ear, and also writing lyrics that verged on the pornographic. The young musician was "a volcano of emotion boiling under the surface," a friend of his said in *People*.

In high school, he played in a band with other musicians—Morris Day (later of the Time) and Andre Cymone—who would later become his creative associates. But his talent outstripped that of his peers, and by the age of eighteen he was already a star waiting to be discovered. Collaborating on a song one day with Minneapolis studio owner Chris Moon, Nelson recorded guitar and vocal tracks, then offered to play keyboards, and continued to work on the recording single-handed by adding bass guitar and drum tracks as an astonished Moon looked on. Word spread quickly about the young musician's wizardry. He soon acquired a manager, advertising executive Owen Husney, who suggested shortening his name to the mysterious single name "Prince."

At a Glance . . .

Born Prince Rogers Nelson on June 7, 1958, in Minneapolis, MN; son of John Nelson and Mattie Shaw; married Mayte Garcia, 1996 (divorced, 2000); married Manuela Testolini, 2001 (separated, 2006).

Career: Recording and performing artist, late 1970s—released double-platinum album, *1999*, 1982; starred in *Purple Rain* and wrote soundtrack songs, 1984; formed Paisley Park label, 1987; changed name to an unpronounceable symbol, 1993, and came to be called The Artist; reversed change of name to Prince Rogers Nelson; established a digital subscription service on the Internet to publish his work through New Power Generation Music Club, 2001–06; signed with Columbia Records, 2004.

Awards: Academy Award for best original song score, 1984; six Grammy Awards; Radio & Records, top urban contemporary artist of the past twenty years; World Music Award for outstanding contribution to the pop industry, 1994; Rock and Roll Hall of Fame, 2004; National Association for the Advancement of Colored People (NAACP) Image Award, 2005; NAACP Vanguard Award, 2005; Black Entertainment Television, BET Award for Best Male R&B Artist, 2006; Golden Globe Award for best original song, 2007.

Addresses: *Web*—http://www.3121.com/main.html.

Signed Record Contract

Working with Moon, Prince assembled a demo tape on which he sang and played all the instruments. This feature intrigued executives at the Warner Brothers label, who not only signed him to a lucrative recording contract in 1977 but also granted him near-total creative control in the studio. This level of control was almost unprecedented for a teenage entertainer in an industry where fledgling careers are usually closely managed and marketed. Writing and producing all the music—as he would continue to do throughout his career—Prince released *For You* in 1978. The album only sold moderately well, but Warner did not have to wait long before its faith in its new prodigy was justified.

Prince's next three albums, *Prince* (1979), *Dirty Mind* (1980), and *Controversy* (1981), all went gold, with sales of over five hundred thousand copies each. "Soft and Wet," the lead single on *For You*, had been only moderately suggestive, but his lyrics soon moved into

sexual territory that was explicit even by the libertine standards of the 1980s. *Dirty Mind*, which included songs about oral sex and incest, inspired some protests and would likely have caused wider outrage had Prince's primary fan base not been young, musically progressive urban listeners.

The sexual element never overwhelmed other facets of Prince's music—he was equally adept with romantic ballads, simple party songs, and even political pieces—but he always carefully managed this segment of his output so as to attract maximum attention, posing nearly nude on the covers of several album releases. According to *Rolling Stone*, Husney had advised Prince at the beginning of his career that "controversy is press," and he took this lesson to heart. However, in interviews, Prince has also indicated that he sincerely believes in the redemptive power of sexuality and that his lyrics often fuse sexual and religious elements.

Made His Own Movie

Prince's commercial breakthrough came in 1982 with the double album *1999*. The enduring title track, with its cheerful exhortation to party in the face of imminent millennial apocalypse, could not have disturbed any censor. The music on *1999* displayed the mature style that made Prince a consistent hit-maker throughout the 1980s: high, intense, almost whispered vocals that could carry the sexual message effectively, startling falsettos, sinuous backup vocal lines (often performed by Prince himself), rock guitar, and always interesting funk percussion parts. As a producer, he was capable of bold, unforgettable strokes, such as the pure vocals-and-bass combination, eliminating any instrumental melody parts on "When Doves Cry," which was released in 1984 on the *Purple Rain* album.

Purple Rain, the soundtrack album for his largely autobiographical film of the same name, sold more than thirteen million copies, becoming one of the best-selling soundtracks of all time. The film, which starred Prince, was one of the top films that year at the box office, despite having been produced on a low budget with a cast of mainly nonprofessional actors, and the soundtrack earned him an Academy Award for Best Original Song Score.

Besides its huge success, the album had unintended consequences when Tipper Gore, the wife of politician and future presidential candidate Al Gore, listened to the lyrics of the sexually explicit song "Darling Nikki." Gore, incensed that she had purchased an album for her eleven-year-old daughter containing overt references to masturbation and other sexual acts without any warning as to its contents, formed the Parents Music Resource Center, which pressured the recording industry to adopt a ratings system similar to the one employed in the movies. This resulted in a voluntary labeling system for albums with "explicit lyrics." For his part, Prince did not oppose the labeling scheme, and became one of many artists to offer "clean" edited versions of their explicit albums.

Career and Popularity Continued to Grow

Meanwhile, Prince was at the peak of his creative powers, producing far more music than his label would allow him to release. Operating with total creative freedom in his Minneapolis studio, Paisley Park, Prince lent his prolific songwriting and producing energies to artists such as Sheena Easton, Chaka Khan, Sheila E., Patty LaBelle, and the Bangles, besides the stable of Minneapolis musicians whose careers he had launched—the Time, Andre Cymone, Vanity, Jill Jones, and others.

Prince's own albums, which were released at a pace of one per year, continued to top the charts in the late 1980s and early 1990s. However, his movie ventures were not as successful; he tried to replicate *Purple Rain*'s cinematic success by directing and starring in two features: *Under the Cherry Moon* (1986) and *Graffiti Bridge* (1990). Even though the soundtracks to both films spawned hit songs, the films themselves were box office failures.

In 1993 dwindling record sales and arguments over creative control soured Prince's relationship with Warner Brothers. For the three years remaining on his Warner Brothers contract, he made public appearances with the word *slave* scrawled across his cheek. He also dropped the Prince name in favor of an unpronounceable glyph; the music press soon dubbed him the Artist Formerly Known as Prince, or simply The Artist. Other than a massive greatest-hits collection released in 1993, his albums during this period were commercial flops, often consisting of old material that had previously been deemed unfit for release.

Continued to Blaze His Own Trail

Prince's relationship with Warner Brothers ended in 1996. His post-Warner plans for his career focused on direct distribution of his music to fans through mail order and the nascent Internet, a controversial idea at the time. "You have to ask yourself, is this artist the kind of mercurial crazy some people say, or is he the wise one who understands where he fits in at the start of a new century?" one industry insider mused in *Forbes* magazine. Clearly, he understood where he fit. His first musical release, a three-CD set of new material, called *Emancipation* (1996), was made through a traditional distribution arrangement with the large Capitol/EMI conglomerate. Despite the set's stiff price and songs featuring a broad range of musical styles, it sold several million copies.

Even though he had retreated somewhat from his independent stance with the release of *Emancipation*,

Prince stuck by his goal of flooding the market with the products of his prolific creativity, planning to release another massive compendium, *Crystal Ball,* in 1997 through his 1-800-New-Funk mail order service and Web site. However, production problems delayed the project, so he decided to turn to traditional distribution methods—a decision that proved unpopular with fans who had preordered the set months earlier, but saw copies arrive in stores at discounted prices before they had been delivered by Prince's direct distribution system.

Despite the problems with *Crystal Ball,* direct distribution remained one of his goals. In May of 2000 he officially resumed use of the name Prince, and in February of 2001—just one month after Apple inaugurated its iTunes online music store—he established the New Power Generation Music Club, an independent digital subscription service. Through the music club, he offered downloads of digital music, as well as backstage videos of the goings on at his Paisley Park studios, concert news, and streaming sneak previews of new recordings.

While Prince was innovating in the world of business and online distribution, his popularity was ebbing. Albums of new material, *Newpower Soul* (1998), *Rave Un2 the Joy Fantastic* (1999), and *The Rainbow Children* (2001), all suffered from underwhelming sales. Regardless, he experienced a major resurgence in 2004, the year he was inducted into the Rock and Roll Hall of Fame. His album *Musicology* was released later that year to critical acclaim and solid sales. The sales of the album were aided by another innovation: the inclusion of a copy of the CD with the purchase of each concert ticket to the *Musicology* tour. According to Pollstar, the tour was the highest grossing tour of 2004, taking in $87.4 million.

Sales of Prince's 2006 follow-up, *3121,* were strong and were accompanied by the opening of his night club in Las Vegas, also named 3121. A song he wrote for the 2006 animated film *Happy Feet* earned him a Golden Globe Award for best original song in 2007. His distribution innovations continued with his next album, *Planet Earth.* When he released the CD in Britain, he had it distributed as a free insert in the Sunday, July 15, 2007, edition of the *Mail* newspaper. As a consequence of this giveaway, there was never a retail release in Britain, and an unusually high level of online piracy of the album resulted. In September of 2007 Prince announced that he would sue the video-sharing network YouTube, the auction site Ebay, and a file-sharing group known as Pirate Bay for copyright infringement and assisting in the illegal distribution of his songs. Similar legal action was contemplated against unofficial fan Web sites that have posted lyrics to his songs, pictures of him, or have used his trademarks, including the glyph he once used as his name.

Selected discography

Albums

For You, Warner Bros., 1978.
Prince, Warner Bros., 1979.
Dirty Mind, Warner Bros., 1980.
Controversy, Warner Bros., 1981.
1999, Warner Bros., 1982.
Purple Rain, Warner Bros., 1984.
Around the World in a Day, Warner Bros., 1985.
Parade, Paisley Park, 1986.
Lovesexy, Paisley Park, 1988.
Graffiti Bridge, Paisley Park, 1990.
Come, Warner Bros., 1994.
Emancipation, EMI, 1996.
Crystal Ball, EMI, 1998.
The Rainbow Children, Redline, 2001.
One Nite Alone ... Live!, NPG, 2002.
N.E.W.S., NPG (Big Daddy), 2003.
Musicology, NPG/Columbia, 2004.
3121, NPG/Universal, 2006.
Planet Earth, NPG/Columbia, 2007.

Sources

Books

Contemporary Musicians, Volume 40, Gale Research, 2003.
Stambler, Irwin, *The Encyclopedia of Pop, Rock, and Soul,* St. Martin's, 1989.

Periodicals

Ebony, January 1997, p. 128.
Entertainment Weekly, December 20, 1996, p. 7; November 10, 2000, p. 59; June 8, 2001.
Esquire, March 1997, p. 39.
Forbes, September 23, 1996, p. 180.
Interview, May 1997, p. 88.
Jet, February 5, 1996, p. 36; May 19, 1997, p. 56; July 9, 2001, p. 64; January 17, 2005, p. 39.
People, November 19, 1984, p. 160; March 7, 1994, p. 72; December 3, 2001, p. 37.
Rolling Stone, August 30, 1984, p. 16.
Vegetarian Times, October 1997, p. 78.

Online

Pareles, Jon, "The Once and Future Prince," *New York Times,* http://www.nytimes.com/2007/07/22/arts/music/22pare.html (accessed December 21, 2007).
"Prince Sites Face Legal Threats," *BBC News,* http://news.bbc.co.uk/2/hi/entertainment/7082684.stm (accessed December 21, 2007).
"Prince Surprises Waiting Fans with a Show," *USA Today,* http://www.usatoday.com/life/people/2006-03-22-prince-surprise_x.htm (accessed December 21, 2007).

—James M. Manheim and Derek Jacques

Rain Pryor

1969—

Writer, comedian, actress, singer, producer

Pryor, Rain, photograph. Michael Germana/UPI/Landov.

Rain Pryor is an author, entertainer, and actor best known for her thought-provoking explorations of her life as the daughter of famed African-American comedian Richard Pryor and Jewish entertainer Shelly Bonis. Pryor has distinguished herself as a versatile performer having produced a critically acclaimed biography, two musical albums of jazz standards, and a one-woman show that mixes comedy and heartfelt drama.

Rain Pryor was born on July 16, 1969, in Los Angeles, California. Her father, Richard Pryor, met her mother, Shelly Bonis, while Bonis was performing as a dancer at a Los Angeles club. Pryor says her parents' relationship started as love at first sight, but by the time Pryor was six months old, her parents had divorced and Pryor was living alone with her mother in Beverly Hills.

Pryor was raised by her mother, who worked at a variety of jobs to support herself and her daughter, including performing as a clown in a local circus and working as a professional photographer. "She's brilliant ... it's disgusting!" Pryor said to *Contemporary Black Biography* (*CBB*), joking about her mother's enviable ability to succeed in any of a long list of disparate vocations and interests. Later in life, Bonis began working as an astronomer, consulting with organizations such as the National Aeronautics and Space Association. Pryor said that her parents' brilliance made her feel a need to be brilliant herself and to succeed at whatever she chose to do.

Besides her mother, Pryor was raised by her maternal grandparents, Herbert and Bunny Bonis, whom she described to *CBB* as "wonderful ... typical white, middle-class grandparents." Pryor began having regular contact with her father when she was about four years old, and after that time her life was divided between two different worlds. Though she lived with her mother, visits with her father introduced her to a different lifestyle. She recalled from a young age witnessing her father's struggles with drugs and alcohol and his tumultuous, often troubling personal life. Though punctuated with drama, Pryor's childhood was also filled with the love and support of her family.

Educated at Beverly Hills High School

Pryor attended Beverly Hills High School, where she was involved in number of extracurricular activities, including the drama club, the school swim team, and the drill team. Despite her extracurricular interests, Pryor described herself as a "bad student." From around age five, Pryor decided that she was going to be an actor; therefore, most of school was a waste of time. This attitude stayed with her through high school, where she told *CBB,* "When I would skip class, they would call to the drama department, because I would go and hang out there."

Pryor's high school drama department was her home away from home, and she played in a number of school productions. She did her first solo performance in high school, a dramatic monologue from the play *Nuts,* just before the Barbara Streisand film hit the theaters in 1987.

Besides working as an actor, Pryor also demonstrated an ability to sing and write music. In 1986, shortly before graduating from high school, she was asked by representatives from Motown Records if she wanted to record an album. Though she was willing to do it, her father staunchly refused, believing that the label executives were trying to take advantage of her. Though Pryor refused the offer, she was determined to make singing and music a large part of her life.

Starred in a Popular Television Comedy

Following high school, Pryor enrolled in community college to pursue an associate's degree in psychology. "I always thought I would either be an actor or a psychologist," Pryor told *CBB.* "People always seem to open up to me." However, in 1988 Pryor attended a general audition for the television series *Head of the Class,* which ran from 1986 to 1991 on the ABC television network. At the audition, Pryor was asked to perform a monologue of her choice, so she decided to write an original presentation. Her performance, in which she portrayed three separate personalities, was a hit with the evaluators, who asked her to return the next day for an additional performance. After her second interview, Pryor was asked to appear on the show.

Pryor's first appearance as Theola June "T.J." Jones on *Head of the Class* was intended to be a one-time guest performance. However, when Pryor received a standing ovation from the audience, the show's producers asked her to stay on as a recurring character. Pryor remained part of the cast from the third until the final fifth season, and even became one of the most popular characters on the program. "It was the stuff Hollywood dreams are made of," Pryor told *CBB.*

At the time, Pryor did not realize how fortunate she had been; having received the first job she auditioned for, she said she "didn't realize that other people were really struggling trying to find work." Pryor went from making minimum wage as a retail sales associate to making almost $7,000 each week and feeling very much like Hollywood royalty. Unfortunately, as Pryor told *CBB,* "When the show ended, I went broke, so I went to the stage."

Worked in Theater and Rehab Clinics

Pryor had a number of appearances on various television programs, including an after-school ABC television special called *Frog Girl,* about a student who refused to dissect frogs in class. Unable to return to television full time, Pryor dedicated herself to stage acting and appeared in a number of theatrical performances around Los Angeles. Many of her productions featured Pryor's singing voice, including the Who's rock opera *Tommy* at the La Hoya Playhouse.

It was during this time that Pryor became more deeply involved in producing her own work. She produced and performed in a production of Bernard Shaw's *Joan of Arc,* which she called *Joan.*

In 1998, Pryor began working as a drug counselor in Beverly Hills. The decision to enter counseling was prompted by watching her father struggle with addiction and recovery throughout her childhood. Pryor started as an assistant and was eventually leading drug counseling classes. She worked first in Beverly Hills' celebrity clinics, but found that she did not prefer the clientele, "I couldn't stand working with celebrities that were messed up," Pryor told *CBB*. "Like, if I have to take you for a manicure after you've just smoked crack?" During her time as a counselor, a number of tabloid journalists inaccurately reported that Pryor was seeking treatment for drug addiction.

Performed a One-Woman Show

In 2001, Pryor developed and performed *Europa*, a one-woman show at a friend's dinner theater in Los Angeles. The show was such a success that she decided pursue a larger audience. After marrying counselor Kevin Kindlin in 2002, one of Kindlin's contacts offered Pryor the opportunity to perform her show to an audience of potential financial backers. Pryor's performance received a standing ovation, and she was offered the chance to open her show at the famed Canon Theatre in Beverly Hills.

Pryor's show, which she called *Fried Chicken and Latkes*, has run continuously since 2002 and has been performed on national and international tours. Pryor's blend of songs, dramatic monologue, and comedy was a critical hit and was, for Pryor, a culmination of her experiences dealing with her relationship with her mother, grandparents, and father. Though Pryor's exploration of her life as "half Jewish, half black," is at the core of the show, her diverse talents are also featured as the show features a number of original songs.

Pryor's father was diagnosed with multiple sclerosis (MS) in 1987, but many treatment options were unavailable until after 1993. As Pryor watched her father's disease progress, she became involved with MS organizations to help spread knowledge of the disease and obtain funding for research. In 2003, Pryor was asked to be a spokesperson for the MS Society, a capacity that she served in for several years, during which she gave as many as fourteen speeches a year to potential funding groups and for educational purposes.

Wrote Biography and Left Los Angeles

Pryor visited her father regularly from 2003 to his death in 2005. Before her father's death, Pryor began working on her biography *Jokes My Father Never Taught Me: Life, Love, and Loss with Richard Pryor*, a telling and intimate look at her life and relationship with her family. She finished the book nine months after her father died and said to *CBB*, "The end was painful ... like giving birth. I cried a lot at the end." Pryor's book met with critical acclaim when it was published in 2006, and was rereleased in 2007. Though Pryor had been approached by publishing companies wanting her to write a tell-all biography about her father, Pryor routinely refused. "I didn't want to write that kind of book," she told *CBB*. "I wanted to

write a book about a father and a daughter and forgiveness, and that father happens to be Richard Pryor."

In 2006 her marriage to Kindlin ended. After that, she felt it was time to leave Los Angeles, so she moved to Baltimore, Maryland. Then she traveled abroad to perform the show *Divas*, which featured Pryor singing jazz standards in the style of famous singers such as Nina Simone and Billie Holliday. The show was a major success with international audiences in China, Ireland, Australia, and England. A live CD that featured music from her show was released after her performances in London.

In Baltimore, Pryor and Yale Partlow, her romantic partner, were expecting a child in April of 2008. Pryor told *CBB* she was busy preparing for motherhood and family life. In addition, Pryor hoped to continue working on stage and was working on the production *Pryor Experience*, which featured a blend of drama, comedy, and jazz music and debuted in November of 2007. For the future, Pryor planned to continue writing and recording music, work in the dramatic theater, and start her own MS foundation headquartered in Maryland. Pryor believed that she has taken strong lessons from her family and experiences. "You have to live an authentic life," she told *CBB*. "If you're living life and you're screwing up: change. There are no excuses. But if you're realistic about your dreams, don't give up and it will happen for you."

Selected works

Albums

Rain Pryor Live in London, Cahoots Theatre Company, 2006.

Fiction

Fried Chicken and Latkes (play), 2004.

Nonfiction

Jokes My Father Never Taught Me: Life, Love, and Loss with Richard Pryor, Harper Collins, 2006.

Sources

Periodicals

Austin American-Statesman, January 13, 2007.
Boston Herald, April 29, 2006.
Cincinnati Post, March 28, 2005.
Liverpool Echo (Liverpool, England), April 13, 2007, 11.
People, April 17, 1989, p. 131.
Weekend Argus (South Africa), January 6, 2007.

Other

Additional information for this profile was obtained through an interview with Rain Pryor on October 23, 2007.

—Micah L. Issitt

Lionel Richie

1949—

Pop singer, songwriter

Richie, Lionel, photograph. Rune Hellestad/UPI/Landov.

The ballads written and sung by Lionel Richie, both as part of the group the Commodores and during an impressive solo career, formed a soundtrack for countless American romances in the late 1970s and early 1980s. Richie achieved a string of successes matched by few other popular songwriters, with his compositions rising to the number-one position on the U.S. pop singles chart at least once in every year between 1977 and 1985. The most successful interpreter of Richie's songs continues to be Richie himself, and for more than a quarter-century the quintessential romantic balladeer has touched Americans of all races and walks of life.

Richie's musical personality was formed at one of the crucial intellectual sites for African Americans: the Tuskegee Institute (now Tuskegee University) in Alabama. He was born on June 20, 1949, and his childhood home was actually on the school's campus, where his father, a U.S. Army systems analyst, lived with his mother, an educator who later became a school principal. Richie's musical education drew on the diverse sonic streams that passed through Tuskegee. His maternal grandmother favored classical music and reacted coolly to her grandson's first forays into pop songwriting. Northern African-American pop and southern soul found their ways to Tuskegee. Hoping at one point to become an Episcopal minister, Richie gravitated toward gospel music. He was also influenced by another tradition whose reach among African Americans is sometimes underestimated: "Because it was the South, it was hard not to hear country music," he was quoted as saying by Irwin Stambler in the *Encyclopedia of Pop, Rock, and Soul.*

Joined Group at Tuskegee

Enrolling at Tuskegee himself, Richie joined forces with a group of other students he met at a talent show; the attraction for the others was that Richie owned a saxophone. Richie, for his own part, was successful in concealing the fact that he barely knew how to play it. A gifted musician who had taught himself to play the piano by ear, Richie made rapid strides as a performer and composer at Tuskegee. The group, first called the Mystics, became the Commodores after the word was

At a Glance . . .

Born Lionel B. Richie Jr. on June 20, 1949, in Tuskegee, AL; son of Lionel Sr. and Alberta Richie; married Brenda Harvey, 1975 (divorced); married Diane Alexander, 1996 (divorced); children: (with Harvey) Nicole; (with Alexander) Miles, Sofia. *Education:* Graduated from Tuskegee Institute, 1974.

Career: Joined the Commodores while in college; began solo production work and composition for other artists, late 1970s—; co-composed and recorded "We Are the World," 1985.

Awards: Selected Awards: Three platinum albums; four gold albums; eighteen Grammy Award nominations and four awards; twelve American Music Awards; five People's Choice Awards for Best Song; numerous other industry awards; Academy Award, "Say You, Say Me," 1986; honorary doctorate, Tuskegee University, 1986.

Addresses: *Web*—http://www6.islandrecords.com/site/artist_home.php?artist_id=342.

picked at random out of a dictionary. Richie discarded his religious ambitions in favor of courses in economics and accounting that proved ideal training for a career in the financially cutthroat music business.

The Commodores struggled for a time, gaining fans across Alabama but losing all their equipment to van thieves on a 1969 trip to New York. Regardless, they bounced back, landing a series of club appearances and signing on with a manager, Benny Ashburn, who would stay with them until his death during Richie's years of solo stardom. Signing briefly to the Atlantic record label, they went nowhere, but when they attracted the attention of Motown Records executive Suzanne de Passe in 1971, they gained wide exposure when she slated them as the opening act for many of the tours of that label's brother-act dynamo: the Jackson Five.

The heavy funk sound of the Commodores did not fit the polished, smoothed Motown mold, however, and the group's first record for the label, *Machine Gun,* was not released until 1974. That album and successors performed solidly, and the group broke through to the pop Top Ten with the ballad "Sweet Love" in 1976. This song, a Richie composition, also marked a new direction musically for the group. Even though earlier singles such as 1975's "Slippery When Wet" had been primarily dance-oriented, the group came to

believe that the secret to long-lasting success lay in the cultivation of romantic balladry. "Sweet Love" proved only the first of a series of romantic numbers from Richie's pen: "Just to Be Close to You" and "Easy" rose into the pop Top Ten.

Most successful of all was 1978's "Three Times a Lady," whose waltz tempo perhaps showed the influence of the country music Richie had heard as a young man. This song, a feature of weddings for years to come, achieved platinum status for sales of one million copies, as did the album *Natural High,* from which it was taken. The song propelled the Commodores and the increasingly dominant Richie to national stardom. The Commodores enjoyed a string of hits between 1978 and 1981, and no ill will arose between the group members. But Richie found himself in demand for his own creative talents alone. He wrote and produced "Lady" for pop superstar Kenny Rogers in 1980, and followed it up with "Endless Love," a duet he recorded with Diana Ross. These songs remained atop the U.S. pop charts for six and nine weeks, respectively.

Whether recorded with the Commodores, by other artists, or on his own, Richie's ballads were instantly identifiable. Simple and seemingly inevitable in their gentle progressions, they hide Richie's considerable craft as a songwriter. For his own part, Richie credited God as his "co-composer" in an interview with *Ebony* writer Robert E. Johnson quoted in *Contemporary Musicians.* Richie played to his strengths on his debut solo album, *Lionel Richie,* which was released in 1982. Its hit singles "Truly" and "You Are" closely followed the style of the Commodores' chart successes.

Co-composed "We Are the World"

Richie's second and third solo albums, 1983's *Can't Slow Down* and 1986's *Dancing on the Ceiling,* broadened his reach. "All Night Long," the lead single from *Can't Slow Down,* was an upbeat, tropical-flavored dance piece that resembled none of the leading rhythm and blues (R&B), disco, and funk dance styles of the time. These albums were among the biggest successes of the 1980s, and *Can't Slow Down* was claimed to be the best-selling release in the history of the Motown label. Gaining Richie even more acclaim and publicity than any of his solo efforts, though, was the all-star recording "We Are the World," which he co-composed with fellow pop superstar Michael Jackson and recorded with an all-star lineup of artists. Profits from sales and performances of the song went toward African famine relief.

By the late 1980s, Richie had few worlds left to conquer. He continued to enter into collaborative efforts, winning an Academy Award for Best Song and notching yet another number-one single for the song "Say You, Say Me" from the film *White Nights.* He tapped the country music vein yet again in a recording he composed for and performed with the country group Alabama, "Deep River Woman."

In 1992 Richie released the *Back to Front* greatest-hits package; it included "Do It to Me," a new song that once again topped the charts. Richie moved to the Mercury label in the 1990s, releasing the modestly successful *Louder Than Words* (1996) and *Time* (1998); these discs largely avoided any updating of Richie's sound with contemporary hip-hop influences. In 2000 Richie raised his profile somewhat when he appeared as the opening act on the farewell tour of soul superstar Tina Turner, and planned a new release, *Renaissance,* that featured the teen-oriented Backstreet Boys.

Continued Being Successful, Despite Family Issues

In 2003 Richie's second wife, Diane, filed for divorce after nearly seven years of marriage. According to CNN, Diane was seeking financial support in keeping with the couple's previously extravagant lifestyle, which included spending as much as $300,000 per month. In official documents released to the court, Diane claimed that she spent as much as $15,000 per month on clothing and $20,000 per year on cosmetic surgery. Shortly after their divorce, Diane and her alleged lover, Daniel Serrano, were accused of using Diane's house to perform illegal plastic surgery procedures involving an injection that was purported to ease the signs of aging. Diane was arrested and charged with two counts of aiding and abetting.

After 2003, Richie's adopted daughter from his first marriage, Nicole Richie, began gaining fame of her own largely owing to her association with Paris Hilton and appearance on the reality television series *The Simple Life.* Nicole's celebrity life was tumultuous, including a widely publicized arrest for possession of heroin in 2003 and a second arrest in 2006 for driving under the influence of alcohol. In addition, after 2006, a number of tabloid journalists speculated that she had developed an eating disorder. Nicole's various problems soon brought Richie's family life into question, and he appeared in numerous interviews defending his daughter's behavior and expressing his hope that she would find a solution to her problems. Richie expressed his regret at not having been a better father, owing to his busy work schedule, but affirmed his intention to help his daughter in whatever way he could.

Richie's 2006 album, *Coming Home,* marked a turning point in his career, as the album was his most popular in more than a decade and debuted at number six in *Billboard*'s top two hundred album rankings. Richie conducted an extensive publicity tour that was followed by a series of concerts in small venues across the United States. With an increasing base of fans and a number-one ranked single, "I Call It Love," Richie was asked to perform at the 2007 Grammy Awards. Richie's 2007 concert series featured songs from the span of his solo career blended with new compositions and classics from his time with the Commodores.

As he neared sixty, Richie had cemented his place as one of the premier R&B artists of his generation. Though his recent life has been filled as much with family strife as with professional success, he continues to be a force in the music industry, by blending his R&B roots with the popular music of a new generation. In a 2006 interview with National Public Radio's Tony Cox, Richie reflected on his career, "It's not where you've been, it's where you're going…. We start out with nothing, then the rest of it in-between is, who did you touch, how did you affect them, and what memories do they have of you?"

Selected discography

Albums

Lionel Richie, Motown, 1982.
Can't Slow Down, Motown, 1983.
Dancing on the Ceiling, Motown, 1986.
Back to Front, Motown, 1992.
Louder than Words, Mercury, 1996.
Time, Mercury, 1998.
Renaissance, 2000.

Sources

Books

Contemporary Musicians, Volume 2, Gale, 1990.
Larkin, Colin, ed., *The Encyclopedia of Popular Music,* Muze UK, 1998.
Romanowski, Patricia, and Holly George-Warren, *The New Rolling Stone Encyclopedia of Rock and Roll,* Fireside, 1995.
Stambler, Irwin, *The Encyclopedia of Pop, Rock, and Soul,* St. Martin's, 1989.

Periodicals

Entertainment Weekly, April 21, 2000, p. 75.
Jet, August 30, 1999, p. 32.
Oakland Tribune, November 28, 2006.
People, July 20, 1998, p. 39.
San Diego Union Tribune, December 4, 2004.

Online

Cox, Tony, "A Tuneful 'Coming Home' for Lionel Richie," *National Public Radio,* http://www.npr.org/templates/story/story.php?storyId=6057529 (accessed December 20, 2007).
"Lifestyle of the Richie and Famous," *CNN Online,* http://www.cnn.com/2004/US/03/03/offbeat.people.richie.reut/index.html (accessed December 20, 2007).

"Lionel Richie: Nicole Made Mistakes," *ABC News Online,* http://abcnews.go.com/Entertainment/wireStory?id=3445473 (accessed December 20, 2007).

—James M. Manheim and Micah L. Issit

Rihanna

1988—

Singer

Rihanna, photograph. © Allstar Picture Library/Alamy.

Rihanna is the rare rhythm and blues (R&B) diva to emerge from the Caribbean world. Though she had made two previous albums, the Barbadian singer debuted a glamorous new look in the spring of 2007 as her latest single, "Umbrella," began to climb the charts. By late summer "Umbrella" was on the verge of becoming the most successful single of the entire year. Craig McLean, a writer for the *Daily Telegraph,* called it "a brilliant pop song, propulsive and sinuous…. Already it is feeling like a defining song of 2007."

Born on February 20, 1988, as Robyn Rihanna Fenty, Rihanna grew up in Bridgetown, the capital of Barbados. Her father, Ronald, was a native of the island, and her mother, Monica, was originally from Guyana, a nation on the northeastern coastline of South America. Along with two younger brothers, Rihanna saw her parents' marriage suffer because of the crack-cocaine addition her father developed. "I knew that my mom and dad would argue when there was foil paper with an ashtray," Rihanna recalled in an interview with Grant Rollings for the *Sun,* a British tabloid. "He would just go into the bathroom all the time. I didn't know what it was."

Monica struggled to support her family by work in the financial-services industry, but Rihanna was fortunate to attend one of the top schools in Barbados, the Combermere School, founded in 1695. She loved to sing at an early age and formed a teen group, called Contrast, with some friends. In 2004, the year she turned sixteen, she won the title of Miss Combermere, though she had been a self-confessed tomboy who cared little about makeup or clothes until that point. Her break into show business came when producer/songwriter Evan Rogers came to Barbados for a vacation with his wife; the mother of a friend of Rihanna's knew Rogers's wife from their school days together, and the mother arranged an introduction. Rogers and his business partner, Carl Sturken, were responsible for making stars out of Kelly Clarkson, Christina Aguilera, N'Sync, and several other top pop acts. Rihanna sang for Evans one of her favorite songs, Mariah Carey's "Hero," followed by the Destiny's Child's track "Emotions." He was impressed enough to sign her to his company, Syndicated Rhythm Productions (SRP), and arrange for her to come to New York City to cut a demo record. Rogers and his wife assured Monica Fenty that Rihanna would

At a Glance . . .

Born Robyn Rihanna Fenty on February 20, 1988, in Bridgetown, St. Michael's Parish, Barbados; daughter of Ronald and Monica Fenty.

Career: Signed to Syndicated Rhythm Productions, c. 2004; signed with Def Jam Records; made television acting debut in Las Vegas, 2005; has endorsement deals with Nike, J. C. Penney, Clinique, and CoverGirl.

Awards: Monster Single of the Year and Video of the Year, MTV Music Video Awards, both 2007, for "Umbrella."

Addresses: *Agent*—Glenn Gulino, William Morris Agency, 1325 Avenue of the Americas, New York, NY 10019.

stay at their home and would be watched over as if she was their own daughter.

The next stop on Rihanna's path to stardom came after SRP contacted Jay-Z, the rapper turned mogul who cofounded Roc-A-Feller Records and who had recently become president and chief executive officer of Def Jam Records. Rihanna was invited to audition in person for Jay-Z in his office, "and that's when I really got nervous," she told Sylvia Patterson in the London *Observer*. "I was like: 'Oh God, he's right there, I can't look, I can't look, I can't look!' I remember being extremely quiet. I was very shy. I was cold the entire time. I had butterflies." The tryout was a success, however, and she was signed to Def Jam, which released her debut album, *Music of the Sun*, in August of 2005. Capitalizing on her West Indian roots, the label positioned the teen as a fresh new voice that merged rap and Caribbean rhythms, which were showcased in the first single released from the album, "Pon de Replay," a dancehall reggae that peaked at number two on the U.S. and British charts.

Subsequent singles from *Music of the Sun* were less successful, but Rihanna's enticing good looks—statuesque and with green eyes—helped her land lucrative endorsement contracts with Nike, Clinique, and J. C. Penney that opened the door to unique cross-marketing deals. In April of 2006 her second album, *A Girl Like Me*, was released, and its first single, "SOS," reached number one on *Billboard*'s Hot 100 chart thanks to a tie-in with Nike. Another release further blurred the line between art and commerce: "Just Be Happy," a song written for her by African-American/Chinese-American rapper Ne-Yo, was available only on her Web site as a part of a special promotional campaign with Clinique and its fragrance, Happy.

Both Ne-Yo and Jay-Z appeared on Rihanna's third album, *Good Girl Gone Bad*, which was released in June of 2007. Its first single was "Umbrella" and had already caused a stir that spring for marking the debut of a new, more grown-up look for the singer. The song wound up spending ten weeks at the number-one spot on the British charts, the longest run for a female artist there since Whitney Houston more than a decade earlier. It also reached number one on the U.S. and European charts, it won MTV's Monster Single of the Year Video honors in September, and its lavishly produced video won Video of the Year at the same ceremony. For part of it, a nude Rihanna was coated in silver paint and then filmed inside a special black box. "The body paint was really oily," she told Elizabeth Sanchez in *Men's Fitness* about the experience. "I couldn't wait to get it off my face. That was the worst part about it—getting it off. I was in the shower for two and a half hours!... Days after, I still had some in my hair, ears, even my belly button."

Good Girl Gone Bad sold well and secured Rihanna's place as a new R&B/pop powerhouse. "The title of the album represents my liberation," she told Sanchez. "Being able to break out of the innocent image I was forced into. Now I'm just being me." World-famous before she was twenty years old, the singer has been romantically linked to musicians Omarion, Chris Brown, and Justin Timberlake, along with actors Shia LaBeouf and Josh Hartnett. She lives in Los Angeles, and she admitted to Patterson that fame had its drawbacks. "With success has come a lotta great stuff, but there's cons, too," she reflected. "Who to trust is a huge one. I always have to keep my guard up. A lot. I'm dealing with fake people. All the time. So I just keep my guard up."

Selected discography

Albums

Music of the Sun, Def Jam, 2005.
A Girl Like Me, Def Jam, 2006.
Good Girl Gone Bad, Def Jam, 2007.

Singles

"Pon de Replay," 2005.
"SOS," 2006.
"Unfaithful," 2006.
"Umbrella," 2007.
"Don't Stop the Music," 2007.

Sources

Periodicals

Daily Telegraph (London, England), May 31, 2007.
Men's Fitness, August 2007.

New York Times, June 4, 2007.
Observer (London, England), August 26, 2007.
Sun (London, England), June 15, 2007.
Times (London, England), January 6, 2007.

—Carol Brennan

Holden Roberto

1923–2007

Political leader

Holden Roberto was the founder of the Frente Nacional de Libertação de Angola (FNLA; National Front for the Liberation of Angola), a militant political organization that played a major role in Angola's struggle for independence from Portugal from the 1950s to the 1970s. After achieving independence in 1975, Roberto's organization competed in an extended civil war that lasted until the major combatants formed a peace agreement in 2002. Roberto remained the leader of the FNLA until shortly before his death in 2007 and was posthumously acclaimed by leading members of the Angolan government as one of the most effective and important leaders in Angolan history.

Holden Roberto was born on January 12, 1923, in a portion of northern Angola known as Sao Salvador (now Mbanza Congo), which bordered the Belgian Congo (later Zaïre and then the Democratic Republic of Congo in 1960). Roberto's family was part of the Bakongo ethnic group, one of the region's largest ethnic groups comprising a population of over ten million throughout Angola and the modern-day Democratic Republic of Congo.

In 1925, Roberto's family immigrated to Léopoldville (now Kinshasa), the Belgian Congo, where Roberto's father, Garcia Roberto, worked as a Baptist minister while his mother, Joana Lala Nekaka, remained in the home to care for the couple's children. Roberto attended Baptist elementary and secondary schools and, after his graduation in 1940, took his first job working for the colonial ministry in Léopoldville.

Co-founded Angola's First Independence Movement

Angola had been under Portuguese control since the mid-seventeenth century, and in the 1950s Portugal changed the status of Angola from colonial territory to overseas province, a political decision intended to allow Portugal to maintain possession of the nation for an extended period. In 1951, Roberto decided to visit Angola. During his visit, he witnessed acts of violence perpetrated by Portuguese police on Angolan citizens. In later statements, Roberto claimed that his visit to his homeland convinced him to become involved in the independence movement.

In 1956, Roberto founded the União das Populações do Norte de Angola (UPNA; Union of the North Angolan Population), which was later renamed the União das Populações de Angola (UPA; Union of the Angolan Population). Roberto served as the head of the organization from 1960 to 1962, during which time he studied independence movements in other African nations. In 1958, Roberto attended a meeting of nationalist leaders in Ghana, during which he met with leaders from other African nations struggling for independence, including Patrice Lumumba of the Congo, who remained one of Roberto's closest friends and allies until Lumumba's assassination in 1961. In addition, Roberto gained strength for his organization by forming an alliance with fellow Angolan revolutionary Jonas Savimbi.

Though Roberto and Savimbi's UPNA is often cited as the nation's first independence movement, at the time

At a Glance . . .

Born Holden Roberto on January 12, 1923, in Sao Salvador, Angola; died on August 2, 2007, in Luanda, Angola; son of Garcia Roberto and Joana Lala Nekaka. *Education:* Attended Baptist missionary schools, 1936–40.

Career: União das Populações de Angola, president, 1960–62; Frente Nacional de Libertação de Angola, president, 1962–2007.

of its foundation, the communist and socialist parties of Angola were also forming an alternative independence group, the Movimento Popular de Libertação de Angola (MPLA; Popular Movement for the Liberation of Angola), which advocated independence under a socialist system. The MPLA, under the leadership of writer and statesman Viriato da Cruz, struggled against the Portuguese government and against Roberto's faction, which advocated transition to a democratic government.

During the 1950s, Roberto met with representatives of the U.S. military and began to receive financial support from the U.S. government. The Angolan independence struggle became part of the wider cold war, in which the United States and other democratic nations supported pro-democracy factions in Africa, whereas China, the Soviet Union, and other communist/socialist nations supported pro-socialist factions.

Fought in the War of Independence

By 1960, Roberto had organized an army of guerrilla fighters. The following year, on February 4, 1961, Roberto and the guerrillas staged a raid against a colonial jail, which later became famous as the first military assault of the war for independence. Roberto continued with a more aggressive attack on colonial forces on March 15, wherein over five thousand militants attacked Portuguese settlements and government buildings.

In April of 1961, Roberto met with U.S. president John F. Kennedy to arrange further support from the United States and organize plans for the movement's future operations. Strengthened by international support, Roberto joined forces with the Partido Democrático and renamed the politically restructured organization as the FNLA. Roberto declared the FNLA as the legitimate successor to the colonial government in Angola and named himself as president with Savimbi serving as foreign minister.

From 1962 to 1964, Roberto and Savimbi led the FNLA against Portuguese forces in a series of guerilla battles throughout the northern portions of the nation. Some FNLA members, including Savimbi, were skeptical of Roberto's reliance on U.S. aid and encouraged him to lead the FNLA away from foreign support. Roberto believed that the success of his movement depended on his ability to maintain strategic political alliances. In 1962, he decided to divorce his first wife and marry the sister-in-law of Mobuto Sese Seko, thereby ensuring the Democratic Republic of Congo's support and obtaining additional troops and armaments for the FNLA. In 1963, Roberto's faction also began receiving military aid from the Israeli government after he traveled to Israel several times to meet with military and government leaders.

In 1964, Savimbi split with Roberto and the FNLA, accusing Roberto of becoming too closely involved with the United States, failing to expand the independence movement from the northern portions of the country, and focusing too heavily on the welfare of the Bakongo ethnic group at the expense of Angola's other ethnic minorities. Savimbi formed the União Nacional para a Independência Total de Angola (UNITA; National Union for the Total Independence of Angola), which became the most radical of Angola's independence organizations and received aid from the People's Republic of China, after Savimbi announced his intentions to install a communist government following independence.

The Portuguese government fought a three-tier struggle against UNITA, the MPLA, and the FNLA from the mid-1960s until the mid-1970s. In April of 1974, the Carnation Revolution took place in Portugal, during which the ruling authoritarian government was overthrown in a popular coup and after two years of transitional turmoil was replaced by a democratic-socialist system. The Portuguese revolution effectively ended the Angolan war for independence, as the transitional Portuguese government quickly negotiated agreements with the nation's former territories. On January 15, 1975, the Alvor Agreement was signed by Portuguese representatives and the leaders of the three independence groups, formally designating Angola as an independent nation. Under the terms of the agreement, UNITA, the MPLA, and the FNLA agreed to form a coalition government; however, during negotiations disagreements between the groups' leadership led to outbreaks of violence and by June of 1975 the conflict had escalated into civil war.

Fought in the Angolan Civil War

At the start of the civil war, UNITA and the MPLA were headquartered in Angola, whereas the FNLA was operating from the Democratic Republic of Congo, where Roberto utilized the Congolese military to supplement his forces. Roberto's refusal to move his headquarters to Angola was criticized by many of his allies as a strategic mistake. Though the FNLA had an initial military advantage in the strategically important city of Luanda, the MPLA gradually overcame FNLA forces in the city by drawing support from the local populace. By July of 1975, the FNLA was losing ground in locations across Angola.

Concerned that an MPLA victory would transform Angola into a communist country, the United States formed an alliance with UNITA and increased financial and military support for Roberto's FNLA. In addition, the U.S. and British governments began actively recruiting mercenaries to bolster FNLA forces. Several hundred British mercenaries joined the struggle in 1975 but, as the FNLA forces were largely outnumbered and without significant popular support, most of the mercenaries were killed or captured and executed by the MPLA. Despite U.S. aid, by the end of 1976 the FNLA was losing the struggle to the MPLA, and as a result, the United States, South Africa, and Britain made a strategic decision to concentrate military aid on Savimbi's UNITA faction.

As the FNLA lost foreign support, relations between Roberto and Mobuto deteriorated, and Roberto was forced to leave the Democratic Republic of Congo. In 1978, Roberto fled to Paris and declared the FNLA as a government in exile. The United States and South Africa continued to support UNITA against the MPLA, which was supported by Cuba and the Soviet Union. The civil war continued until 1991, when Savimbi and José Eduardo dos Santos of the MPLA met and signed the Bicesse Accords, an agreement that called for a transition to multiparty elections and a coalition socialist government.

Returned to Angola

Roberto returned to Angola in 1992, when several FNLA members took part in the first multiparty election. However, because of the FNLA's extended absence, the party received only 2 percent of the popular vote and placed five members in the nation's newly formed parliament. Refusing to take part in the government, Roberto became one of the most vocal critics of the MPLA.

Shortly after the 1992 election, Savimbi refused to acknowledge the presidential election, in which he was defeated by dos Santos, and led UNITA in an armed revolt against the government. Though Roberto declined to join UNITA or Savimbi, he also criticized dos Santos for corruption and mismanagement of economic resources. Violence between UNITA and the MPLA government continued for an additional decade, though occasionally this violence was punctuated by short-lived cease-fire agreements. Following Savimbi's death in February of 2002, the new leadership of UNITA was able to renew a peace agreement with the MPLA that lasted through 2007.

In the 1990s, the FNLA became divided along political and regional lines, with part of the organization remaining with Roberto, and the other part forming under the leadership of political activist Lucas Ngonda. Negotiations to reunite the party under a single leader repeatedly failed. In 2007, Roberto announced he was retiring from politics and bade the next generation of leaders to reunite the FNLA and attempt to transform the organization into a relevant force in Angolan politics.

Roberto was flown to Paris in 2007 to receive treatment for a heart condition. He recovered well enough to return to Luanda, but suffered a fatal heart attack on August 2, 2007. An August 9, 2007, news dispatch from the Africa News Service noted that President dos Santos praised Roberto as "one of the pioneers of the national liberation struggle, who has been an incentive to a generation of Angolans to follow the path of resistance and fight for the independence of Angola." At the time of his death, Roberto had reportedly been working to complete his memoirs, though the book was never finished.

Selected writings

Nonfiction

"Angola's Agony," *Wall Street Journal,* March 30, 1984, p. 27.

Sources

Books

Hauser, George M., *No One Can Stop the Rain: Glimpses of Africa's Liberation Struggle,* Pilgrim Press, 1989.
Marcum, John A., *The Angolan Revolution,* Massachusetts Institute of Technology Press, 1978.

Periodicals

Africa News Service, August 9, 2007.
Guardian (London, England), August 8, 2007.
The Independent (London, England), August 8, 2007.
Newsweek, January 26, 1976, p. 28.
New York Times, August 4, 2007.
Philadelphia Daily News, June 1, 1991.
The Times (London, England), August 13, 2007.

—Micah L. Issitt

John T. Scott

1940–2007

Artist, teacher

The vigorous, expressive, and abstract artworks created by sculptor John T. Scott can be found in museums and public areas in historic cites such as Boston and Washington, D.C. However, they are perhaps most at home in the parks and civic buildings of New Orleans, Louisiana, where Scott grew up, absorbing the jazz rhythms and rich cultural mix that inspired his artistic style. Colorful and dynamic, Scott's art blends influences from Africa, the Caribbean, and the American South, along with social commentary and a strong sense of African-American identity. Many of Scott's sculptures have moving parts, inspiring critics to compare their random movement to music. Scott made that comparison himself in *Circle Dance: The Art of John T. Scott,* "I would like to do with visual language what African American artists have done with gospel, blues and jazz. And if I can move somebody's spirit, I'd like that, too."

John Tarrell Scott was born in the Gentilly area of east New Orleans. He spent his early years on a farm that provided produce for Kolb's, a famous New Orleans restaurant. His father, Thomas Scott, worked as a driver for the owners of Kolb's, and later as a cook in other local restaurants. His mother, Mary Mable Holmes Scott, worked in the home, caring for Scott and his five sisters and brothers. When young John was seven years old, the family moved to the Lower Ninth Ward, a largely black, working-class district of the city.

Demonstrated Artistic Talent Early

Growing up with little money, Scott learned the values of hard work, resourcefulness, and creativity from his parents. He learned to make the things he could not afford, a union of practicality and creativity that would appear frequently in his later art work. He learned carpentry from his father, and, from his mother, who put painstaking effort into the everyday items she made for her family and friends, he learned the patient art of embroidery.

Even in elementary school Scott's teachers recognized his extraordinary artistic talent, and his high school teachers encouraged him to go on to college. After his graduation from Booker T. Washington High School in 1958, he entered Xavier University of Louisiana, a historically black Catholic college in New Orleans. In the fine arts department at Xavier, Scott's teachers helped him gain the confidence to exceed the limits placed on African-American artists in the segregated South. They also urged him to continue his education and pursue a master's degree.

Scott graduated from Xavier in 1962 and entered graduate school at Michigan State University, where he was a teaching assistant for two of his professors, the well-known artists, Charles Pollock and Robert Weil. He earned his master's of fine arts in 1965, then returned to take the job of professor of fine arts at Xavier University. Soon after, he married his longtime girlfriend Anna Rita Smith. Along with caring for his family and creating his own art, he continued to teach and mentor young artists as an art professor at Xavier for the rest of his life.

At a Glance . . .

Born John Tarrell Scott on June 30, 1940, in New Orleans, LA; died on September 1, 2007; son of Thomas and Mary Mable Holmes Scott; married Anna Rita Smith, 1965; five children: Ayo, Maria Scott-Osborne, Tyra Joseph, Lauren Kannady and Alanda Rhodes; six grandchildren. *Education:* Xavier University of Louisiana, BA, 1962; Michigan State University, MA in Fine Arts, 1965.

Career: Xavier University of Louisiana, fine arts department, professor, 1965–2007; professional artist, 1965–2007.

Memberships: Orleans Gallery; Phi Kappa Phi National Scholastic Honorary Fraternity.

Awards: City of New Orleans, Second Annual Mayor's Arts Award, 1980; Youth Leadership Council, Role Model Award, 1988; John D. and Catherine T. MacArthur Foundation, MacArthur Fellowship, 1992; National Conference of Artists, Outstanding Art Contributor Award, 1995; Loyola University of New Orleans, honorary doctorate in humane letters, 2007.

Although Scott created many paintings and prints, he is best known for his collages and mobile sculptures, energetic combinations of a variety of materials often assembled out of everyday items that could be found around the house and neighborhood. His pieces are characterized by bright colors and geometric shapes, which echo the patterns found in the art of Africa and the Caribbean, the cultural roots of the slaves who were the ancestors of many African Americans.

Influenced by the Catholic culture of Louisiana and the religious atmosphere at Xavier, Scott created many works of religious art during his early career in the 1960s. In 1967 he created *Stations of the Cross* as a commission for an order of Josephite priests and monks, and in 1969 he created *Resurrection of the Risen Christ* for a New Orleans Catholic high school. His early work showed such promise that he became one of the youngest artists invited to join the Orleans Gallery, an artist's cooperative.

Inspired by the Civil Rights Movement

By the 1970s the civil rights and black nationalist movements had instilled a new sense of pride in African-American identity. Scott began to reflect this in his art, creating pieces with titles such as *Marcus Garvey* and *Jackson State Murder* that stressed his dedication to the struggle for racial equality. His work also began to demonstrate the deep connections he felt among the people of Africa and the many people of African ancestry who had been scattered around the world, largely by the slave trade. In pieces such as *Ritual of Oppression Series,* a collection of tiny sculptures created in 1976, he explores the pain of this diaspora.

In 1983 Scott received a fellowship to study with George Rickey, a New York artist famous for his work in kinetic, or moving, sculpture. During his six-week residency in Rickey's studio in East Chatham, New York, Scott met and exchanged ideas with many members of the East Coast art community. Influenced by Rickey, Scott began to add more movement and drama to his work. His *Diddlie Bow* series, created in 1983–84, demonstrates an increased playfulness in movement, along with Scott's characteristic interest in the ties between black American culture and African themes. The diddley bow is an American folk musical instrument that traces its origins to Africa. Often used in traditional blues music, the original diddley bow was also employed as a weapon. Scott's *Diddlie Bow* sculptures are filled with the movement of the bow shape as it changes from instrument to weapon to boat.

In 1984 Scott took part in a cooperative art project about black history, titled *I've Known Rivers.* His contribution to the piece combined his characteristic bright colors with geometric symbols that suggested the culture of ancient Africa. Also during the 1980s, Scott began working with a New England art gallery and received a commission for a public sculpture that was placed in a Boston train station.

Created Works Inspired by New Orleans

By the 1990s he was also creating large public art pieces in his home city of New Orleans. *River Spirit,* commissioned by the Port of New Orleans for their main office building, is a three-dimensional mural depicting the boats, workers, and music that make up the culture of the Mississippi delta. Other Scott sculptures were placed in the city's Woldenberg Park, City Park, and Museum of Art.

In 1992 Scott was awarded a fellowship from the John D. and Catherine T. MacArthur Foundation. Nicknamed the "Genius Grant," the MacArthur Fellowship is a prestigious award, given to creative individuals to help them in their work. As an African-American artist who had worked hard for his place in the artistic community, Scott was somewhat skeptical about qualifying for the title of "genius," but he appreciated the

$315,000 grant that accompanied the award, using the money to expand his studio.

In 2005 the New Orleans Museum of Art presented a retrospective show of Scott's work, titled *Circle Dance.* Named for one of his characteristic sculpture series, the term *circle dance* also describes a certain kind of folk dance, common in Africa, and brought to the United States by African slaves. The rhythmic sense of music, movement, tradition, and change suggested by the term *circle dance* is perhaps the most common characteristic of Scott's vast body of artworks.

Shortly after the end of the *Circle Dance* retrospective, the city of New Orleans was hit by the devastating force of hurricane Katrina. In the early morning hours of August 28, 2005, as the powerful storm approached the city, Scott and his family evacuated to the nearby city of Houston, Texas. His home and studio were badly damaged by strong winds and flooding, though the eight major art pieces he had installed around the city were unharmed.

Scott never returned home to New Orleans. He was in poor health, having suffered for several years from pulmonary fibrosis, a lung disease possibly caused by cigarette smoke and the fumes and particles from decades of welding his sculptures together. He underwent two full lung transplants in Houston, but did not recover and died there on September 1, 2007.

Sources

Books

Powell, Richard J., and John Tarrell Scott, *Circle Dance: The Art of John T. Scott,* University Press of Mississippi/New Orleans Museum of Art, 2005.

Periodicals

Black Collegian, March–April 1992, p. 33; October 1998, p. 147.
Black Issues Book Review, January–February 2006, p. 29.
Jet, September 24, 2007, p. 17.
New Orleans City Business, September 8, 2007.

Online

Adams, Noah, "Prized Sculptures Survive Katrina, Stolen by Thieves," *National Public Radio,* http://www.npr.org/templates/story/story.php?storyId=6692039 (accessed December 28, 2007).
"Circle Dance: The Art of John T. Scott," *Traditional Fine Arts Organization,* http://www.tfaoi.com/aa/5aa/5aa313.htm (accessed December 28, 2007).
Cotter, Holland, "John T. Scott, New Orleans Sculptor, Dies at 67," *New York Times,* http://www.nytimes.com/2007/09/04/arts/design/04scott.html?_r=2&adxnnl=1&oref=slogin&adxnnlx=1198854422-RT/JzlFSYnAyrIpaCunvFg (accessed December 28, 2007).
Elie, Lolis Eric, "Scott Led War for Soul of the City," *Times-Picayune,* http://www.nola.com/news/t-p/index.ssf?/base/news-0/1188799370218160.xml&coll=1 (accessed December 28, 2007).
"John T. Scott," *St. James Guide to Black Artists,* St. James Press, 1997. Reproduced in *Biography Resource Center,* http://galenet.galegroup.com/servlet/BioRC (accessed December 28, 2007).
MacCash, Doug, "Renowned Artist Stayed Close to N.O. Roots," *Times-Picayune,* http://www.nola.com/news/t-p/frontpage/index.ssf?/base/news-9/1188713831303400.xml&coll=1 (accessed December 28, 2007).

—Tina Gianoulis

Kiron K. Skinner

1962(?)—

Academic, author

Kiron K. Skinner is a professor and political analyst with two *New York Times* best sellers to her credit. A scholar of post–World War II U.S. foreign policy, she teaches history at Carnegie Mellon University in Pittsburgh, Pennsylvania, and is also a fellow of the Hoover Institution at Stanford University. In 2003 and 2004 Skinner coedited a trio of newly discovered writings from Ronald Reagan, the U.S. president credited with ushering a new era of political conservatism in America. Together, the titles make up "a primary source for all future historians and political scientists who evaluate the 40th president," asserted *National Review* writer Steven F. Hayward. "No appraisal of Reagan can be complete without reckoning with the self-discipline and seriousness that is revealed here."

Born in the early 1960s, Skinner earned an associate's degree from Sacramento City College before heading to Spelman College in Atlanta, Georgia, for an undergraduate degree in political science. She earned a master's degree and a doctorate from Harvard University, focusing on political science and international relations in her studies. Her area of interest was U.S. foreign policy in the decades that followed the end of World War II in 1945, and she was particularly fascinated by the historic changes that occurred during the Republican administration of Reagan, a onetime Hollywood actor who was elected governor of California in 1966. During Reagan's first term in the White House in the early 1980s, tensions between the Soviet Union and the United States reached an all-time high, but less than a year after the end of his second term, much of the Communist bloc in Eastern Europe had crumbled. The Soviet Union would itself collapse in 1991, bringing an end to the cold war that had dominated the postwar political discourse.

Skinner won a prestigious fellowship at Stanford University's Hoover Institution and began researching the Reagan era. "There's been so much written about the end of the Cold War from the standpoint of the old Soviet Union, but very little from the American side," she explained in a report that appeared in a *Grand Rapids Press* article by Bob Hoover. "Most of the focus has been on activities in Russia, but I was curious to know what was happening in Washington." At the time Skinner began her research, Reagan was still alive but suffering from Alzheimer's disease and had been out of the public eye for some time. Skinner wrote Nancy Reagan, the former first lady, to request permission to conduct research at the Reagan Presidential Library in Simi Valley, California. Nancy granted the request, and it was there that Skinner discovered a forgotten sheaf of yellow legal pads from the 1970s filled with Reagan's handwritten speeches.

After his second term as California governor ended in 1975, Reagan wrote a twice-weekly syndicated newspaper column and gave a daily weekday radio commentary that was picked up for syndication by some three hundred U.S. stations. Reagan scholars knew the newspaper columns had been ghostwritten, and the radio addresses were assumed to have been penned by another hand, too. The yellow legal pads that Skinner found proved otherwise: Of the 1,027 "Viewpoints" that Reagan broadcast between 1975 and 1979, Skin-

At a Glance . . .

Born c. 1962. *Education:* Sacramento City College, AA; Spelman College, AB; Harvard University, AM, PhD.

Career: Carnegie Mellon University, associate professor of history and political science; Stanford University, Hoover Institution, W. Glenn Campbell Research Fellow; member of the executive panel of the Chief of Naval Operations, the Defense Policy Board of the U.S. Department of Defense, the National Security Education Board, and the Council on Foreign Relations.

Addresses: *Office*—Hoover Institution, 434 Galvez Mall, Stanford University, Stanford, CA 94305-6010.

ner found handwritten notes from Reagan for 682 of them. Annelise Anderson and Martin Anderson, Hoover Institute researchers, helped her shape them into book form, and the result was *Reagan, in His Own Hand: The Writings of Ronald Reagan That Reveal His Revolutionary Vision for America,* published in 2001. "They are raw drafts, with Reagan's self-editing apparent, and reveal a writer adept at marshaling a philosophical argument in a listener-friendly, conversational style," wrote William Safire in the *New York Times Magazine.* "In today's age of composition on computers and writing by government committee, we are struck by the workings of one man's mind expressed through a pen in his hand."

Other commentators in conservative-leaning publications were equally effusive in their praise, with Hayward declaring that "the remarkable range and depth of Reagan's writings suggests that he was arguably the best-prepared person to enter the White House in modern times." Hayward also contended that Skinner's book "marked a watershed in the public's knowledge and estimation of Reagan. It proved that Reagan was no mere creature of speechwriters and handlers, as his detractors had long alleged, but was in fact the prime mover of his public career." Indeed, Skinner viewed the speech drafts as a rebuke to the tongue-in-cheek nickname—"The Great Communicator"—that Reagan was given by wary pundits early on in his first administration. An audience estimated at twenty million were likely listening to those weekday radio commentaries, and with those, "Reagan probably reached more people as a private citizen than anybody before Oprah," the *Grand Rapids Press* article quoted Skinner as saying. "What he was doing was expanding his political base. By the time he ran for president, a lot of people knew his message."

In 2003 Skinner and her coeditors, Annelise Anderson and Martin Anderson, issued *Reagan: A Life in Letters,* which also spent a couple of weeks on the *New York Times* nonfiction best-seller list. The trilogy ended in 2004 with *Reagan's Path to Victory: The Shaping of Ronald Reagan's Vision: Selected Writings.* Two other titles appeared in 2007: *Strategy of Campaigning: Lessons from Ronald Reagan and Boris Yeltsin,* written with a team of coauthors that included U.S. secretary of state Condoleezza Rice, and *Turning Points in Ending the Cold War,* for which Skinner served as editor.

To some, Skinner may appear to be following the career path of Rice, the first African-American woman to serve as U.S. national security advisor as well as U.S. secretary of state, but in a 2004 interview with radio host Tavis Smiley, Skinner claimed to be a registered Democrat. She also offered a long-range, nonpartisan view of the war in Iraq. "War is extremely difficult, and I think we forget that," she told Smiley. "If you think back to World War II, the reconstruction in Germany, the Germans were starving in 1946. It took a long time to get the country up and running. We had the Berlin airlift. War is extremely difficult. It rarely goes well, even when you 'win,' and reconstruction is especially difficult. I think now in this kind of instant age of television and communications we want to see things going well very quickly, but it doesn't happen that way."

Selected writings

Books

(With Annelise Anderson and Martin Anderson, eds.) *Reagan, in His Own Hand: The Writings of Ronald Reagan That Reveal His Revolutionary Vision for America,* Free Press, 2003.

(With Anderson and Anderson, eds.) *Reagan: A Life in Letters,* Free Press, 2003.

(With Anderson and Anderson, eds.) *Reagan's Path to Victory: The Shaping of Ronald Reagan's Vision: Selected Writings,* Free Press, 2004.

(With Serhiy Kudelia, Bruce Bueno de Mesquita, and Condoleezza Rice) *Strategy of Campaigning: Lessons from Ronald Reagan and Boris Yeltsin,* University of Michigan Press, 2007.

(Editor) *Turning Points in Ending the Cold War,* Hoover Press, 2007.

Sources

Periodicals

Grand Rapids Press (Grand Rapids, MI), March 4, 2001.

National Review, November 8, 2004.

New York Times, January 5, 2004; January 19, 2004.

New York Times Magazine, December 31, 2000.

Online

"Dr. Kiron Skinner," *The Tavis Smiley Show*, http://www.pbs.org/kcet/tavissmiley/archive/200410/20041029_skinner.html (accessed December 26, 2007).

"Kiron K. Skinner," Hoover Institution, http://www.hoover.org/bios/skinner.html (accessed December 26, 2007).

—Carol Brennan

Jimmy Lee Sudduth

1910–2007

Artist

Alabama artist Jimmy Lee Sudduth was one of the leading folk artists of the American South, but his death in 2007 at the age of ninety-seven marked another closing chapter in a remarkable discovery and resurgence of outsider art in twentieth-century America. Sometimes called "primitive" or "vernacular" art, outsider art refers to artists who are entirely untrained and largely removed from the history of and contemporary trends in the visual arts. "Sudduth's art often depicted everyday life in Alabama—portraits of houses, people, farm animals and his dog, Toto," wrote Margalit Fox in the artist's *New York Times* obituary. "But it also ranged over the architecture of faraway places, as in his paintings of Washington landmarks and his geometric scenes of New York City skyscrapers."

Born in 1910, Sudduth spent his entire life in northwest Alabama, with the exception of trips he took to New York and Washington, D.C., once he became well known. He was born on a farm near Caines Ridge, Alabama, and certain details of his background have been lost over time: He may have been born into a family named Wilson and adopted by the Sudduths as an infant. His adoptive parents worked as itinerant farmhands, and the family moved frequently as a result. He had just a few years of formal schooling as a youngster and was probably functionally illiterate, though he did sign his paintings later with a practiced hand, as "Jim Sudduth"; some sources cite his first name as "Jimmie."

Sudduth's adoptive mother was a folk remedy expert, and he went with her on her plant-gathering trips into the woods. It was there he first drew a picture on a tree stump using mud. When he and his mother returned to the woods a few days later, the image was still there, which she considered to be a divine message that her son should continue painting. He painted on tree stumps, plywood, old doors, or pieces of sheet metal, and he concocted his own paint by using mud with various ingredients, such as coffee grounds, crepe paper he had wetted and squeezed out, colored chalk, leftover house paint, brick dust, rose petals, pine needles, turnip greens, axle grease, chimney soot, elderberries, grass, tobacco, or egg yolk. Mud was an impermanent material, however, and early on Sudduth realized that he had to add other ingredients to lend his pigments some staying power. Sugar was the best, he discovered, but he also mixed his tinted muds with molasses, honey, sorghum syrup, or Coca-Cola.

Like most practitioners of outsider art, Sudduth worked with whatever materials were available to him; he applied his paints with a sponge only much later in life. His finger was the ideal brush, he was fond of saying. "I paint with my finger 'cause that's why I got it, and that brush don't wear out," Fox's *New York Times* obituary quoted him as saying. "When I die, the brush dies." For many years, his subject matter was relegated to images of his own world in northwestern Alabama: local landmarks, animals such as roosters and cows, a pot of flowers or a barn, and his beloved dog. Long a local fixture for his paintings as well as his harmonica playing, he had spent much of his life in humble jobs, including working in a grist mill and a lumberyard, and was "discovered" by the arts establishment when he was in his late fifties while working as a gardener for the director of the Fayette Art Museum.

The first exhibition of Sudduth's "sweet mud" paintings, as he called them, was held in 1968 at Stillman College in Tuscaloosa, Alabama, followed a few years later by a show at the Fayette Art Museum. National recognition came in 1976, when he was included in the annual Festival of American Folklife at the Smithsonian Institution. "The popularity of vernacular art exploded in the 1980s, and Sudduth of Fayette in northwest Alabama was prominent among that wave of self-taught makers with original visions," wrote Howard Pousner in the *Atlanta Journal-Constitution.* His works were regularly included in group exhibitions of American outsider art, including the show *Bearing Witness: African-American Vernacular Art of the South,* held at the Schomburg Center for Research in Black Culture in Harlem in 1997, and *Testimony: Vernacular Art of the African-American South,* which opened at the Kalamazoo Institute of Arts in 2000 and toured several cities.

Prices for Sudduth's paintings rose on the art market over the years, and some were sold for as much as $5,000. His works were also acquired by several major museums, including the Smithsonian Institution, the Museum of American Folk Art in New York City, and the High Museum of Art in Atlanta, Georgia. Susan Mitchell Crawley, a curator at the High Museum, wrote a book on him, *The Life and Art of Jimmy Lee Sudduth,* in 2005. Interviewed by Pousner for the *Atlanta Journal-Constitution,* Crawley extolled Sudduth's art, noting that "he reached the height of his powers in the 1980s when he was exploiting the texture of mud and the fluidity of paint; at the same time, his drawing, which was once very tight and precise, had become free and expressive. Although he's most famous for his use of mud and other natural materials, he is a gifted painter with remarkable formal skill. His work reveals a wide range of subject matter, amazing technical ingenuity, and a fine eye for color."

Sudduth had spent so many decades working in mud that he claimed to be able to recognize thirty-six different shades of dirt in Alabama soil alone; as his fame grew, fans sometimes sent him samples of dirt from around the country. In the early 1900s, with his health declining, Sudduth was no longer able to gather the plants he needed for his mud paint, and so he switched to acrylics, which he applied with a sponge. His last years were spent in a nursing home in Fayette, where he died on September 2, 2007.

Sources

Books

Crawley, Susan Mitchell, *The Life and Art of Jimmy Lee Sudduth,* Montgomery Museum of Fine Arts, 2005.

Periodicals

Art in America, July 2003.
Arts & Activities, September 2004.
Atlanta Journal-Constitution, August 13, 2006; September 9, 2007.
Boston Herald, February 14, 1997.
New York Times, February 14, 1997; June 29, 2003; April 4, 2004; May 13, 2005; September 9, 2007.

—Carol Brennan

Oumou Sy

1952—

Fashion designer, teacher, author, artist

Sy, Oumou, photograph. Djibril Sy/Maxpp/Landov.

Since her debut on the European fashion scene in 1982, Senegalese artist Oumou Sy has become one of Africa's best-known designers of clothing, jewelry, and hairstyles. Her designs combine the traditional and the contemporary to create whimsical styles that capture the spirit of modern Africa. However, Sy was not satisfied to be merely a high fashion designer creating clothing for the elite. Determined to make fashion accessible to everyone in a way that was compatible with African culture, she founded a workshop to produce affordable ready-to-wear clothing and initiated a carnival parade to bring her high-fashion creations to the streets, where everyone could enjoy them. Raised in a strict Muslim family that did not believe that formal education was necessary for girls, Sy is a self-educated woman who stresses the importance of accessible schools. In her home city of Dakar, she started two respected schools of fashion, one for designers and one for models.

Perhaps Sy's greatest contribution to Senegal and to Africa has been her work to spread the availability of Internet technology. Feeling strongly that the ordinary citizen of Africa must not be left out of the information and communication revolution represented by the Internet, she helped found the first cyber café in West Africa. She also worked with a rural Internet project, traveling to remote villages to demonstrate the many practical uses of information technology and to help residents explore alternative power sources.

Oumou Sy was born in 1952 in Podor, a village in the northern part of the West African nation of Senegal. Her mother had come from the southern province of Casamance, and her father was part of an elite clan of religious leaders of the Toucouleur people. The Toucoulours are Muslims with an ancient history in northern Senegal. Though, as a girl, Sy was not permitted to attend school, she had a close relationship with her father, who encouraged her creativity and curiosity. The young Sy showed a flair for design at an early age, making dolls and other toys of clay and twigs. She especially loved playing with scraps of fabric, feeling their textures and finding ways to combine them with other materials.

When she was only five years old, her father died. Though she had lost one of her greatest supporters, her father's death filled her with a determination to be worthy of his belief in her. Though her chosen career

At a Glance . . .

Born Oumou Sy in 1952, in Podor, Senegal; married Michel Mavros; twelve children.

Career: Fashion designer; École des Beaux Arts de Dakar, teacher; Metissacana Association, cofounder, 1996; Atelier Leydi, founder, 1998; Made in Africa, founder; Atelier Macsy, founder.

Memberships: Aicha Association.

Awards: Prince Claus Fund for Culture and Development, Art of African Fashion Award, 1998; Radio France International, RFI Net Award, 2001; Government of France, Légion d'Honneur, 2006.

Addresses: *Office*—Metissacana, 30 rue de Thiong, BP 6491 Dakar, Senegal.

would require much hard work, she would continually be inspired and encouraged by her father's example of kindness and public service.

Learned Traditional Fabric and Metalworking Techniques

The child who loved playing with fabric swatches soon became the young woman who loved sewing them together to make beautiful clothing and pieces of art. From the craftspeople of her village, she learned traditional techniques of dying, weaving, and embroidering fabric. She also learned metalwork and began making jewelry, updating simple but dramatic tribal designs. Sy's signature style developed with her creative use of unlikely materials, both traditional and modern. Her dresses combine fabric with feathers, beads, vinyl, wicker, and traditional woodcarvings to create a modern look with the flavor of ancient African culture. She called her blending of fabric, style, and culture *metissage,* French for "hybrid" or "mixture," feeling that this concept represented Africa itself, with its blending of native and colonial cultures. Typical of Sy's blend of modern sensibility with historic African tradition is her ongoing project of imagining and creating royal costumes for the kings and queens of ancient Senegal, which once was divided into many kingdoms.

When she reached adulthood, Sy moved to Dakar, Senegal's bustling capital city. Dakar has a thriving design industry, with hundreds of small shops where couturiers create their individual fashions. Sy became part of this vigorous atmosphere of creativity, and her

designs soon became famous throughout Senegal. In 1982 she began displaying her clothes in European fashion shows, where they were warmly received. By the 1990s she had begun designing costumes, makeup, and hairstyles for films and clothing for some of Senegal's most popular musicians, such as Youssou N'Dour and Baaba Maal. She became a respected teacher at Dakar's École des Beaux Arts (School of Fine Arts).

Although she continued to present her work at European fashion shows, Sy's deepest interest lay in creating a support structure for the fashion industry in Senegal and throughout Africa. When Senegal gained access to the Internet during the 1990s, Sy saw immediately that the new technology could not only help her fashion business but could also connect Africa with the rest of the world as never before. In 1996, only six months after the arrival of Internet technology in Senegal, Sy, along with her husband, business manager Michel Mavros, and financial expert Alexis Sikorsky, opened an Internet café in Dakar. They named it Metissacana, or "the metissage is coming" in Bambara, one of Senegal's native languages.

Metissacana was not only the first Internet café in Africa, outside of South Africa, but also it was a cultural association and fashion center. Offering food, drinks, and computer access in its courtyard restaurant, the center had a boutique of Oumou Sy ready-to-wear fashions and a haute couture, or high fashion, showroom, with a rooftop gallery for fashion shows. In 1997 Sy initiated an annual fashion week to highlight Dakar's contribution to the world of haute couture. In conjunction with the fashion week, she launched a carnival procession of flamboyant costumes and extravagant floats to bring the celebration of fashion to all the people of the city.

Supported Economy and Education

Sy was not only determined to increase the accessibility of fashionable clothing in Africa, she was also convinced that the continent should manufacture the goods it needed. Disturbed to see that much of the clothing purchased by working-class Africans was made in Asia, she established her own workshop to manufacture affordable ready-to-wear clothing from African materials. By doing so, she provided many jobs for workers and injected pride into African fashion with her "Made in Africa" label.

As a self-educated woman, Sy had a special awareness of the importance of accessible schooling. During the late 1990s, she established two schools to teach young designers the skills, both traditional and modern, that she had painstakingly learned on her own. The Ateliers (studio) Leydi was a design school, both for couturiers, or fashion designers, and for designers of all sorts of innovative products, and the Ateliers Macsy was a school for models.

In 1998 Sy received international recognition for her contributions to her country when she became the recipient of the Art of African Fashion Award, given by the Prince Claus Fund for Culture and Development, a charitable organization in the Netherlands. Her work as a designer was acclaimed throughout Europe, and she opened shops in Geneva and Paris.

Pioneered Internet Access in Senegal

She also continued her work to spread the use of Internet among the people of Africa. Metissacana continued to be successful as an Internet café, boasting over two thousand subscribers and twenty computers by 2001. The café's Internet service was the first in Africa to broadcast live radio Webcasts, and in 2001 it became the first to link a live Senegalese concert to a music festival in France. During Senegal's 2000 presidential election, Metissacana offered unprecedented online political coverage, including debates and opinion polls.

When privatization threatened public access to the Internet, Sy and her partners traveled throughout Senegal to introduce rural people to the usefulness of the Web. They visited villages without electricity or phones, unrolling hundreds of yards of telephone cable to make hookups. They then set up a large-screen monitor and took questions from fascinated audiences, on every subject from crop prices to sports scores, and demonstrated how answers could be found quickly by searching the Web. The founders of Metissacana began exploring alternative energy sources, such as solar technology, to power Internet connections in rural areas, and sought partners in other African nations in hopes of connecting all of Africa.

Sy's very public role in trying to keep the Internet free and open has angered some powerful people in her home country. Some of her supporters believe that it was Sy's work combating private control of the Internet that led to her arrest, along with a number of her models, on sex trafficking charges. A flood of outraged international support followed, and the charges were dropped. When Sy was released after being detained for thirty-three days, she was more determined than ever to continue her work.

Through her shops, her international shows, and her Internet connections, Sy has continued to work for greater communication within Senegal, across Africa, and throughout the world. Her haute couture fashions have brought Africa's mix of ancient and modern cultures to the notice of the world, and her pioneering work in Internet access has helped bring the rest of the world to Africa.

Sources

Books

Levin, Alan, *The Wonder Safaris: Journeys of Miracles and Surprises,* Struik Publishers, 2004.

Periodicals

New African (London, England), November 2005.
Print (Rockville, MD), July–August 1999, p. 12.

Online

"Fashion Show by Oumou Sy," *Documenta 12,* http://www.documenta12.de/1367.html?&L=1 (accessed December 28, 2007).
"Internet: Motor of Development: An Interview with Oumou Sy," *World-Information.org,* http://world-information.org/wio/readme/992006691/1019572356 (accessed December 28, 2007).
Mavros, Michel, "Metissacana," *Ars Electronica,* http://www.aec.at/en/archiv_files/20021/E2002_158.pdf (accessed December 28, 2007).
"Metissacana Closes Its Doors," *Unplugged: Art as the Scene of Global Conflicts,* http://www.aec.at/unplugged/update/artikel.asp?id=238&lang=e (accessed December 28, 2007).
Mustafa, Hudita, "The African Place," *Archis R.S.V.P. Events,* http://pro.archis.org/plain/object.php?object=323&year=&num= (accessed December 28, 2007).
Ondego, Ogova, "Top French Award for Senegalese Fashion Designer,"*ArtMatters: Flaunting Arts and Culture in Africa,* http://www.artmatters.info/fashion/articles/frenchaward.php (accessed December 28, 2007).
"Oumou Sy," *Internet Movie Database,* http://french.imdb.com/name/nm0842928/maindetails (accessed December 28, 2007).
"Portrait: Oumou Sy," and "Fashion Made in Africa," *CulturCooperation,* http://www.culturcooperation.de/site/s3_3_1e.htm (accessed December 28, 2007).

—Tina Gianoulis

Rosetta Tharpe

1915–1973

Gospel singer, songwriter

Tharpe, Rosetta, photograph. AP Images.

Rosetta Tharpe was one of the first gospel singers/songwriters to transcend her genre and gain international popularity as a performer. At the height of her popularity, she was one of the best-known performing artists, of any genre, in the world and conducted international tours, which raised the popularity of gospel music to previously un-achieved levels. Though Tharpe's career was largely forgotten by the 1980s and 1990s, her guitar playing and singing style influenced a number of popular artists, in-cluding Elvis Presley, Chuck Berry, Little Richard, and Jerry Lee Lewis.

Tharpe was born Rosetta Nubin on March 20, 1915, in Cotton Plant, Arkansas, a small, primarily African-American community. Tharpe's mother, Katie Nubin, was a gospel singer and mandolin player who traveled with the Church of God in Christ Ministry and played for the Holiness Church in Cotton Plant. After divorc-ing her husband, Nubin raised her daughter with the help of the Pentecostal church community and continued her work as a traveling preacher and musician.

Sang Gospel Blues

Tharpe learned the basics of how to play a piano and man-dolin from her mother. She was given her first guitar when she was about four or five years old and soon learned to accompany herself while sing-ing. By age six, Tharpe was accompanying her mother in churches throughout Arkan-sas, Mississippi, Florida, Ten-nessee, and Georgia and trav-eling with the revival tour of evangelist P.W. McGee. While still a child, Tharpe was billed as the "Little Sister," or the "Pint-Sized Guitar-Playing Miracle," and she eventually became known as one of the most popular acts in the touring gospel circuit. In 1920, Tharpe and her family relocated to Chicago, but they continued working with McGee's traveling show and toured the country from 1923 to the early 1930s.

From 1920 to the late 1930s, Tharpe's playing and performance style was largely influenced by classic gospel, her mother's mandolin playing, and the piano playing of Arizona Dranes, a blind pianist who traveled with McGee in the 1930s. In Chicago, Tharpe was exposed to urban blues and jazz, and she soon began to

At a Glance . . .

Born Rosetta Nubin on March 20, 1915, in Cotton Plant, AR; died on October 9, 1973, in Philadelphia, PA; married Thomas J. Thorpe, 1934 (divorced); married Forrest Allen (divorced); married Russell Morrison, 1951.

Career: P.W. McGee's revival show, performer, 1920–36; Decca Records, recording artist, 1936–38; self-employed musician, songwriter, performer, 1938–73.

adopt traces of these "new" sounds into her repertoire. By the time she reached adulthood, she had begun to craft a unique method of playing gospel music, with a distinct urban appeal.

Tharpe relocated to New York City in the early 1930s, where she joined the Holiness Church in Harlem and began performing with the church choir. In 1934, she married Thomas J. Thorpe, the pastor of Holiness Church. When the marriage ended, reportedly because Thorpe wanted his wife to cease touring and performing, she kept her husband's name but changed the spelling, thereafter performing as "Sister Rosetta Tharpe."

In 1936, representatives from Decca Records—a British label that opened a U.S. branch in 1934—offered Tharpe a recording contract after watching her perform at a club in New York. Tharpe was the first gospel singer to receive a recording contract with a major recording company. Her first recordings were released in 1938 and met with critical and popular acclaim. Almost immediately, she received offers to perform at major venues and, in December of 1938, she headlined the historic "From Spirituals to Swing" concert held at Carnegie Hall, alongside Benny Goodman and Count Basie.

As Tharpe began performing for larger audiences, she interspersed her traditional gospel songs with secular music and nontraditional versions of spirituals done with jazz and blues overtones. Some of the members in the Pentecostal community were troubled by Tharpe's departure from strict gospel tradition, whereas many in the secular audience were enthusiastic about the new, crossover sound. Tharpe was among the first gospel artists to play at Harlem's internationally famous Cotton Club, where she shared the stage with Cab Calloway. Her first major radio hit—"Rock Me," which was a remake of a gospel spiritual changed into a love song—gained her further criticism from strict Pentecostal audiences but became a national hit and made Tharpe the most popular recording artist in gospel history.

Toured the United States and Europe

The 1940s was the pinnacle of gospel popularity in the United States, and Tharpe was one of the genre's leading women. During the late 1930s, she began transitioning from her finger-picked acoustic guitar to an electric guitar. "When Rosetta Tharpe switched to the electric guitar primarily as a performer ... she enjoyed a loud, kind of noisy, dirty sound," said biographer Gayle Wald in a 2007 interview with New York Public Radio. Wald noted that Tharpe's electric guitar was unique in the gospel world and a forerunner of the pop gospel that was popularized in later decades. "She's doing a praise song to god and yet it has this noisy, dirty sound to it."

By the mid-1940s, Tharpe had reached an unprecedented status for a gospel singer. She was one of only two gospel performers asked to record V-disks, which were sent overseas to U.S. soldiers fighting in World War II. During this time, Tharpe was also featured on three short television performances, in which she showcased her ability to perform visually as well as vocally. Tharpe's movements, poses, and guitar-playing style were reminiscent of later artists in the rock-and-roll genre, including Presley, Lewis, and Pete Townshend.

In 1947, Tharpe's record managers decided to make a series of duet records featuring Tharpe and young gospel singer Marie Roach Knight. The duo proved to be more popular than had been expected, and their radio and record singles reached the top of the sales charts. Tharpe and Knight continued performing and touring together off and on for next twenty years. It was during her collaborations with Knight and pianist Samuel Blythe Price that Tharpe reached superstar status, with sold-out concerts across the nation and record sales that outpaced those of any other gospel artist.

Between touring and performing, Tharpe met and married her second husband, gospel booking agent Forrest Allen. By 1950, the couple had divorced, and Tharpe decided to reunite with her mother for a national tour. Tharpe and Nubin recorded a number of songs that were featured on the radio and performed at the Apollo Theater in New York, in the show *Spirituals in a Modern Manner*.

In 1951, Tharpe married Russell Morrison, a manager and promoter of gospel and rhythm and blues. Tharpe's promotional team decided to couple the wedding with a concert held at Griffith Stadium in Washington, D.C. Over twenty thousand people purchased tickets to see the concert/wedding. A recording of the concert was sold following the show.

In 1952, Tharpe became the first gospel singer to tour Europe, where she stayed for over a year playing concerts at churches and other venues in England,

Spain, Germany, and France. She returned to England in 1957 for an extended tour. Her popularity grew rapidly in Europe, where American gospel music was only beginning to spread. Tharpe played to sold-out crowds at most of her appearances and was often hailed in the European media for her ecstatic performances.

Influenced a Variety of Singers

Though Tharpe continued playing spiritual music, her blend of secular gospel was never fully accepted by the Pentecostal community, so she eventually joined a Baptist church. By the mid-1960s, the American popular music scene was changing, and Tharpe's style, while still controversial among the religious community, was no longer at the forefront of American popular music

Tharpe continued touring Europe and the United States during the 1960s and still had the popularity to draw large crowds at major venues. In 1967, she was one of the headlining acts at the Newport Folk Festival, and the following year she was asked to perform at the Paris Jazz Festival. Tharpe was still touring Europe when her mother died in 1969. The following year, Tharpe suffered her first stroke and was hospitalized for several months. Even though her leg was amputated due to complications from her stroke, she recovered sufficiently to make short appearances on tours in 1972 and early 1973. In October of 1973, while she was in Philadelphia preparing to record a new album, she suffered a second and fatal stroke. Tharpe was buried in an unmarked grave in Philadelphia as, for unknown reasons, Morrison was unwilling to purchase a gravestone.

Tharpe's career was largely forgotten for nearly two decades, though her influence on popular music remained strong. Musicians such as Presley, Little Richard, Lewis, and Isaac Hayes cited Tharpe among their influences, and her blues guitar style influenced countless musicians in the 1970s and 1980s blues/rock scene. Wald noted in her biography of Tharpe that country and folk legend Johnny Cash called Tharpe his "favorite artist." In reference to Tharpe's legacy, Wald wrote: "[Tharpe] was a woman before her time in a number of ways: as a woman guitarist, as a Gospel 'crossover' star, as an artist willing to follow her own artistic vision. She figured out ways to work a guitar to bring an audience—even a huge, stadium size audience—to its feet."

In the twenty-first century, Tharpe's relevance has been resurrected, and her music continues to influence artists in the gospel, rhythm and blues, and folk genres. In 2003, MC Records released the first Rosetta Tharpe tribute album, *Shout, Sistah, Shout,* which featured a number of mainstream artists singing renditions of Tharpe's most popular recordings. Tharpe's rise to superstardom, her struggle to remain relevant as a popular artist while maintaining her roots in the religious community, and her bravery and innovation as a musician and a performer highlight issues that remain central to music, artistry, and the evolution of culture.

Selected Works

Albums

Gospel Train, Polygram, 1956.
Sister Rosetta Tharpe/The Same Price Trio, Decca, 1958.
Gospel Train, Vol. 2, Lection, 1960.
Live in 1960, Southland, 1960.
Sister on Tour, Verve, 1962.
Live in Paris: 1964, French Concerts, 1964.
Live at the Hot Club de France, Milan, 1966.
Great Gospel Music, Universal Special Products, 1995.
In Concert, Nesak, 1995.
Precious Memories, Savoy, 1998.

Sources

Books

Wald, Gayle F., *Shout, Sister, Shout!: The Untold Story of Rock-and-Roll Trailblazer Sister Rosetta Tharpe,* Beacon Press, 2007.
Yanow, Scott, *Swing,* Miller Freeman Books, 2000.

Periodicals

American Quarterly, Vol. 55, September 2003, pp. 387–416.
Philadelphia Inquirer, February 27, 2007.
Sing Out!, Vol. 47, 2004, p. 47.
Washingtonian, Vol. 42, 2007, p. 45.

Online

"The Gospel of Sister Rosetta Tharpe," *All Things Considered,* http://www.npr.org/templates/story/story.php?storyId=1603597 (accessed December 14, 2007).
"Life and Legacy of Rosetta Tharpe," *New York Public Radio,* http://www.wnyc.org/shows/soundcheck/episodes/2007/06/06 (accessed December 15, 2007).

—Micah L. Issitt

Clarence Thomas

1948—

Supreme court justice, appeals court judge, federal official

Thomas, Clarence, photograph. Roger L. Wollenberg/UPI/Landov.

Clarence Thomas was sworn in as a justice of the U.S. Supreme Court in November of 1991, following what was perhaps the greatest furor over such an appointment in modern history. A conservative jurist with experience in the education department under President Ronald Reagan, Thomas had also served as the assistant secretary of the U.S. Department of Education's Office of Civil Rights and headed the Equal Employment Opportunities Commission, during which he had allegedly sexually harassed a staff member, Anita Hill. Hill's accusations surfaced only after Thomas's nomination to the nation's highest court by President George W. Bush; Hill was by this time a law professor. The Senate confirmation hearings that dealt with these charges had enormous political and social ramifications above and beyond Thomas's suitability for the Supreme Court.

Thomas's appointment was a watershed for the Bush administration, which needed to replace retiring black justice Thurgood Marshall. The choice of an African-American conservative effectively stymied Democratic opposition to Thomas, who suspended his lifelong criticism of racial politics long enough to call his confirmation hearings a "high-tech lynching." This remark is representative of the many contradictions embodied by this controversial figure. Indeed, *Newsweek* noted that "Thomas is an intense opponent of affirmative action, yet has benefited from it throughout his life…. The very reason he was named to succeed Thurgood Marshall on the Supreme Court is because of his race."

Thomas was born in 1948 in Pin Point, Georgia, a tiny coastal hamlet named for the plantation that once stood there. His mother, Leola, was eighteen at the time of his birth; his father, M. C. Thomas, left the family two years later. Leola, her two children—Clarence and his older sister Emma Mae—and her Aunt Annie Graham occupied what *Newsweek* described as "a one-room wooden house near the marshes. It had dirt floors and no plumbing or electricity." Their destitute life was struck by further misfortune five years after M. C. walked out on the family, ostensibly headed for Philadelphia: the house burned down, so the family moved near Leola's parents, Mr. and Mrs. Myers Anderson. Having in the meantime married a man who did not want to raise the children—there was now a third child, Myers, who went by the name Peanut—Leola agreed

At a Glance . . .

Born Clarence Thomas on June 23, 1948, in Pin Point, GA; son of M. C. Thomas and Leola Anderson; married Kathy Grace Ambush, 1971 (divorced, 1984); married Virginia Lamp, 1987; children: (with Ambush) Jamal; (legal guardian of) Mark Martin Jr. *Education:* Holy Cross College, Worcester, MA, 1971; Yale University Law School, JD, 1974.

Career: Held summer jobs in legal aid and at Hill, Jones, and Farrington (law firm), c. 1971–74; offices of Missouri Attorney General John Danforth, staff member, 1974–77; Monsanto Corporation, legal counsel, 1977–80; U.S. Department of Education, Office of Civil Rights, assistant secretary, 1981–82; Equal Employment Opportunity Commission, chairman, 1982–89; Federal Appeals Court, judge, 1990–91; U.S. Supreme Court justice, 1991—.

Memberships: Holy Cross College, Black Student Union, founder, 1971; advisory board of the *Lincoln Review,* member.

Addresses: *Office*—U.S. Supreme Court, 1 First St. NE, Washington, DC 20543-0001.

was to teach us to fend for ourselves and to do that in an openly hostile environment," Thomas noted in a 1987 speech before the Heritage Foundation, published in *Policy Review* in 1991.

Clarence performed duties as altar boy and crossing guard at St. Benedict's, and though not remembered by his teachers as an outstanding student, he excelled at sports. After school he and his brother helped their grandfather on his delivery rounds. Clarence's favorite retreat was a blacks-only library in Savannah—the Savannah public library was for whites—funded by the Carnegie family. His browsing there helped formulate his ambition: he would one day have the sophistication to understand magazines such as the *New Yorker.*

He graduated from St. Benedict's in 1962, spent two years at St. Pius X High School, and then transferred—at his grandfather's insistence—to a white Catholic boarding school called St. John Vianney Minor Seminary. Clarence did well in school, but experienced for the first time the hostility of racism. His schoolmates' derisive remarks came as a shock—his segregated youth had ironically provided some insulation from everyday racism—but he kept his composure. Following St. John's, Clarence went to Immaculate Conception Seminary in Conception, Missouri, to study for the priesthood. As one of only four blacks there, Thomas was again made acutely aware of the double standards of white Christian society. One incident, however, caused him to give up on the seminary for good: the voice of a fellow seminarian cheering the news that civil rights leader Martin Luther King Jr. had been shot in 1968. "I knew I couldn't stay in this so-called Christian environment," he remarked later.

Struggled with Race and Identity

In 1968 Thomas began his studies at Holy Cross, a Jesuit college in Worcester, Massachusetts. This period saw an intensification of Thomas's struggle with his identity, his background, and the politics of race. He joined the Black Student Union, a militant group on campus that succeeded in using its political and rhetorical energies to make some changes, including an all-black dormitory, more courses relevant to black students, and increased financial aid. The atmosphere of questioning and empowerment was exhilarating for Thomas, though unlike many of his contemporaries he never abandoned his earliest sources of strength: "Thomas still spoke the conservative maxims of his grandfather and the nuns far more often than the chic of the left," reported *Newsweek.* Though he adopted some of the language, style, and arguments of the radical Black Panther Party's leaders, he remained a skeptic and was often the sole dissenter among his revolutionary circle. This tendency would serve him well as he learned what he would later call "the loneliness of the black conservative."

During his sophomore year, Thomas met Kathy Grace Ambush and began a relationship that would lead to

to let the Andersons care for the two boys and sent Emma Mae to live with Aunt Annie in Pin Point.

Raised by His Devout Catholic Grandfather

Myers Anderson exercised a huge influence on Clarence's life. A devout Catholic who created his own fuel oil business in Savannah in the 1950s, he provided the example of self-motivation in the face of segregation that would inspire his grandson. Through hard work and a refusal to submit to the poverty and degradation of menial work, he "did for himself," as one of his favorite expressions went. He fed and cared for Clarence and Peanut and paid for their education at St. Benedict the Moor, an all-black grammar school where white nuns exercised firm discipline. The racist vigilante group known as the Ku Klux Klan often threatened the nuns, who rode on the backs of buses with their students and demanded hard work and promptly completed assignments. Clarence's grandfather took him to a meeting of the National Association for the Advancement of Colored People (NAACP), of which Anderson was a member, and read the boy's grades aloud. "The most compassionate thing [our grandparents] did for us their 1971 marriage. In 1973 their son, Jamal, was born. Thomas had registered for the draft in 1966, at age eighteen, but had a student deferment. When he graduated in 1971 and discovered that his number in the conscription lottery was low, he braced himself to being a likely candidate for military service in Vietnam. However, he failed his physical examination. He had applied to Yale, Harvard, and the University of Pennsylvania law schools—all of which had accepted him—and decided on Yale because of the financial support it offered him. Thomas was a beneficiary of Yale's new affirmative-action policy, which offered opportunities to minority students. Though he benefited from this policy, it raised in Thomas—perhaps for the first time—doubts about whether he had succeeded on his own merits. These doubts would trouble him throughout his career and would motivate a deep distrust of what conservatives like to call "entitlements" or "handouts."

Thus, he strained to demonstrate his qualifications, to prove that something other than his blackness had brought him into the Ivy League. While at Yale he held some summer jobs; he assisted a small legal-aid establishment, which brought him into contact with welfare cases, and he spent a summer at the law firm of Hill, Jones, and Farrington. In the latter job Thomas could exercise his skill at developing both sides of an argument. As a law student, he dedicated himself to areas of legal study less often associated with blacks—tax and corporate law—rather than civil rights. His eagerness to dissociate himself from the stereotypes that surrounded beneficiaries of affirmative action was a strong determining factor here. Yet, when he began to look for work as his graduation drew near, he found few law firms interested him. The pay they offered was demonstrably lower than what white graduates would have been offered, and they tended to assume Thomas wanted to do social rather than corporate law. Once again, he found himself pigeonholed by race.

Joined Staff of Missouri Attorney General

Rather than accept what he considered an insufficient salary from the firm where he'd done his summer work, Thomas accepted a position on the staff of John Danforth, attorney general of Missouri. Danforth had attended Yale himself and, as an Episcopal minister and Republican, he saw in Thomas a promising young conservative. Thomas worked hard under Danforth and specialized in tax law. He achieved a victory when he appealed a decision against the state regarding the governor's banning of personalized license plates, and won in a higher court. Danforth's office had thought the case unwinnable because a lot of wealthy people had these so-called vanity plates; Thomas felt it necessary to prove that the privileged few could not control the law.

Yet, Thomas himself sought status symbols; he bought a BMW automobile while working in Danforth's office, though he told fellow workers that a Mercedes-Benz was the car for a "gentleman" to drive. This affection for status symbols no doubt grew out of Thomas's fondness for the ideology of self-help. He took a large step in the direction of greater financial stability when Danforth left Missouri to take a Senate seat; Thomas landed a job as legal counsel for the Monsanto Corporation. There, as *Time* phrased it, he "shepherded pesticides through government registration."

Monsanto's chemical empire supported him comfortably until he decided to move on to Washington. He returned to Danforth's staff and worked on energy and environmental issues, but was at the same time struck by the work of a handful of black conservatives. The writings of right-wing African-American economists Thomas Sowell and Walter Williams, as well as the African-American conservative journal, the *Lincoln Review,* had a galvanizing effect on Thomas. He joined the advisory board of the *Review,* which has created waves in the African-American community by taking some very unpopular—some would say reactionary—stands. The journal's editor, Jay Parker, argued on behalf of the government of South Africa, while the journal itself opposed a holiday for Martin Luther King Jr.; questioned the extent, if not the existence, of racial discrimination; and referred to abortion as a plot to "slaughter" blacks. Parker and Thomas chatted on the phone in 1980; the controversial editor would soon be looking for interested African-American conservatives to join the administration of President Ronald Reagan.

Accepted Posts with High Political Visibility

Thomas's first offer from Reagan's people was a position as a policy staffer on energy and environmental issues, but he turned this job down, accepting—in spite of his previous aversion to such matters—a place at the head of civil rights under the secretary of education. Ten months later, he was put in charge of the Equal Employment Opportunity Commission (EEOC), an agency charged with enforcing civil rights laws. Why Thomas accepted these jobs remains unclear, because they are the sort of classically "African-American" appointments he had resolutely avoided in the past. Some observers speculated that Thomas merely took the positions with the highest political visibility, whereas others suggested that his recent infatuation with ultraconservative African-American thinkers such as Sowell and Parker had awakened in him a new political enthusiasm and that he wished to tackle affirmative action and other issues head on.

In any case, Thomas's years at the EEOC were fraught with conflict. He was a demanding supervisor and often dealt with employees harshly. He allegedly settled petty scores in harsh ways, argued inconsistently on issues such as hiring quotas for minorities—he both opposed and supported them over the course of his tenure—and reportedly avoided prosecuting thousands of age discrimination cases. Although less doctrinaire than "the other Clarence"—Reagan's fiery Civil Rights Commission chair Clarence Pendleton, another conservative African American who alienated much of the civil rights community—Thomas made his self-help philosophy well known. He remarked to Lena Williams in a *New York Times* profile that "race-conscious remedies in this society are dangerous. You can't orchestrate society along racial lines or different lines by saying there should be 10 percent blacks, 15 percent Hispanics." He also made waves by remarking in 1984 that civil rights leaders just "bitch, bitch, bitch, moan and whine."

Despite the discontent he evoked from civil rights activists, Thomas was granted a second term at EEOC in 1984. He did not stand uniformly behind the administration's decisions, however. His was a dissenting voice—though reportedly not a very loud one—when the U.S. Department of Justice argued that religious institutions such as Bob Jones University, which practices various kinds of discrimination, should remain tax-exempt. "A fellow member of the administration said rather glibly that, in two days, the furor over Bob Jones would end," Thomas remarked in a 1987 speech. "I responded that we had sounded our death knell with that decision. Unfortunately, I was more right than he was."

Divorced and Remarried

It was a difficult period for Thomas, who had separated from Kathy in 1981; the two divorced in 1984, and Clarence retained custody of Jamal. The circumstances of the marriage and the divorce remain a well-guarded secret, and allegations of abuse made at the time returned to haunt Thomas during his confirmation hearings years later. Thomas became a stern taskmaster at home, pressuring Jamal to succeed at school just as Myers Anderson had pressed him in his own youth. In 1986 he met Virginia Lamp, a white fellow law school graduate active in conservative causes. The two fell in love and married in 1987. Virginia was a U.S. Department of Labor lawyer when Thomas was nominated for the Supreme Court.

Thomas's private regimen is as interesting a mix as his frequently contradictory public statements. He began lifting weights while at college and continues his bodybuilding to this day, yet he also smokes cigars—not, some would say, the best habit for someone in weight training. Earning $71,000 a year under Reagan, Thomas was chauffeured around in a limousine that, according to *Time,* stopped at a Catholic church every morning so he could pray. Yet, despite his lifelong piety, he was accused by Hill of a fascination with pornography and bizarre sexual practices such as bestiality. He has long opposed affirmative action, but bases this opposition on a distrust of white institutions that he believes keep African Americans begging for jobs and other economic opportunities.

In a critical 1987 speech before the conservative Heritage Foundation, Thomas articulated his feelings about the perils of "entitlement" programs, job quotas, and—most notoriously—welfare. He had some years earlier shocked listeners by criticizing his sister for her dependency on welfare, though, according to *Time's* Jack E. White, "she was not getting welfare checks when he singled her out but [was] working double shifts at a nursing home for slightly more than $2 an hour." But in this Heritage Foundation speech, he articulated more specifically his concern about the "welfare mentality." Though Reagan and others on the right had rankled African Americans and civil rights proponents with derisive references to "welfare queens," Thomas's criticisms may have been harder for his opponents to dismiss—or so the administration hoped.

Embraced Vision of African-American Conservatism

The Heritage Foundation speech also outlined Thomas's plan for bringing more African Americans into the ranks of conservatism. "I am of the view that black Americans will move inexorably and naturally toward conservatism when we stop discouraging them; when they are treated as a diverse group with differing interests; and when conservatives stand up for what they believe in rather than stand against blacks," he proclaimed. He went on to suggest that the "unnecessarily negative" approach of the Reagan administration had been more alienating than its political philosophy toward welfare and affirmative action. Many critics have attacked Thomas for this ardent individualism. Bruce Shapiro represented many of Thomas's opponents when he wrote in the *Nation* of Thomas's "far-reaching commitment to unravel the fabric of community and social responsibility."

Perhaps the most important strand of the Heritage Foundation speech was Thomas's invocation of natural law. This discussion provided the most substantial evidence of his judicial philosophy, and was particularly worrying to civil rights advocates and many people concerned about the fundamental separation of church and state. The alarm of these constituencies was magnified by Thomas's citing of Heritage trustee Lewis Lehrman's argument on behalf of the rights of the fetus as grounded in the Declaration of Independence as "a splendid example of applying natural law." In brief, natural law depends on applying a perception of God-given rights and rules—as, indeed, the Declaration and other founding documents of the American republic do, at least rhetorically—to human law. "Without such a notion of natural law," Thomas claimed in his speech, "the entire American political tradition, from Washington to Lincoln, from Jefferson to Martin Luther King, would be unintelligible." Thus, against what he perceived as the abstractions and inhumanity of the welfare state, he promoted a philosophy that "establishes our inherent equality as a God-given right."

Yet, many critics have expressed grave reservations about the implications of such a belief.

The Republican Party, however, which saw potential in Thomas early on, began to see him as a good prospect for the nation's highest court. President Bush nominated him to the federal appeals court in 1990, and he was confirmed by the Senate in March of that year. The appeals court is a common stop on the route to the Supreme Court, and this was a route in which Thomas had expressed no uncertain interest. In 1991 Bush nominated him for the Supreme Court. Still, his performance on the appeals court wasn't exactly impressive. "As Supreme Court nominees go," reported Margaret Carlson in a 1991 *Time* profile, "Thomas has little judicial experience. He is not a brilliant legal scholar, a weighty thinker, or even the author of numerous opinions." Shapiro was more blunt in the *Nation,* by saying that Thomas was "among the more scantily qualified Supreme Court candidates in recent memory."

Supreme Court Nomination Created Controversy

The stage was set for an ideological battle over Thomas's appointment even before Hill went public with her accusations. The NAACP, after lengthy discussion and much internal upheaval, voted to oppose Thomas's confirmation. The chairman of the organization, William F. Gibson, read a statement featuring a seven-point argument for opposing Thomas. This statement, which was printed in its entirety in *Crisis,* reasoned that "Judge Clarence Thomas's judicial philosophy is simply inconsistent with the historical positions taken by the NAACP." The criticisms centered on Thomas's performance at the EEOC and what Gibson characterized as the judge's "reactionary philosophical approach to a number of critical issues, not the least of which is affirmative action." Oddly enough, the NAACP stressed the importance of looking past race in this instance—though it believes fervently in the importance of having African Americans on the Supreme Court—to focus on Thomas's record. Thus, an organization traditionally affiliated with the "entitlement" sensibility Thomas so disliked had actually judged him on his merits. It found him wanting. Similarly, the Congressional Black Caucus (CBC) voted 20–1 to oppose Thomas's confirmation. The lone dissenter was also the CBC's only Republican.

Jesse Jackson, perhaps the most vocal black activist in the United States, was particularly critical of Thomas. *In These Times* quoted Jackson's remarks to a Chicago meeting of his organization, Operation PUSH: "He is a prime beneficiary of our [civil rights activists'] work. He got public accommodations, the right to vote, open housing because of civil rights marches and activism; yet he stood on our shoulders and kicked us in the head." John B. Judis, writing for *In These Times,*

asserted that Thomas's praise for Lehrman's antiabortion article "puts him on the fanatic fringes of the abortion debate and could prove politically embarrassing to Republicans in 1992." Judis remarked on Thomas's celebration of former National Security Aide Oliver North—who had lied to Congress about his involvement in the famed Iran-Contra scandal—and concluded a lengthy examination of Thomas's legal thinking by declaring simply "that Clarence Thomas is not fit to be a Supreme Court justice."

Bush expressed his support for Thomas largely on the basis of the judge's character. His life story, a real-world example of the conservative ideal, appeared in virtually every endorsement. Bush made no mention of Thomas's judicial temperament, nor of his decisions on the appeals court; it was clear that this appointment was a symbolic one. Strangely enough, Thomas's patron had chosen him because he was a successful *African-American* man. Whether Thomas privately considered himself a beneficiary of a White House "quota" remains unknown. In any case, Thomas's personal odyssey from Pin Point to the pinnacle of Washington, D.C., success, or some version of that odyssey, would always serve as an endorsement. Lena Williams's *New York Times* article concluded by referring to Thomas's "difficult childhood and his ability to succeed against the odds," an angle that the Bush administration would exploit to the utmost in its presentation of Thomas the judicial candidate.

Allegations of Sexual Harassment Surfaced

The Senate's confirmation hearings appeared to be moving along smoothly when Hill's allegations were made public. On October 8, Hill—a professor at the University of Oklahoma Law School—held a press conference, in which she made public the main points of the testimony she had previously given the Federal Bureau of Investigation (FBI). The FBI report had been reviewed by the confirmation committee but not made public, and on the day of Hill's press conference the Thomas vote was scheduled to move to the Senate floor. A wave of protest by women's groups and other activists led the committee, headed by Delaware's Joseph Biden, a Democrat, to review Hill's charges. Her testimony accused Thomas of badgering her for dates while she worked with him, and of accosting her with stories of pornographic film scenes and his own sexual prowess. The accusations fit the paradigm of sexual harassment in the workplace: the male superior uses sexual banter and other discomfiting tactics as a means of exercising power over a female underling. Hill claimed that Thomas's constant harassment made it difficult for her to do her job, and even caused her anxiety to manifest itself in the form of physical distress.

The televised hearings, during which Hill, Thomas, and several witnesses on both sides testified about the allegations, were among the most widely viewed political events in television history. Thomas denied any wrongdoing, but stopped short of calling Hill a liar. Most of Thomas's political allies on the committee—Republican senators Strom Thurmond, Arlen Specter, Alan Simpson, and Orrin Hatch—interrogated Hill mercilessly, and suggested that Hill was either being cynically manipulated by liberals or was lying outright. *Spy* magazine reported that numerous young researchers had been recruited by the White House staff to find embarrassing or otherwise damaging disclosures about Hill and her testimony. The partisan battle over the confirmation became so vicious that following the vote considerable press attention was devoted to Congress's political game-playing and the painful divisions it left among various constituencies.

Thomas himself remarked during the course of the televised hearings that the process had been a harrowing personal ordeal for him and his wife. Indeed, he claimed, he would have preferred "an assassin's bullet to this kind of living hell," and he would have withdrawn from consideration earlier had he known what lay ahead. Lewis Lapham's column in *Harper's* the following month attacked Thomas as a hypocrite: "He had the gall to present himself as a victim, a man who had been forced to endure the unspeakable agony of sitting comfortably in a chair for two weeks and being asked a series of facile questions to which he gave equally facile answers." Lapham asserted that Thomas displayed "contempt for the entire apparatus of the American idea—for Congress, for the press, for freedom of expression, for the uses of democratic government, for any rules other than his own."

Confirmation Followed Heated Hearings

Many African Americans had supported Thomas and followed the Republicans' theory that Hill was part of a campaign to smear him. Many women who opposed Thomas and believed Hill vowed to defeat Thomas's backers in the next elections. Another ramification of the Hill-Thomas debacle was the major attention suddenly afforded the previously neglected question of sexual harassment; the phrase entered the mainstream political vocabulary almost overnight. In any event, the verdict—in the minds of the committee and in the press—was that both witnesses were credible and that determining the truth of what had taken place nearly a decade before was nearly impossible. The president urged Congress to give Thomas the benefit of the doubt, arguing that he was innocent until proven guilty. Others argued that Thomas was not on trial for harassing Hill, and that any doubt was sufficient to disqualify him. In the end, Thomas was confirmed by a 52–48 margin. To those who complained about the confirmation hearings' focus on these "personal" matters, the *New Republic* replied that "the Bush administration promoted Mr. Thomas's nomination as a matter of

character, not of professional qualifications; and it has reaped a bitter reward."

Following the confirmation, Virginia Thomas told her story to *People,* recounting the tension of the confirmation fight and speculating that Hill was in love with Thomas. She referred to the struggle to get Thomas confirmed as "Good versus Evil." Meanwhile, Alisa Solomon of the *Village Voice* argued that Hill was attacked for showing the same qualities for which Thomas was celebrated: her ability to argue, her aggressiveness, and her self-sufficiency. Thomas, Solomon wrote, "seems unable to see women as a class, and therefore unable to recognize the importance of rulings that affect us."

Thomas had made it to the top, and his defiant individual style and renegade opinions had left him with many admirers and detractors. The question on most observers' minds was this: Would Thomas be the gadfly on a conservative court, or would he fall in line with its prevailing right-leaning tendencies? His experience before his confirmation guaranteed that he would be watched just as closely after he donned the robes.

Judicial Decision Brought Criticism

During the first few years after his appointment to the Supreme Court, Thomas remained quiet and out of the limelight that had shone on him for most of his career. He did not ask questions during oral arguments, he wrote few decisions or dissension to these decisions, and most often followed the lead of other conservative justices such as Sandra Day O'Conner and Antonin Scalia. Then, starting in 1994, Thomas came into his own as a justice as he became the deciding vote in numerous controversial cases, many dealing with issues of race and free speech. One specific case that many minorities took to heart was *Adarand Constructors Inc. v. Pena,* where a white owner of a construction company sued the state of Colorado for unfair hiring practices due to affirmative action. Randy Pech, the plaintiff in the case, argued that the state had awarded an Hispanic-owned company the job of redoing highways based purely on the fact that the company was Hispanic owned and run. Pech contended that he was the victim of reverse-racism and that this was not the purpose of the affirmative action program. The issue was contested heavily both within the court as well as in the media, where many people felt that if Pech won his case that it would be the beginning of the deconstruction of the affirmative action program that greatly helped many minorities secure jobs and education. When the final decision came down, in favor of Pech by one vote, 5–4, it was discovered that Thomas had voted in favor of the majority.

Another example of Thomas's controversial decision making came from the case *Missouri v. Jenkins.* In this case, the state of Missouri was suing a district judge for forcing it to "waste" money to bring more white students into predominately black city schools that were receiving fewer funds from their community than suburban schools that were mainly made up of white students. Once again, the case was heavily disputed in the Court; in the end, the decision came out in favor of the plaintiff, with the court split 5–4. Many critics of the decision felt that this was a major blow to the idea that desegregation, whether natural or forced, would bring equality to educational institutions, but Thomas shot back with his own views, which were summed up later in *Insight on the News* magazine: "He added that a school's majority black status is not a constitutional violation in and of itself and wondered why there was an assumption that 'anything that is predominantly black must be inferior.'"

Both of these decisions outraged many in the African-American community, who felt that Thomas had turned into an "Uncle Tom," completely controlled by the conservative right who traditionally downplayed the needs of minorities. Yet, Thomas felt that it was his job not to play favorites to any one community, but instead to show impartiality in his decisions and to try and follow the letter of the law. As he told *Jet* magazine, "I cannot do to White people what an elite group of Whites did to Black people, because if I do, I am just as bad as they are. I can't break from ... law just because they did. If they were wrong in doing that [using law to discriminate] to us, then I am wrong in doing it to them."

Gained Respect Along with Criticism

Since 1994, Thomas has continued to make decisions that were not popular in the African-American community. However, as he remained constant in his decisions, he also gained the respect of many people in the field who assumed the worst of him after the Anita Hill hearings. Ronald Rotunda, a professor at the University of Illinois said to the Knight Ridder/Tribune News Service, "He thinks independently and it's unfair to think of him as a knee-jerk conservative." However, many people still feel that Thomas has somehow "betrayed" the needs of minorities, specifically those of the African-American community. Yet, as Thomas told *Newsweek,* "It pains me more deeply than any of you can imagine, to be perceived by so many members of my race as doing them harm.... All the sacrifices and all the long hours of preparation were to help not to hurt."

One area in which Thomas receives little criticism in is his family life. It is clear that Thomas is devoted to his wife and to fostering a healthy relationship. Even more evident is Thomas's love for his extended family. In 1997 he took custody of his grandnephew, Mark Martin Jr., to give him the opportunity to succeed, something he would not have received with his parents.

The *American Lawyer* explained the circumstances: "Mark Sr., Thomas's nephew, had been in prison on cocaine-trafficking charges. And Mark Jr.'s mother Susan was struggling with her own problems, raising four children, including young Mark Jr., on her own. Thomas believed that the boy would face lifelong trouble if he were not removed from his environment soon, and the parents agreed." According to a friend in the same *American Laywer* article, "He was paying back his own grandfather by taking care of Mark."

An *Ebony* magazine article stated that "Thomas's struggle against the tradition of Supreme Court Justice Thurgood Marshall and his exile from mainstream Black America is one of the strangest stories of our time." Yet, many critics wondered if the controversy around his decisions would fade as time went by and he remained a steady advocate for more conservative justice. Apparently, this was not the case. By 2002, institutions in the African-American community had begun to question his methods and protested his appointment to the highest court in the nation. Five professors at the University of North Carolina School of Law at Chapel Hill boycotted a visit that was to be given by Thomas to allow students to discuss and interact with the justice. The *New Jersey Law Journal* noted the reason the protestors gave was that "for many people who hold legitimate expectations for racial equality and social justice, Justice Thomas personifies the cruel irony of the fireboat burning and sinking ... his visit adds insult to injury." Thomas, however, takes comments such as these in stride, for as he told *Newsweek,* he has the "right to think for myself." He went on to say that he refused "to have my ideas assigned to me as though I was an intellectual slave because I'm black."

In June of 2003 Thomas dissented from the Supreme Court's decision to uphold affirmative action, and called the policy a "cruel farce" that leaves African Americans with a lifelong stigma suggesting that they only succeed because of their skin color. The Court ruling addressed two separate cased concerning admissions policies at the University of Michigan undergraduate and law schools. In his dissenting opinion, Thomas criticized the Court for maintaining discrimination under the guise of aiding minority students. "The law school tantalizes unprepared students with the promise of a University of Michigan degree and all of the opportunities that it offers," Thomas said in his written opinion. "These overmatched students take the bait, only to find that they cannot succeed in the cauldron of competition."

Policies at the University of Michigan's Ann Arbor College of Law were upheld by a vote of 5–4 as being consistent with the goal of maintaining student body diversity, whereas policies at the undergraduate college, which award a blanket point value (20 out of 150 points) to minority applicants, was found to be more problematic. The Michigan case was the first time that the Supreme Court ruled on an affirmative action case since the 1978 case of *Regents of the University of California v. Bakke,* in which the Court struck down the use of quota systems in promoting minority students.

In October of 2007 Thomas published his autobiography *My Grandfather's Son: A Memoir,* in which he wrote about his upbringing with his grandfather and the successes and struggles of his early life. Critical reception of the book was sharply split along ideological lines. Some criticized Thomas for failing to address his failures and successes as a justice, whereas others lauded him for his honest and telling accounts of his childhood and the hardships he was forced to overcome in succeeding to the Supreme Court. Though his biography revealed little regarding the details of the Anita Hill controversy, Thomas wrote about the turmoil that the episode caused in his life and in the lives of his family and friends.

Even though *My Grandfather's Son* provided an inside look at Thomas's life, for some critics there remain questions about Thomas's judicial performance. In an interview with *Newsweek Online,* Thomas said about his years on the bench and his general approach to his position, "I made a decision when I first got here: I will only do what is necessary to discharge the responsibilities under my oath. I will not do things for histrionics. I will not do things so people will think well of me. The job is important, it's not about me." Despite statements to the contrary, some critics believe that Thomas's judicial positions are governed more by his mentors and leaders in the conservative community than by his personal duty. In interviews, Thomas expressed the hope that his book and stories of his upbringing would shed light on his decision-making process, showing that his role as a justice is a product of his upbringing and experience and not with the overall trend of the conservative community. "I assume people will say that I am conservative," Thomas said to *Newsweek,* "But the reason I wrote the book about my grandfather is that my views are consistent with his."

Selected writings

My Grandfather's Son: A Memoir, Harper, 2007.

Sources

Periodicals

American Lawyer, August 2001, p. 76.
American Spectator, October 1991.
Crisis, August/September 1991.
Daily Telegraph (London, England), June 26, 2003.
Economist, October 4, 2007.
Harper's, December 1991.
In These Times, July 24, 1991; August 7, 1991; October 23, 1991.
Insight on the News, September 4, 1995, pp. 8–10.
Jet, November 28, 1994, p. 22; September 11, 1995, p. 8.
Knight Ridder/Tribune News Service, July 2, 1995.
M2 Best Books, January 10, 2003.
Nation, September 23, 1991; October 14, 1991; October 28, 1991; November 4, 1991; November 11, 1991.
New Jersey Law Journal March 18, 2002, pp. 6-7.
New Republic, October 28, 1991.
Newsweek, September 16, 1991; October 21, 1991; October 28, 1991; August 10, 1998, p. 53; October 14, 2007.
New York Times, February 8, 1987; October 8, 1991; June 24, 2003; June 25, 2003.
People, October 28, 1991; November 11, 1991.
Policy Review, Fall 1991.
Spy, December 1991.
Time, September 16, 1991; October 28, 1991.
U.S. News & World Report, October 21, 1991.
Village Voice, October 22, 1991.

Online

"Clarence Thomas: The Justice Nobody Knows," *60 Minutes,* http://www.cbsnews.com/stories/2007/09/27/60minutes/main3305443.shtml (accessed December 20, 2007).
Weymouth, Lally, "A Justice's Candid Opinions," *Newsweek Online,* http://www.newsweek.com/id/43358/output/print (accessed December 20, 2007).

—Simon Glickman, Ralph G. Zerbonia, and Micah L. Issit

Isiah Thomas

1961—

Basketball player, entrepreneur

Thomas, Isiah, photograph. AP Images.

To many sports fans and writers, Isiah Thomas was the best "small man" ever to play professional basketball. The six-foot-one-inch Thomas served as a point guard for the Detroit Pistons from 1981 to 1994, earning a spot on the All-Star roster for twelve consecutive years and leading his team to back-to-back National Basketball Association (NBA) championships in 1989 and 1990. Thomas, who joined the Pistons when he was just nineteen, was a ruthless competitor on the court but dedicated himself to civic causes and social issues in his spare time.

Detroit Free Press columnist Charlie Vincent called Thomas "the spirit and the heart and the soul of a team that wormed its way into our hearts. He came with a smile that made us all think he was a choirboy but showed us, in time, that—on the floor—he could be an assassin." Vincent added that Thomas "showed a generation of Detroit fans how a winner behaves. He has given us memories of glory and of leadership and courage." Thomas retired from the court on May 11, 1994. He later became an entrepreneur, a television commentator, and a basketball executive and coach.

"I'm in love with basketball," Thomas once told *Sports Illustrated*. "It's my release. It's my outlet. If I get mad, I go shoot. It's my freedom. It's my security. It's my drug; it's my high." Thomas's love of the game has at times bordered on obsession. As a rookie Piston point guard in 1981, he set a goal of being part of an NBA championship team. At times, that goal seemed out of reach no matter how hard Thomas played as an individual. Time and maturity seasoned his game, however, and he finally led the Pistons to their first-ever championship in 1989. *Sport* magazine contributor Johnette Howard wrote, "Like many other superstars—at least the smart ones—Thomas learned long ago that piling up statistics is less intriguing than chasing or craving what he cannot guarantee. Like winning. By that measure, regardless of what anyone else says, he is an unqualified success."

Was His Family's Last Hope

Isiah Lord Thomas III grew up in the heart of Chicago's West Side ghetto, the youngest of seven boys and two girls born to Mary and Isiah Thomas II. "He was well behaved, but spoiled," Mary Thomas told *Sports Illustrated*. "I can't say I didn't treat him special. He was the baby. He got special attention." Isiah II was a plant supervisor who pushed his children to read, barred them from watching anything but educational television, and lectured them to stick together and protect one another. When Thomas was an infant, his father lost his job as a supervisor at International Harvester and could not find comparable work elsewhere. He was forced to work as a janitor at extremely reduced wages, and the stress of his disappointment caused friction in the family. "My father was frustrated by his intelligence," Thomas told *Gentleman's Quarterly*. "He was a black man coming up in the Twenties, Thirties and Forties. Being very intelligent and not being able to express that intelligence made him a very angry man. Sometimes he took that anger out on our family."

Eventually, Isiah II and Mary separated, and the child-drearing duties fell primarily to Mary. She was a strict disciplinarian who required her children to be home by the time the street lights came on. Born a Baptist, she turned the family toward Catholicism and thus came under the wing of a local church, Our Lady of Sorrows, and its schools. Fearlessly protective of her family, there was little that Mary would not do to shield her children from the gangs that prowled their neighborhood's streets. Once she chased gang members from her front porch with a shotgun when they came to recruit her sons. Her courage and determination—especially where Thomas was concerned—were the subject of a 1987 made-for-television movie.

Thomas spent most of his free time playing basketball at the tiny Gladys Park, next to Chicago's Eisenhower Expressway. According to Ira Berkow in the *New York Times,* the young Thomas was a "prodigy in basketball the way Mozart was in music. At age three, Amadeus was composing on a harpsichord; at three, Isiah could dribble and shoot baskets." Thomas was tutored by his older brothers, some of whom were top-notch players in their own right. Thomas recalled those days fondly in *Sports Illustrated*: "Go anywhere on the West Side and say, 'Meet me at the court,' and they'd know what you were talking about," he said. "That's where I really learned to play. There were some basketball players there. You could always get a game there. Any time of day, any time of night. Me and my brothers used to go over there with snow shovels in the winter so we could play."

When Thomas was twelve, the street gangs began moving in more ferociously, and some of his older brothers succumbed to the lure of drug abuse and crime. Mary moved the family five miles west to Menard Avenue, but trouble seemed to follow. "Those were probably the worst times as a kid," Thomas told *Sports Illustrated*. "We very rarely had heat. We had an oil furnace but no money to buy oil. In the winter, it was always cold, and you had to sleep all the time with your clothes on. Everything broke down in the house once we bought it. … I mean everything was a disaster." Sleeping in a closet and eating food donated by concerned church members, Thomas was tempted to follow the lead of his brothers and turn to drug dealing as a way out of poverty. His brothers and his mother convinced him otherwise. They told him that he might well lead the family into better circumstances with his basketball skills.

Most of the coaches in the Chicago area considered Thomas too small to have any significant impact on a basketball program, but Thomas's brothers persuaded coach Gene Pingatore of St. Joseph High School to give Isiah a sports scholarship. St. Joseph was located in a white suburb of Chicago. Thomas had to commute three hours each way to and from school, taking three buses and arriving home well after dark. He struggled to acquire discipline in the classroom and on the court and, by his junior year, he led St. Joseph to a second-place finish in the state high school championship tournament. As a senior, Thomas was one of the most coveted college prospects in the nation.

From College to the Pros

More than one hundred colleges recruited Thomas. His family wanted him to stay home and attend DePaul

University, but he chose to go to Indiana University and play for temperamental coach Bob Knight. Thomas made All–Big Ten his freshman year and was named a consensus All-American as a sophomore. That year he led the Hoosiers to the National Collegiate Athletic Association (NCAA) championship game, where Indiana routed the North Carolina Tar Heels 63–50. With twenty-three points in the championship match, Thomas was named NCAA tournament most valuable player (MVP). Despite his All-Star performance as a freshman and sophomore, Thomas was not happy at Indiana. He and Knight clashed frequently. Finally, in 1981—on the advice of his friend Magic Johnson—Thomas decided to leave college and apply for the NBA draft.

Thomas was selected second in the opening round of the 1981 NBA draft by the Detroit Pistons, a hopelessly foundering organization that had won only 37 of 164 games the previous two seasons. At the tender age of nineteen, Thomas became responsible for rescuing the NBA's worst team. A *Detroit News* headline hailed him as "Isiah the Savior," and Pistons season ticket sales jumped 50 percent. Even the club brass talked about making the NBA Finals as they announced Thomas's four-year, $1.6 million contract. Undaunted by the expectations, Thomas turned in a successful rookie season, averaging seventeen points per game and leading his team in assists and steals. He improved further in his second season, averaging nearly twenty-three points and eight assists per game. Both years he represented the Pistons at the All-Star Game.

Through his first four years in Detroit, Thomas consistently outplayed his teammates. He was the first player in league history to be voted to the All-Star team in his first five seasons, and in 1984 and 1986 his performances in the All-Star game were so spectacular that he was named the contest's MVP. By 1984, he had managed to guide the Pistons to their first winning record in seven seasons, and he was given a new ten-year, $12 million contract that was specifically designed to keep him in Detroit for his entire career. He responded to this vote of confidence in the 1984–85 season by compiling an NBA record of 1,123 assists, an average of 13.1 per game.

In addition to shining on the court, Thomas also earned the affection of basketball fans everywhere—and especially in Detroit—for his well-publicized anticrime work, his open dedication to his family, and his accessibility to the media. Howard noted of Thomas, "Half the beat reporters in the NBA had his home phone number, and it wasn't uncommon for him to sit for an hour after a practice, talking about some societal issue such as racism or his latest take on the game." Perhaps inevitably, however, pressures began to mount on the affable superstar as the Detroit Pistons became a legitimate playoff contender in 1986. A turning point in the evolution of Isiah Thomas occurred during the 1987 Eastern Conference finals against the Boston Celtics.

Fame Brings Its Own Problems

Under new head coach Chuck Daly, the Detroit Pistons improved enough to challenge for the 1987 NBA championship. That year, Thomas averaged almost twenty points per game in the playoffs as the Pistons advanced to an Eastern Conference showdown with the Celtics. The winner of the best-of-seven series would advance to the NBA playoffs—something the Pistons had never done. The series was hard-fought and seethed with emotion. By Game Five, each team had won twice, and as Game Five drew to a close, the Pistons clung to a one-point lead and had possession of the ball. With one second left to play, Thomas inbounded the ball. His pass was stolen by Larry Bird of the Celtics. Bird lobbed the ball to teammate Dennis Johnson, who scored the winning basket as the buzzer sounded. The dramatic loss stunned the Pistons, who went on to lose the series in seven games.

Just after Detroit's loss to the Celtics, another Piston, rookie Dennis Rodman, told reporters that Larry Bird was "overrated" because he was white. Asked to comment on his teammate's statement, Thomas responded that while Bird was a "very, very good basketball player," if he were black he would be "just another good guy." The backlash among media and fans was immediate. Even though Thomas apologized to Bird at a press conference—and clarified his remarks by explaining that he felt an inherent racial bias existed in basketball—his reputation was severely damaged. Howard wrote in 1992 that in the wake of that controversy, "neither [Thomas] nor his image has ever been the same." Howard added, "Looking back on it now, Thomas' greatest sin might've been that his thinking and candor put him ahead of his time."

Thomas's honeymoon with the media ended just as the Pistons achieved their greatest success. Beginning in 1987, the Pistons adopted surly tactics both on- and off-court that led to their being nicknamed the "Bad Boys." With Thomas as team captain, the "Bad Boys" turned in a strong 1987–88 season and capped the year with an Eastern Conference Finals victory over the Celtics and a bruising, seven-game championship run against the Los Angeles Lakers. Playing with a jammed finger, a bruised eye, facial cuts, and a badly sprained ankle, Thomas threatened to steal the series for the Pistons, especially in Game Six, when he scored forty-three points and eight assists. Los Angeles won the championship in seven games, but the Pistons—and Thomas—had finally shed their losing image. The next two seasons would belong to Detroit.

Back-to-Back Titles

With Thomas at the height of his ability, the Pistons won the NBA championship in 1989 and again in 1990. These championship teams were often embroiled in controversy, both for their aggressive style of play and for their combative attitudes off-court. *Rolling Stone* contributor Jeff Coplon wrote that the "Bad Boys" were perceived nationwide as "goons, thugs, terrorists…. When they took the court, a hockey game broke out. Normally placid opponents … blew up bumps into scuffles, scuffles into brawls. In the cultish NBA, if the Celtics were white America's team, and the Lakers were Club Hollywood, the Pistons belonged to Qaddafi…. Piston-bashing was suddenly a blood sport—especially among those most threatened by Detroit's rise." In 1988–89 Detroit compiled the best regular-season record in the NBA, winning sixty-five of eighty-two games. A six-game Eastern Conference Finals victory against Michael Jordan and the Chicago Bulls set the stage for another showdown with the Lakers. This time, the Pistons swept Los Angeles in four games and returned to Detroit with the championship.

Even greater triumph awaited Thomas the following year as Detroit's "Bad Boys" advanced again to the championship series, this time against the Portland Trail Blazers. In a series remembered for its physical play, the Pistons won in just five games to clinch back-to-back championship victories. *Sports Illustrated* correspondent Jack McCallum credited the strong Detroit showing to Thomas. The Piston captain, wrote McCallum, "kept the tempo at a controlled, even pace, which disrupted the fast-breaking … Trail Blazers. And when he wasn't doing that, he was creating something from nothing, with long-distance jump shots, body-twisting drives and steals in the open floor…. By the time the Pistons had beaten the Blazers … to clinch their second straight championship … there was only one great guard still playing basketball—Isiah Lord Thomas III."

Thomas was named MVP of the 1990 championship series. Returning home to celebrate with his wife, he discovered that he was the target of media scrutiny for alleged gambling improprieties. Even though no formal charges were brought against him, the negative publicity only alienated him further from the media and fans he had once courted so gallantly. As regular-season play began in the 1990s, Thomas's statistics fell off somewhat, and he began spending more time alone with his family. He was sidelined in the 1991–92 season after receiving a blow to the head in a game against the Utah Jazz. Also, Thomas was probably the best-known NBA player who was not selected for the celebrated 1992 U.S. Olympic basketball team, allegedly because of pressure from reigning basketball superstar Michael Jordan, with whom Thomas had long feuded. This omission was particularly difficult for Thomas, because he had been a member of the 1980 Olympic basketball team that was forced to boycott the Olympics by President Jimmy Carter.

Through these and other controversies, Thomas remained the Pistons' team captain. He also served a four-year stint as the president of the NBA Players Association. As he ended his eleventh season in the NBA, Thomas reflected on his career in *Sport* magazine: "You gotta understand. I'm 6-1. If I was 6-9, I could be 'nice.' If I was 6-9, or 6-6 and could jump out of the building, I could be nice. But being 6-1, having to try to be successful in a league where everyone else is 6-7, 6-8, 6-9, you've got to have a little fire in your gut, or you'll be like every other 6-1 guy is supposed to be in the league—average. I didn't want to be average…. You have to do what you have to do. And I had no problems doing that."

Retired in Style

As a team, the Pistons' fortunes ebbed, whereas those of the Chicago Bulls rose. The Pistons were defeated by the Bulls in the Eastern Conference Finals in 1991, crushing their hopes for a third straight NBA title and prompting calls for "rebuilding." In December of 1993 rumors suggested that Thomas was about to leave the Pistons for the New York Knicks. Instead, on January 7, 1994, the Pistons called a press conference to announce that Thomas had signed a long-term contract that would take him past retirement. "This is one of the happiest days of my career, and one of the happiest days of my life," Thomas told the *Detroit Free Press* when the agreement was announced. Soon after the contract was signed, more rumors circulated that Thomas would retire at the end of the season.

On April 19, 1994, Thomas played his last game as a Detroit Piston, although his retirement would not become official until May 11. Thomas left his final game in the third quarter with a torn Achilles tendon, after scoring twelve points and serving up six assists against the Orlando Magic. Reflecting on his years in the NBA, Thomas told Vincent, "I have no regrets. As a basketball player, you gave everything to your sport, gave everything to the organization and to the team you played for. You leave it all out on the floor. So it's not disappointing to me at all." Following his retirement party, Thomas ended rumors about his taking a front-office position with the Pistons franchise, telling reporters, "All the jobs were full."

Thomas met many of the goals he set for himself as a rookie in the NBA—and exceeded even his own sky-high expectations. The leader in every category in the history of the Pistons' franchise, Thomas also left the game as the fourth all-time NBA leader in assists and steals, and the twenty-eighth all-time leader in scoring. He retired with 18,822 career points, 9,061 assists, and 1,861 steals in 979 games. Thomas told *Jet* magazine, "I'm living the dream I had since I was a little boy. How many kids, especially kids who grew up as poor as I did, ever live to see their dreams come true? I'm just lucky I've had the opportunity."

Following his retirement from the NBA, Thomas turned his attention to becoming a successful businessman and entrepreneur. Along with his business partners, he purchased American Speedy Printing Centers, Inc. With Thomas serving as principal shareholder and co-chairman of the board of directors, American Speedy Printing Centers emerged from bankruptcy to become a highly profitable company. In 1994 he became a principal investor in OmniBanc Corp, the nation's first multistate African-American-owned bank holding company. The goal of OmniBanc was to revitalize economically disadvantaged inner-cities communities. As Thomas remarked in *American Banker,* "Anytime you have the chance to revitalize the community that you came from ... it's a very exciting challenge and a very exciting opportunity."

Moved to Toronto

On May 24, 1994, Thomas was introduced as the vice president of basketball operations for the expansion Toronto Raptors, the first NBA franchise located outside the United States. As part of his duties, he was charged with helping to shape the team, which debuted during the 1995–96 season. At a press conference in Toronto at the time of this announcement, Thomas remarked, "I think it's the dream of most professional athletes ... to make this kind of cross-over once the playing days are over.... I'm so excited to get on with the job at hand."

In late 1997 Thomas abruptly resigned from his position with the Toronto Raptors and left town. Rumors circulated that his relationship with Raptors majority owner Allan Slaight had soured after Thomas failed to purchase sole ownership of the team. Even though Thomas owned a 9 percent share of the Raptors, he wanted complete control of the organization. His sudden departure dealt a severe blow to the team's morale. As Raptors forward Walt Williams told *Maclean's,* "Isiah is a big part of why a lot of the guys are here."

Shortly after leaving the Raptors, Thomas signed a deal with NBC in December of 1997 to become an analyst for NBA games. With experience as both a player and an NBA executive, NBC felt that Thomas would bring an interesting perspective to the job. Even though Thomas was excited about the new opportunity, he had almost no experience as a broadcaster and realized that he had much to learn. As quoted by *Jet* magazine, Thomas remarked, "I understand that I come into this as a rookie, that I'm very young and very green. I don't come into this professing to be the top guy, but as a young guy with a lot of talent."

Became Owner of the CBA

Thomas had long professed a desire to purchase his own NBA franchise. That goal had gone unfulfilled. However, in 1999, he purchased the nine-team Continental Basketball Association (CBA). Suddenly, he was the sole owner of nine franchises scattered across the United States. Thomas voiced his plans for the CBA in *Black Enterprise,* "My goal is to one day form an official affiliation with the NBA where each team will have its own CBA team and you can call up or send down players, similar to what they have in baseball." He also planned to expand the CBA and increase its visibility through increased promotion and marketing. "Our goal is to continue to grow the league through acquisitions and mergers. We've looked at some cities ... and there's considerable interest in smaller cities wanting to have the second-best league in the world playing in their towns."

In May of 2000 Thomas was elected to the Basketball Hall of Fame in his first year of eligibility. This distinction placed him alongside other Detroit sports legends such as Al Kaline, Ty Cobb, and Gordie Howe. At a press conference held at the Palace of Auburn Hills, the same arena where Thomas led the Pistons to championship glory, his trademark competitiveness shone through. As reported in the *Detroit Free Press,* Thomas remarked, "I kid Magic and Jordan all the time that if I was taller, they never would've gotten the championship from me. If I had been 6-5 or 6-6, I would have killed all of those guys all of the time." The press conference also featured a five-minute video highlighting some of Thomas's greatest moments on the basketball court. After watching the video, Thomas quipped in the *Detroit Free Press,* "I look at that video and I think to myself, 'Man, I was good.'"

Thomas was asked to serve as head coach for the Indiana Pacers in 2000, replacing Larry Bird, who remained with the organization as president of basketball operations. Thomas's first two seasons with the Pacers were disappointing as the team was eliminated before the conference finals. In 2003 Bird made the decision to replace Thomas as head coach, though Thomas had a full year left on his contract. Bird reported, in interviews, that he felt dissatisfied with Thomas's recent performance and was also concerned that he and Thomas were failing to communicate effectively. In December of 2003 Thomas was hired as president of basketball operations for the New York Knicks. Thomas made radical changes to the Knicks' line up, but the team fared poorly in the 2004 and 2005 seasons. In 2006 he decided the serve as both president and head coach for the team in hopes that his more direct leadership would help the team to improve its performance.

In January of 2006 Anucha Browne Sanders, a former women's basketball player and executive for the Knicks, alleged that Thomas had sexually harassed her during her time as a member of the Madison Square Garden (MSG) management team. Browne Sanders accused Thomas of using profanity and making sexual advances. The three-week trial ended in favor of Browne Sanders, and the MSG was ordered to pay more than $11 million in damages. Thomas was not found to be personally liable to Browne Sanders and claimed that while he was guilty of using inappropriate language in Browne Sanders's presence, he never intentionally insulted her.

Thomas's performance as a basketball player gained him praise and acclaim throughout his tenure, whereas his postplaying career was fraught with difficulties. With his sexual harassment suit settled, Thomas renewed his conviction to continue working toward a championship as head coach of the Knicks. In March of 2007 MSG management renewed Thomas's contract for an unspecified period as both head coach and president of the franchise. "I feel there's a lot of work still yet to be done," Thomas said in an interview with Howard Beck of the *New York Times*. "I feel good that the uncertainty about my professional situation is cleared up. But the most important thing is that we keep our team moving forward and we stay focused and continue to try to get into the playoffs."

However, the team's performance continued to disappoint the Knicks owner, management, and fans. Game after game during the last months of the 2007-08 season, Thomas was greeted with chants of "Fire, Isiah!" Looking at the end of another dismal season the Knicks organization took steps to stop the team's losing streak. On April 2, 2008, long-time basketball executive Donnie Walsh was hired to replace Thomas as president of basketball operations. The Knicks ended the 2007-08 basketball season with a record of 23 wins and 59 losses—finishing in last place in the Atlantic Division of the NBA's Eastern Conference.

Sources

Periodicals

American Banker, October 20, 1994, p. 6.

Black Enterprise, November, 1999, p. 28.

Boston Globe, November 1, 1981; April 26, 1985; June 7, 1987.

Chicago Tribune, February 8, 1987.

Detroit Free Press, April 25, 1987; April 28, 1987; January 4, 1994; January 8, 1994; April 20, 1994; May 12, 1994; May 25, 2000.

Detroit News, October 11, 1981.

Dollars & Sense, May 1994, pp. 21–22.

Ebony, May 1990.

Gentleman's Quarterly, February 1988, pp. 190–193, 238–242.

Inside Sports, April 1984, p. 64; November 1987, p. 21; June 1994, pp. 38–39.

Jet, December 11, 1989, pp. 36–38; October 22, 1990, p. 48; October 14, 1991, p. 49; January 31, 1994, p. 48.

Los Angeles Daily News, June 19, 1988.

Los Angeles Herald Examiner, June 6, 1987.

Los Angeles Times, February 10, 1986; June 7, 1988; June 11, 1988; June 20, 1988.

Maclean's, December 1, 1997.

Newsday, June 2, 1987; May 30, 1988.

Newsweek, December 14, 1981, p. 130.

New York Daily News, September 12, 2007.

New York Times, April 27, 1981; June 2, 1987; January 8, 1994; January 9, 1994; March 12, 2007.

Oakland Press (Michigan), April 3, 1994; April 4, 1994; April 18, 1994; April 24, 1994.

Philadelphia Daily News, June 15, 1988.

Philadelphia Inquirer, June 7, 1988.

Rolling Stone, May 4, 1989.

Sport, February 1986, p. 59; May 1988, p. 24; June 1992, pp. 66–70.

Sports Illustrated, January 19, 1987; May 18, 1987; June 25, 1990, pp. 32–36; January 21, 1991, p. 46; January 17, 1994, p. 71.

Online

"Jury: Isiah Thomas Sexually Harassed Colleague," *National Public Radio,* http://www.npr.org/templates/story/story.php?storyId=14945034 (accessed December 20, 2007).

"Jury Rules Thomas Harassed Ex-executive; MSG Owes Her $11.6M," *ESPN Online,* http://sports.espn.go.com/nba/news/story?id=3046010.

"Knicks Fire Brown, Name Thomas New Coach," *ESPN Online,* http://sports.espn.go.com/nba/news/story?id=2496106 (accessed December 20, 2007).

"Thomas out with One Year Left on Contract," *ESPN Online,* http://sports.espn.go.com/nba/news/story?id=1604235 (accessed December 20, 2007).

—Mark Kram, David G. Oblender, and Micah L. Issit

Trisha R. Thomas

1964—

Author

Trisha R. Thomas's debut novel, *Nappily Ever After,* touched an emotional chord with African-American readers, among them film star Halle Berry, who acquired the rights to the 2000 book. Eight years later, Berry was set to play the role of Venus Johnson in the film version of Thomas's story, whose heroine in a single day becomes fed up with her high-maintenance, chemically processed hair and her commitment-phobic boyfriend and embarks on a journey of personal growth that will change her life. Venus, said Thomas, is "like many thirtysomething women I know," she told *Essence* writer Robin D. Stone. "She's still trying to figure out what's right, what's wrong and what will get you the success that you've been told you deserve."

Thomas was born in 1964 and graduated from California State University at Los Angeles in 1988 with a bachelor of science in business administration. She spent the next decade in various professions, including marketing consultant, bridal-store owner, artist, and middle-school teacher, and along the way married and became mother to three children. She was living in northern Virginia in the mid-1990s when she began writing *Nappily Ever After,* and she soon became so absorbed in the plot and the life of her fictional character that "I would forget to pick up the children from school," she confessed in an *Essence* interview with Patrik Henry Bass. "I would look up and think, Where are my kids?"

Nappily Ever After was rejected by nearly three dozen publishers and literary agents before Crown Publishers signed Thomas and helped her craft it toward its final version. The story is set in Washington, D.C., and begins when thirty-four-year-old advertising executive Venus Johnson, exhausted by the time-consuming and costly regimen necessary to maintain her long, straight hair, tells her hairdresser to cut it all off, which leaves her with a short, fuzzy—also called "nappy"—Afro that stuns coworkers, family, and friends alike. It also empowers her to challenge her boyfriend of four years, Clint Fairchild, to end his perpetual skittishness about commitment; Venus has supported him through medical school and is ready to move forward now that he has become a physician. When he balks, she cuts him loose.

Earned Terrific Reviews

The rest of *Nappily Ever After* follows Venus through several life changes and challenges, including trouble at work and knowledge of Clint's new girlfriend, Kandi, whom he suddenly seems ready to marry. Thomas's debut novel won a number of impressive reviews, with *Booklist*'s Vanessa Bush asserting that the work "places her in a league with Terry MacMillan and Bebe Moore Campbell." Delorese Ambrose, a critic for *Black Issues Book Review,* noted that "Thomas delivers up a powerful, funny and sensitive coming-of-age novel. She is, without doubt, a talented newcomer to the fiction scene." A *Publishers Weekly* contributor conceded that Thomas's examination "of an African-American woman's journey to self-acceptance is not without flaws ... but Thomas refuses to let her characters slide into stereotype, and she keeps the pace fast and funny."

At a Glance . . .

Born on May 28, 1964, in San Diego, CA; married; children: Tahira, Tiffany, Quinlan. *Education:* California State University at Los Angeles, BS in business administration, 1988.

Career: Worked as a marketing consultant, artist, and designer; owned a bridal store; middle-school teacher until 1999; signed to a book deal with Crown Publishers, c. 1999.

Addresses: *Agent*—Marie Brown Associates, 625 Broadway, New York, NY 10012.

Thomas was struck by the fact that the concept of "nappy" had resonated so deeply with readers. She had originally titled the story "Dreamin Lye," after the caustic chemicals used to relax black hair, but decided to use a different pun for the title as a way to show that Venus's story was a journey of self-discovery that ended on a positive note. African-American booksellers told her the title was a big selling point, and in an interview she gave to the GRITS Online Reading Club, she reflected that the word seemed to tap into a common theme for African-American women: "Going natural is like a dream inside all of us, being free of the pressures, living for oneself, and not feeling obligated to have a certain look."

Thomas's second novel was an abrupt departure from her first, in both subject matter and tone. Published in 2002, *Roadrunner* is the fictional tale of a once-celebrated baseball player named Dell Fletcher who was known as the "Roadrunner" because of his speed around the bases. Fletcher's life has begun to unravel, however, with persistent injuries leading to a substance-abuse problem that is ruining what was a happy home life with his devoted wife and two children. When an argument turns physical, his wife, Leah, calls 911, and the arresting cop is shocked to see how far the athlete he idolized as a kid has fallen. On the way to the police station, Officer Lopez decides to give Dell a tour of some of Los Angeles's seamier streets as a way to show him where drug addicts eventually wind up. Lopez and Dell end up in an altercation and the car crashes, and in the chaos Dell shows he can still live up to his nickname and takes off running. In the ensuing weeks, Lopez is drawn to Leah, while the missing and possibly amnesiac Dell becomes the target of a quasi-romantic predator himself. In a *Black Issues Book Review* critique, Robin Green-Cary pronounced it "even better" than *Nappily Ever After,* noting that "Thomas weaves a wonderful story of love, betrayal and redemption."

Venus Returned in 2004

Thomas's readers, however, clamored for a Venus Johnson update, which was satisfied by *Would I Lie to You? The Journey of Venus Johnston* in 2004. This novel finds Venus now the head of a marketing firm in D.C. and engaged to a software entrepreneur, Airic Coleman. On a business trip to Los Angeles, however, she meets former-rapper-turned-business-mogul Jake Parson, and the attraction is both instant and mutual, despite their ten-year age difference. Back at home, however, Venus's mother is hospitalized, and the medical crisis reunites her with former boyfriend Clint. When Airic comes under federal investigation for financial wrongdoing, she battles with her feelings for the much-younger Jake and the lingering anger she feels toward Clint. In the end, Airic is acquitted, but she leaves him anyway and begins a new chapter in her life—that of mother. In *Nappily Married,* published in 2007, Venus is married to Jake—who is a dutiful father to a daughter who may or may not be his, but a decidedly less faithful husband. When Venus catches him cheating, she returns to the hair salon and demands they straighten her hair. Once again, Thomas gives her protagonist career challenges, too, with a mysterious series of events plaguing the struggling community hospital to which Clint has lured her to come on board as its much-needed public-relations executive.

The film rights to Thomas's debut, *Nappily Ever After,* were snapped up by Halle Berry just before she won an Academy Award for her role in the 2001 film *Monster's Ball.* Other work commitments and Berry's 2007 pregnancy pushed her starring role as Venus Johnson up to a 2008 release for the film. Thomas bowed out of the offer to write the screenplay, feeling that was best handled by more experienced professionals, and she did admit that she had some reservations about Venus's story being translated for the big screen. "I never thought *Nappily* could be a movie," she told the GRITS Online Reading Club, because it had "too much feeling and thinking. It's a deeply layered story, very character driven, so I just couldn't picture it, but then I was convinced by one of the producers that it was also very entertaining." She was buoyed when she learned that the Hollywood studio executive most interested in bringing the novel to the screen had also made *Legally Blonde,* which she had seen and thought that "there was a great message hidden in all the laughter."

Thomas, who lives in Washington state with her family, is working on a fourth installment, *Nappily Faithful,* planned for a 2008 publication date. She finds it hard to give up the character who enthralled her so much that her children were left waiting at school. "I love Venus," she told Mika Ono Benedyk in *Essence.* "She is imperfect. We're indoctrinated to be invincible, but we're all going to make mistakes."

Selected writings

Fiction

Nappily Ever After, Crown, 2000.
Roadrunner: A Novel, Crown, 2002.
Would I Lie to You? The Journey of Venus Johnston, Crown, 2004.
Nappily Married, St. Martin's Griffin, 2007.

Sources

Periodicals

Black Issues Book Review, January 2001; September–October 2002; March–April 2004.

Booklist, November 15, 2000; June 1, 2002.
Daily Variety, January 29, 2002.
Ebony, March 2004.
Essence, June 2002; February 2004; October 2005; August 2007.
Publishers Weekly, November 6, 2000; January 12, 2004.

Online

"Interview with Author, Trisha R. Thomas," *GRITS Online Reading Club,* http://www.thegritsbookclub.com/Interviews/TrishaThomas.html (accessed December 26, 2007).

—Carol Brennan

LaDainian Tomlinson

1979—

Professional football player

LaDainian Tomlinson is one of the most critically acclaimed football players of the twenty-first century. Since his 2001 professional debut with the San Diego Chargers, he has broken numerous league records and received honors from the Associated Press, ESPN, and the Professional Football Writers of America. Having risen from an underprivileged background, Tomlinson dedicates part of his time to working with children in Texas and California.

LaDainian Tomlinson was born on June 21, 1979, in Rosebud, Texas, a small community located near College Station and Waco. Tomlinson was the oldest of three children born to Oliver Tomlinson, a construction worker, and Loreane Chappell, a pastor. Tomlinson also has five half-siblings from Oliver's previous relationships.

In 1983, a back injury left Oliver unable to work at his previous job, placing the family under severe financial strain. Unable to recover from the stress of financial burdens, Tomlinson's parents divorced in 1986, leaving his mother to care for Tomlinson and his younger siblings, Londria and LaVar. After their divorce, Oliver left Rosebud and was absent for most of Tomlinson's childhood. To support the family, Loreane worked as a pastor for the Greater Life Gospel Church.

Wanted to Play Football

Despite being estranged from his father at a young age, Tomlinson reported that his interest in football was inspired by the time that he and his father spent together watching football games on television. In his official biography, Tomlinson reports that he slept with his football from childhood until his junior year in college. In a 2007 interview with *Time*'s Sean Gregory, LaVar Tomlinson recalled, "I can never remember that ball being on the floor."

At nine years old, Tomlinson joined the Pop Warner League, where he played until reaching high school. In the early 1990s, Tomlinson attended a summer football camp, where he had the chance to meet and learn from Emmitt Smith of the Dallas Cowboys. Tomlinson later reported that Smith was one of his most important role models, especially given the fact that both Tomlinson and Smith are short in stature when compared to the average football player.

Tomlinson attended Waco University High School, where he played four years for the school team. Before his senior year, Tomlinson's mother moved to Dallas, but allowed him to remain in Waco to complete his senior year. Tomlinson turned out a spectacular season to win most valuable player (MVP) honors and was named Super Centex Offensive Player of the Year. Over the course of his high school career, Tomlinson scored thirty-nine touchdowns and ran for over twenty-five hundred yards.

Played for the Horned Frogs

Despite a strong senior performance, Tomlinson's first three seasons in the high school league were unremarkable, so he received few offers for college placement.

At a Glance . . .

Born LaDainian Tomlinson on June 24, 1979, in Rosebud, TX; son of Oliver Tomlinson and Loreane Chappell; married LaTorsha Oakley, 2003. *Education:* Waco University High School, Waco, Texas, 1993–97; attended Texas Christian University, 1997–2000; received BA in general studies, 2005.

Career: San Diego Chargers, running back, 2001—.

Selected awards: Professional Football Writers of America, National Football League (NFL) Most Valuable Player (MVP), 2006; Best NFL Player ESPY Award, 2006; Best Record-Breaking Performance ESPY Award, 2006; Best Male Athlete ESPY Award, 2006; Associated Press, NFL MVP, 2007.

Addresses: *Office*—San Diego Chargers, PO Box 609100, San Diego, CA 92160-9609.

He chose Texas Christian University (TCU) in Fort Worth because it was close to his mother and siblings in Dallas and, after interviewing, Tomlinson felt comfortable with the school's coaching staff.

His rookie season with the TCU Horned Frogs was a disappointment as the team fared poorly and Tomlinson was unable to achieve noteworthy scores. Between seasons, he invested his time in strength training and conditioning in hopes of improving his performance for the upcoming season. In addition, the school undertook a complete reorganization of the coaching staff, including the employment of a new head coach, Dennis Franchione.

Under Franchione's leadership, the Horned Frogs improved during the 1998 season, and the following year it achieved an 8–4 record, the team's best in more than a decade. Tomlinson's training regimen was also a success, allowing him to finish his sophomore season with 8 touchdowns and 717 yards, establishing his position as one of the team's top players. His performance continued to improve during his junior season, in which he scored 18 touchdowns and became a league leader with 1,850 yards in gains.

In July of 1999, Tomlinson and a TCU basketball player were arrested for possession of marijuana. Tomlinson appealed and was later cleared of the charges. Despite proving his innocence, the incident reduced Tomlinson's attractiveness to major league scouts, and he felt that the local media treated him poorly by extensively reporting on his arrest and never covering his victorious appeal.

Tomlinson decided to remain with the team for a fourth season, partially to honor his mother, who wanted him to finish college, and also to increase his standing for the professional drafts. The Horned Frogs performed well during the first half of the season but declined in later games. Tomlinson finished his season with 2,158 rushing yards, which was a record for the program and the fourth-best rushing achievement in college football history.

Tomlinson entered the draft before completing his college degree. During his senior year, he reconciled with his father. He later said that this was one of the most important achievements of his time at college. In addition, just before entering the draft, Tomlinson and his long-time girlfriend, LaTorsha Oakley, became engaged; they were married in 2003.

Drafted by the San Diego Chargers

Tomlinson was chosen in the first-round draft by the San Diego Chargers, who were impressed by his work ethic, catching, and running abilities. The Chargers signed Tomlinson for a six-year, $38 million contract, which transformed Tomlinson's life overnight. He immediately purchased new homes for his mother and sister, as well as buildings for his mother's real estate business and his sister's day care center. For himself and his fiancée, Tomlinson purchased new vehicles and a condominium in San Diego.

Tomlinson impressed his coaches and the team's fans by picking up over one hundred yards in each of the team's first three games and also achieved a personal milestone when the Chargers won a close victory over Emmitt Smith and the Dallas Cowboys. Though the Chargers finished with an unimpressive 5–11 record, Tomlinson scored 10 touchdowns and 1,236 yards and was a contender for the Offensive Rookie of the Year Award. During his second season, even though the team again had a poor overall performance, Tomlinson broke the Charger's record for yardage and was voted the team's MVP.

His third season with the Chargers was disappointing, as the team finished with a 4–10 record. Despite the team's poor performance, Tomlinson again scored the team's only significant achievements by obtaining 2,370 yards, which was second in league history to Marshall Faulk's 1999 performance with the St. Louis Rams. In 2004, the Chargers agreed to renegotiate Tomlinson's contract, renewing an eight-year commitment with a pay increase to $60 million. It was during his fourth season when the team emerged from their three-year slump with a surprising bid for the playoffs. Though the Chargers lost in the first round to the New York Jets, the season catapulted Tomlinson to national prominence.

Tomlinson achieved a career record in the 2005 season by scoring twenty touchdowns, but could not help the team to avoid early elimination before the playoffs. The following season, he set a National Football League (NFL) record with nineteen touchdowns in six games. He also achieved a league record for yards achieved within a player's first six seasons. Tomlinson's 2006 season was more impressive, and as a result he was awarded the coveted Associated Press trophy as the MVP in the NFL and the Professional Football Writers of America's MVP Award. Tomlinson was also honored with ESPN's ESPY Award for Best Male Athlete. By the close of the 2006 season, he had set thirteen NFL records.

By week six of the 2007 regular season, the Chargers had achieved a 3–3 record and in interviews, Tomlinson expressed his disappointment and concern for his future on the team. Though Tomlinson played an important role in the team's three victories, he had been limited in offensive effectiveness and only passed the one-hundred-yard mark in one of the team's first six games.

Placed Family and Community First

Tomlinson uses much of his free time to get involved in community activities in San Diego and Waco. He and his wife organized the Tomlinson Touching Lives Foundation, which sponsors children's football and golf camps in both Texas and California. He also supports numerous charitable foundations, including programs that provide food and gifts to underprivileged children and children suffering from illnesses.

In 2005, LaTorsha miscarried, which came as a blow to the hopeful couple. Tomlinson has often expressed in interviews his desire to become a father. "You think you have got life planned out and you've got it all dialed in and you know how it's supposed to go," Tomlinson said in a 2005 interview with *San Diego Union-Tribune*'s Kevin Acee. "We're going to have a baby. It's going to be great. Then God says, 'Not yet. This is not the time.'" Though Tomlinson's successes in football continued to mount, he consistently held that his family and life outside of football were more important

than his career. "What's important to me is my faith in God, my family, then football."

In February of 2007, Tomlinson received the unfortunate news that his father and brother-in-law had been killed in a fatal car accident resulting from an exploded tire. Tomlinson's father was pronounced dead at the scene. "My father and I had a great relationship, and I am devastated by his passing," Tomlinson said in a brief press release shortly after his father's death. "I will miss him."

Sources

Periodicals

San Diego Union-Tribune, September 9, 2004; August 4, 2005; February 24, 2007; September 24, 2007.

Online

Gregory, Sean, "The Best Back Ever," *Time Online Edition,* http://www.time.com/time/magazine/article/0,9171,1574162,00.html (accessed December 17, 2007).

"LaDainian Tomlinson," *JocksBio.com,* http://www.jockbio.com/Bios/Tomlinson/Tomlinson_bio.html (accessed December 17, 2007).

"LaDainian Tomlinson's Bio," *LaDainian Tomlinson Online,* http://ladainiantomlinson.com/bio.htm (accessed December 17, 2007).

Pressman, Stacey, "Coffee with LaTorsha Tomlinson," *Special Report for NBC Sports.com,* http://www.nbcsports.com/nfl/716786/detail.html (accessed December 17, 2007).

Silver, Michael, "Lightning Rod," *Sports Illustrated Online Edition,* http://sportsillustrated.cnn.com/2004/writers/michael_silver/09/03/silver.tomlinson/index.html (accessed December 17, 2007).

"#21 LaDainian Tomlinson," *San Diego Chargers Official Site,* http://www.chargers.com/team/roster/ladainian-tomlinson.htm (accessed December 17, 2007).

—Micah L. Issitt

Neil deGrasse Tyson

1958—

Astrophysicist

Known as both an eminent astrophysicist and a writer who makes complex scientific concepts accessible to the layperson, Neil deGrasse Tyson has been a highly visible figure in the scientific community through his writings, research efforts, and television appearances. As the director of the famed Hayden Planetarium in New York City, he helps bring a greater knowledge and appreciation of astronomy to thousands of people each year.

Studied to Become an Astrophysicist

Tyson's interest in pursuing a career in astronomy was sparked when he was a young boy. Around age ten, he asked to look through a friend's binoculars, which he had used previously only at sporting events. When his friend asked him to look up, he pointed the binoculars at the moon and was startled by the details of the lunar surface revealed to him. Since then, his fascination with the cosmos never waned. "All of a sudden there was this place out there," remarked Tyson in a interview with *Contemporary Black Biography* (*CBB*). "From then on, I've just been looking up."

The young Tyson took advantage of every opportunity available for pursuing his interest in astronomy in the New York City of his boyhood. He acquired a telescope, joined astronomy clubs, and spent many hours at the Hayden Planetarium. He told *CBB*, "I remember looking at the star-filled dome at the Hayden Planetarium and thinking it was a hoax." At the plan-etarium, Tyson attended various astronomy courses for young people, as well as sky shows with specially focused subject matter. He also spoke with officials there whose knowledge of stars he yearned to make his own. While in junior high, he heeded the advice of the chairman of the Hayden Planetarium, who told him to take extra mathematics courses in high school to prepare for an astronomy career.

Promoted Positive Images of African Americans

After graduating from the highly regarded Bronx High School of Science in New York City, Tyson entered Harvard University and pursued a major in physics. He told *CBB* that he got a taste of social consciousness while on the school's wrestling team. A black teammate told him, "The black community of the nation cannot afford to have you study astrophysics." Up to this time, Tyson had not really considered that he had any obligation to better the condition of his community with his intellect. "Those words sat heavily with me, because here I was just following my love of the universe, without any particular reference to the plight of society," remembered Tyson.

Years later as a graduate student, Tyson had a revelation while watching a prerecorded television interview of him discussing a recent explosion on the sun. While watching himself, he suddenly realized that he had never before seen an African American on television discussing a subject that was not an African-American

At a Glance . . .

Born Neil deGrasse Tyson on October 5, 1958, in New York, NY; married Alice Young, 1988; children: Miranda. *Education:* Harvard University, BA, 1980; University of Texas at Austin, MA, 1983; Columbia University, PhD, 1991.

Career: University of Maryland, Department of Astronomy, lecturer, 1987; Princeton University, Department of Astrophysics, postdoctoral research associate, 1991–94; American Museum of Natural History, Hayden Planetarium, staff scientist, 1994–95, acting director, 1995–96; Princeton University, Department of Astrophysical Sciences, visiting research scientist and lecturer, 1994–2003; American Museum of Natural History, Hayden Planetarium/Rose Center for Earth and Space, astrophysicist and Frederick P. Rose Director, 1996—, project scientist, 1997–2000; American Museum of Natural History, Department of Astrophysics, chair, 1997–99, research associate, 2003—.

Memberships: American Astronomical Society; American Physical Society; Astronomical Society of the Pacific; International Planetarium Society; National Society of Black Physicists; New York Academy of Sciences (fellow).

Awards: National Aeronautics and Space Administration, Distinguished Public Service Medal, 2006; named one of *Time's* Top 100 Intellectual and Social Leaders, 2007.

Addresses: *Office*—American Museum of Natural History, Hayden Planetarium and Department of Astrophysics, Central Park West at Seventy-ninth St., New York, NY 10024.

the source of his great inspiration as a child by becoming an assistant astronomer at the Hayden Planetarium, eventually becoming director there in 1996. As a project scientist at the Hayden, Tyson was involved with the $210 million reconstruction of the facility that was completed in 2000.

Maintained a Prolific Writing Career

Tyson's prolific writing career branched out of esoteric research and into the realm of popular reading when he began writing a question-and-answer column for *Star Date* magazine in 1983. Over time, his columns attracted the attention of Columbia University Press, and Tyson was approached about publishing a compilation of his columns. The result was *Merlin's Tour of the Universe*, which entered the bookstores in 1989, while Tyson was still in graduate school.

In 1995 he began writing the monthly column "Universe" for *Natural History* magazine, while still continuing his contributions to *Star Date*. Even though he found the deadlines of magazine work challenging, he refused to rely on formula writing. "I try to have my writing say more than just convey information," noted Tyson to *CBB*. "I try to add a dose of personality, a dose of unusual points of view that could truly reach the heart of the readers and give them insights that they might not have ever had." Over the years, Tyson's articles have covered everything from black holes and the structure of the solar system to the possibilities of life elsewhere in the universe.

Tyson really hit his stride as a writer with his *Universe down to Earth*, which was published in 1994. This collection of informative yet entertaining explanations of scientific methods and phenomena has been acclaimed for breaking down complicated information into language readily understood by the average person. As he noted in the preface, "The book's objective is to convey ideas that etch deeply enough on the mind so that the concepts are not just remembered—they are absorbed into one's intuition." *Universe down to Earth* demystified stellar evolution, conservation of energy, the electromagnetic spectrum, gravity, thermodynamics, and a variety of other topics. None other than acclaimed science writer Carl Sagan called the book a "sprightly, easy-to-read introduction to some key ideas of physics and astronomy." Noted physicist Freeman Dyson added, "Tyson writes in a simple style with a lightness of touch, which can come only to one who is absolute master of his subject."

Besides working at the Hayden, Tyson appears regularly at scientific colloquia and is frequently interviewed on television as a scientific expert. As a consultant with the Committee for the Scientific Investigation of Claims of the Paranormal (CSICOP), he helps to debunk fraudulent reports of paranormal observation. He has

issue. The experience made him see his career in a new light, as one that helped promote positive images of African Americans. "It occurred to me that whatever stereotypes are harbored in the United States, one way to explode them is to march along and provide counterstereotypes whenever that's possible," he said to *CBB*.

After earning a doctorate in astrophysics at Columbia University, Tyson became a postdoctoral research associate in the Department of Astrophysics at Princeton University in 1991. Three years later, he returned to also been involved with programs to promote science education among disadvantaged children in New York City.

Tyson feels privileged to be working in astronomy. "Every period has its discoveries to be proud of," he told CBB. "What might distinguish modern times is the pace of those discoveries—that they're happening almost weekly." As director of the Hayden Planetarium, he makes a point of being available to children visiting the facility who have a budding interest in astronomy like he did as a child. "That's part of the payback for my career," said Tyson.

Became a Widely Recognized U.S. Astrophysicist

Through his position as director of Hayden Planetarium, popular writings in books and magazines, and appearances on television, Tyson has become one of the most popular scientists and astrophysicists in the United States. His ability to illuminate complex philosophical and scientific subjects to the general reader has helped him transcend traditional barriers to enter the realm of pop science. In addition, his accessible nature and personal charisma has helped him become an ambassador for science to popular culture. In 2000 *People* magazine named Tyson the "Sexiest Astrophysicist," an accolade that Tyson addressed with humorous appreciation.

In 2001 Tyson was named by President George W. Bush to serve on the Commission on the Future of the U.S. Aerospace Industry, where he helped craft federal policies toward aerospace research. In 2004 he also served as a member of the Bush administration's Commission on Implementation of the United States Space Exploration Policy. During this same period, Tyson led a controversial campaign to demote the status of Pluto, the former ninth planet, to that of an astrological object. Tyson and allied scientists put forth a wealth of scientific data indicating that Pluto failed to meet the, as then poorly defined, definitions for planethood. In 2006 the International Astronomical Union, which is composed of astronomical organizations from around the globe, agreed to reclassify Pluto as a dwarf planet. That same year, Tyson was awarded the National Aeronautics and Space Administration's Distinguished Public Service Medal, which is the highest honor bestowed on civilians by the administration.

While continuing his work as a lecturer and research director, Tyson co-published in 2004 *Origins: Fourteen Billion Years of Cosmic Evolution,* which was the companion to a Public Broadcasting System (PBS) television series exploring cosmic phenomena. As Tyson's popularity grew, he was asked to appear on a number of popular television programs including Comedy Central Network's *The Daily Show.* Besides becoming the host of PBS's *NOVA Science Now* program, he also published, in 2007, a collection of essays, *Death by Black Hole, and Other Cosmic Quandaries,* which entered the *New York Times* best-seller list.

Even as he became one of the nation's leading ambassadors for science education, Tyson remained rooted in his background as a researcher and worked with the American Museum of Natural History to establish a center for astrophysics research. In 2007 *Time* magazine chose him as one of the magazine's top one hundred intellectual and social leaders. In his interview, Tyson explained to *Time*'s Michael D. Lemonick his passion for science education, "If we ever needed a scientifically literate population, it's now. I get enormous satisfaction from knowing I'm doing something for society."

Selected writings

Nonfiction

Merlin's Tour of the Universe, Columbia University Press, 1989.
Universe down to Earth, Columbia University Press, 1994.
Just Visiting This Planet: Merlin Answers More Questions about Everything under the Sun, Moon, and Stars, Doubleday, 1998.
The Sky Is Not the Limit: Adventures of an Urban Astrophysicist, Doubleday, 2000.
(With Charles Liu and Robert Irion) *One Universe: At Home in the Cosmos,* Joseph Henry Press, 2000.
(With Steven Soter, eds.) *Cosmic Horizons: Astronomy at the Cutting Edge,* Norton, 2001.
(With Donald Goldsmith) *Origins: Fourteen Billion Years of Cosmic Evolution,* Norton, 2004.
Death by Black Hole, and Other Cosmic Quandaries, Norton, 2007.

Sources

Periodicals

Natural History, July 1995, p. 14; October 1995, p. 20; June 1996, p. 70.

Online

"A Conversation with Neil DeGrasse Tyson," *Nova Online: Origins,* http://www.pbs.org/wgbh/nova/origins/tyson.html (accessed December 22, 2007).
Lemonick, Michael D., "Neil DeGrasse Tyson." *Time,* http://www.time.com/time/specials/2007/time100/article/0,28804,1595326_1595329_1616157,00.html (accessed December 22, 2007).

Other

"Tavis Smiley Show," *National Public Radio,* September 27, 2004, February 6, 2007.

Additional information for this profile was obtained through an interview with Neil deGrasse Tyson, and through materials supplied by the Hayden Planetarium.

—Ed Decker and Micah L. Issit

Michael Vick

1980—

Football player

Vick, Michael, photograph. AP Images.

As a quarterback for the National Football League's (NFL) Atlanta Falcons, Michael Vick changed the prospects for that franchise and the game of football itself. In the history of the game, there have been few players who have been able to combine the classic characteristics of a great quarterback—a strong and accurate throwing arm and the intelligence and work ethic to master a complicated offensive system and think on his feet—with the stunning athleticism most often associated with a running back or cornerback as well as Vick. Vick could throw the ball accurately more than sixty yards, and in his second year in the NFL, he threw only eight interceptions against sixteen touchdowns. But what made Vick so special might not even show up on the statistics sheet. Even though he rushed for 777 yards in the 2002 season on 113 attempts, the plays he made evading opposing defensive players to avoid sacks or turning a short gain into a long gain were what captured the imagination of football fans across the country. As he told Michael Silver of *Sports Illustrated,* "Sometimes, I swear I think my body moves on its own, and I amaze myself." Vick's career was cut short and his reputation irrevocably tarnished in 2007 when he was convicted of running an illegal dog-fighting operation.

Excelled at Football Early

Michael Vick was born on June 26, 1980, to Michael Boddie and Brenda Vick in Newport News, Virginia. Vick's mother was sixteen when she gave birth to her first son. With her mother's help, Brenda raised Vick and his three siblings by herself because Boddie spent two and a half years in the army and then traveled to various other locations looking for work. Vick grew up with his siblings and his mother in the Ridley Circle housing project. Even when Boddie moved back with the family, he worked long hours in the Newport News shipyards and rarely saw his family. One thing he did have time for was teaching his son the game of football, introducing Vick to the game at the age of three.

Even though Vick excelled at baseball and basketball, by the time he arrived at Warwick High School in 1994, he had given up all other sports to pursue his passion: football. As a child growing up in an urban housing project, Vick saw plenty of other kids his age

At a Glance . . .

Born Michael Dwayne Vick on June 26, 1980, in Newport News, VA; son of Michael Boddie and Brenda Vick; children: Michael Jr. *Education:* Virginia Tech University, 1998–2000.

Career: Atlanta Falcons, quarterback, 2001–06.

Awards: All-American, 1997; *Sporting News* First Team All America, 1999; Big East Offensive Player of the Year, 1999; Archie Griffin Award, 1999; ESPY Award, top college football player, 1999; Gator Bowl MVP, 2000.

Addresses: *Office*—Atlanta Falcons, 4400 Falcon Parkway, Flowery Branch, GA 30542.

go down the wrong path, but he was always focused on athletics as he told Paul Attner of the *Sporting News,* "Sports kept me off the streets. It kept me from getting into what was going on, the bad stuff. Lots of guys I knew have had bad problems. But if I had to, I would go fishing even if the fish weren't biting. Just to get out of there."

As a freshman in high school, Vick started at the quarterback position on the junior varsity. But after throwing twenty touchdown passes in his first six games, he was promoted to the starting quarterback of the varsity team. Vick proved he belonged at that level in his second game as a varsity starter, throwing for 433 yards on only 13 completions. Vick's coach Tommy Reamon, a former running back in the NFL, knew that he had a special player. In the off-season he sent the young prodigy to camps and worked with Vick alone. Reamon also gave Vick the freedom to make plays on his own—a trait that would serve him well as a quarterback at Virginia Tech and later in the NFL.

Became a Star at Virginia Tech

By the time he was a senior, Vick was considered one of the top high school prospects in the nation. When he finished his high school career, he had thrown for 4,846 yards and 43 touchdowns. Not only did he excel as a passer but also he ran for 1,048 yards and scored 18 touchdowns. Vick was one of the most heavily recruited prospects in the country and narrowed his choices to Syracuse and Virginia Tech. He liked the idea of following in the footsteps of Donovan McNabb, another mobile quarterback who would go on to the NFL, but Vick was swayed by his high school coach, who wanted him to go to Virginia Tech, and by the

school's proximity to home. In the end, he joined Frank Beamer's Virginia Tech Hokies for the fall of 1998.

Beamer red-shirted the freshman for his first year, which gave Vick the time to learn the offense and adapt to college life. The eighteen-year-old got homesick at times, including one occasion when he called his mother at 4:00 in the morning, imploring her to pick him up and let him spend the weekend at home. Even so, he persevered through his freshman year and eventually saw the value of sitting out a full season as he told *Sports Illustrated*'s Lars Anderson, "Before I took my first snap, I wanted to be in control of the offense, know where the players were, how to read defenses. These are all things I learned when I sat out."

Vick began the quest for a starter's job in the spring of his freshman year. Physically, he was unmatched by anyone on the team and easily overshadowed any of the other quarterbacks. He ran a 4.3-second forty-yard dash and recorded a kangaroo-like vertical leap of forty and a half inches. In the spring practice game, he completed just three of ten passes, but he impressed his coaches and teammates with his ability to improvise and make something out of nothing. He won the job as the team's starting quarterback and was fit into a unit that was deep on offense and quick and aggressive on defense. Vick proclaimed his place in college football in his first game—a 47–0 defeat of James Madison. The game included a spectacular play in which Vick scored a touchdown on a diving somersault into the end zone. The vault was played on every sports station across the country.

The Vick legend continued to grow as the Hokies racked up victory after victory, including leading his team on a game-winning scoring drive from its own fifteen-yard line with a little more than a minute remaining in a game against rival West Virginia. Vick led his team to an undefeated regular season as the giants of college football fell one after another. By the end of the season, only two undefeated teams were left standing: Vick's Hokies and college football juggernaut Florida State University.

Impressive Bowl Game Followed by Injury

Even though Florida State won the Sugar Bowl 46–29, the player who made the biggest impact on the game was Vick. Virginia Tech trailed at one point early in the game by three touchdowns until Vick took the game over and led his team to a 29–28 lead. Vick told Silver about his reaction to his team's falling flat in the biggest college football game of the year, "We went down 28–7 and I gathered everyone around and said, 'Yo, it ain't going down like this. Somebody's got to step up. I guess it's going to be me.'" Despite Vick's unsuccessful efforts to lead his team to a victory, his improvisational brilliance was seen by the whole country in college football's biggest game. In his first year as a starter, Vick threw for 1,840 yards and 12 touchdowns and set an National Collegiate Athletic Association record for passing efficiency by a freshman (180.37). As a rusher, he gained 585 yards and added 8 touchdowns. Vick was made a member of the *Sporting News* All-America team and was named the Big East Offensive Player of the Year. He finished third in the Heisman Trophy voting and, as a nineteen-year-old, attended his first ESPY Award show to receive acclaim as the nation's top college football player.

After the glory of his first season as Virginia Tech's signal caller, Vick was asked to top his freshman achievements, which proved to be a difficult task. In his sophomore season, Vick led his team to a 6–0 start, but then he sprained his ankle against Pittsburgh and was sidelined against the powerful Miami Hurricanes. Vick's team lost 41–21 without their leader, and a chance for another undefeated season was lost. Virginia Tech would go on to win the Gator Bowl, and Vick would be named the team's most valuable player, but after an injury-riddled season in which defenses were prepared mostly just for him, his numbers were down. Vick completed 87 of 161 passes with 8 touchdowns and rushed for another 607 yards. After the season, Vick was continually asked about his status for the following year. Because he did not have the season that he and everyone else who followed college football expected him to have, Vick's initial leaning was to return to Virginia Tech for one more season. However, when he learned that he would be the top pick of the NFL draft, he decided to forego his final season and declared that he would be leaving school to join the NFL for the 2001 season.

Joined the Atlanta Falcons

The Atlanta Falcons moved aggressively to trade up to the number-one pick in the draft to ensure that they would get Vick. The organization followed through with their plan, making Vick the first pick overall of the 2001 draft and signed him to a six-year deal worth up to $62 million. Falcon's coach Dan Reeves planned to bring Vick along slowly in his first season and use him in certain situations and with a limited amount of plays, but when starting quarterback Chris Chandler was injured, Vick was forced into the starting lineup. He started against Dallas and St. Louis and played in five other games. Even though the Falcons saw glimpses of greatness in his first year, Vick turned the ball over too often. Part of the problem was the rookie had trouble memorizing all the plays in Reeves' complicated offense. Vick commented on this aspect of his difficult rookie season to Silver, saying, "There was so much verbiage, and instead of studying routes or coverages, I came to practice just worried about getting the names of the plays out. As the backup [to Chandler] I'd get eight reps, and I'd hold up practice because I screwed up six of them."

In his next year in Atlanta, the Falcons made it clear that it was Vick's time to shine. The club released Chandler and handed the reins of the offense over to the talented youngster. Reeves also simplified the playbook to ease the second-year player's time not only learning the offense but also learning the terms used in the offense. Vick told *Sports Illustrated*'s Josh Miller about his own preparation for the new season: "I always knew I had the physical ability to perform, but my confidence wasn't where it needed to be. I knew that I had to work the entire off-season to prepare. I studied my playbook every day, even if it meant locking myself in my bedroom when Mom came to visit. I watched all my plays from last year. It's what I had to do." Vick led his team to the playoffs in his first year as a starter and was talked about as the new prototype for the quarterback of the future. The improved defense and new quarterback led the Falcons from a 6–10 team to a 9–7 team. At one point in the season, Vick led his team to a seven-game unbeaten streak, and the Falcons and their quarterback were the hottest topic in the NFL. Even though the team hit a tough part of the schedule at the end of the season, the Falcons made the playoffs. However, their reward for such a fine season was a trip to Green Bay, Wisconsin, to play the Packers—a team that had never lost a playoff game on their frigid home turf. Vick led his team up north and did what many thought was impossible. Atlanta did not just beat the Packers, rather they destroyed the heavily favored Green Bay team 27–7. The Falcons lost the following week to the Philadelphia Eagles, but Vick had led his team to a playoff win and respectability.

In the beginning of the 2003 season, Vick was sidelined due to a fractured fibula and was unable to play for the first eleven games of the season. When Vick returned in December, the Falcons were suffering from a losing streak of 2–9. The Falcon's regained prominence with Vick's return, but they were unable to achieve a spot in the 2003 divisional playoffs and came in fourth in the Southern Division of the National Football Conference. Vick was named to the 2004 pro bowl for his performance at the end of the regular season. The following season, with the team at full strength, the Falcons achieved a record of 9–6 and won the divisional playoffs against the St. Louis Rams before losing in the divisional championships to the Philadelphia Eagles.

Even though Vick continued to perform well, the team had a disappointing 2005 season, with a final record of 8–8. Regardless, Vick continued to win accolades for his performance and was named to a third pro bowl in 2005. In December of 2004 the Falcons offered Vick the most lucrative contract to that point in NFL history: $130 million over ten years. By the end of his 2006 season, Vick had achieved a number of league records, including the record for the greatest number of rushing yards in a single season.

Found Guilty for Dog Fighting

In June of 2007 a federal grand jury indicted Vick on charges of operating an illegal dog fighting and gambling operation in Virginia. The indictment came after investigators raided Vick's Bad Newz Kennels to search for evidence of dog fighting and seized dozens of animals as evidence. Even though Vick initially denied the charges, over the course of the investigation witnesses came forward claiming to have seen Vick executing dogs and handling proceeds from gambling operations. In August of 2007 Vick pled guilty to breeding dogs for illegal fighting and for executing a number of dogs that failed to perform. Vick was faced with a maximum penalty of up to five years in prison and $250,000 in fines. In the wake of his plea, the Atlanta Falcons announced the Vick would be removed from the team's roster on permanent suspension. Shortly thereafter, his promotional contracts, including an endorsement deal with Nike, were also suspended.

Even though most analysts believed that Vick would receive no more than twelve months' imprisonment, the case abruptly ended his promising career and brought national attention to dog fighting and animal rights issues. Many of his supporters defended him by saying that he was a product of his environment. However, as news spread about the cruelty with which he executed animals for Bad Newz Kennels, he became a widely reviled public figure. And even though Vick released public apologies to both his fans and animal rights enthusiasts, many analysts felt that there was little Vick could do to rehabilitate his reputation or return to the public's good favor.

In December of 2007 Vick was sentenced to twenty-three months' imprisonment for his role in the Bad Newz Kennels controversy. Even though there is no chance for parole in the federal legal system, with time reductions for good behavior, Vick may be potentially eligible for release in as little as three months. As for his potential to return to the NFL, officials said that they would consider that at a later time. John P. Goodwin, manager of animal fighting activities for the Humane Society, told Juliet Macur of the *New York Times,* "I think the judge sent a strong message to dogfighters that this is a dead-end activity, and for professional athletes, it's a career-killer."

Sources

Periodicals

Jet, January 17, 2005.
New York Times, November 6, 2003; December 1, 2003; August 21, 2007; August 28, 2007; December 11, 2007.
Sports Illustrated, January 13, 2000; September 2, 2002; December 2, 2002.
Sporting News, April 9, 2001.

Online

"Michael Vick," *Jock Bio,* http://www.jockbio.com/Bios/Vick/Vick_bio.html (accessed December 21, 2007).

—Michael J. Watkins and Micah L. Issit

Eric Eustace Williams

1911–1981

Prime minister, historian

Eric Eustace Williams served as prime minister of Trinidad and Tobago for more than two decades until his death in 1981. Before entering politics, Williams had been a respected historian on Caribbean topics and continued to write about the region during his time in office. "Perhaps one of the strongest tributes to the liberal democratic society he built over 25 years," noted his 1981 *Times* of London obituary, "was the smooth, efficient and constitutional transfer of power to a successor in the 12 hours after his death."

Williams was born in 1911 in Trinidad and Tobago's capital city, Port of Spain, whose name reflects Trinidad's earlier status as a Spanish colonial possession. The country's population, however, is a mixture of French and other European groups, along with blacks whose ancestors were slaves either on the island or settled there later. The country that Williams would later rule was actually two islands: Trinidad, named by Christopher Columbus after the Holy Trinity, and the much smaller Tobago. Trinidad became a possession of Britain in 1797, and Tobago followed in 1814; in 1888 the two islands were made into a single crown colony.

Trinidad is a predominantly Roman Catholic country, a legacy of the Spanish era when colonial authorities allowed any European to move there, provided they were of that faith, to encourage settlement. Williams's family was Roman Catholic, and he was the first of twelve children. His father, Thomas, was a postal clerk, and at the age of eleven Williams won a scholarship to

Queen's Royal College, a private academy founded in 1870 with a rigorous curriculum. A top student, he won one of the so-called Island Scholarships to Oxford University in England, where he earned an honors degree in history from St. Catherine's College in 1935. He went on to pursue a doctorate at the college, submitting a dissertation on slavery and its role in the economic history of the British West Indies that earned him his doctorate, again with first-class honors, in 1938. Williams put forth a rather radical idea in his dissertation, arguing that Britain's abolition of slavery in its colonies came about because of economic necessity, not from any great moral awakening.

Spent the 1940s in America

Jobs for black academics were scarce in the late 1930s, and Williams took a teaching position at Howard University, a historically African-American college in Washington, D.C. He became a full professor of social and political science in 1947 and, through his published works, became known as one of the foremost experts on the Caribbean world. He returned to Trinidad in 1952, when he was named deputy chair of the Caribbean Commission, established by the United States, Britain, the Netherlands, and France to create a development plan for the region. He grew dissatisfied with the commission's progress, however, and came to believe it was unable to move forward in a way that would be best for the citizens, not the colonial masters. In 1955 he resigned from Howard University's faculty

Born on September 25, 1911, in Port of Spain, Trinidad and Tobago; died of a heart attack on March 29, 1981, in St. Anne, Trinidad; son of Thomas Henry Williams and Eliza Boissiere; married Elsie Ribeiro, c. 1939 (divorced, 1951); married Soy Moyeau, c. 1951 (divorced, 1953); married Mayleen Mook-Soong, 1957 (divorced, c. 1958); children: (with Ribeiro) Alistair, Pamela, (with Moyeau) Erica. *Education:* Attended Queen's Royal College, 1922–31; St. Catherine's College, Oxford, BA (first-class honors), 1935, DPhil (first-class honors), 1938.

Career: Queen's Royal College (Trinidad and Tobago), acting master, and acting lecturer for the Government Training College for Teachers, 1931; Howard University, assistant professor, 1939–44, associate professor, 1944–47, professor of social and political science, 1947–55; Caribbean Commission, deputy chair, 1952–55; adviser to Trinidad government, 1954–55; People's National Movement, founder, 1956; chief minister and minister of finance, planning, and development of Trinidad and Tobago, 1956–61; first prime minister of independent state of Trinidad and Tobago, 1962–81, also minister of external affairs, 1961–64, 1973–74, minister of community development, 1964–67, minister of Tobago affairs, minister of finance, planning, and development, and minister of national security, 1967–71, minister for finance, beginning in 1975.

Memberships: Historical Society of Trinidad and Tobago (former president).

Awards: Made Privy Councillor of the British Commonwealth, 1964; Companion of Honour, 1969.

government corruption, aid for sugar cane workers, universal, secular and compulsory education, birth control and economic and industrial development," wrote C. Gerald Fraser in the *New York Times.*

With the 1956 PNM win, Williams became chief minister of Trinidad and Tobago, a position similar to that of prime minister but used in places that were still British Crown colonies. For the next five years, he also served as the country's minister of finance, planning, and development. One of the first major acts of his government was to abolish school fees and make education compulsory but free of charge. This proved to be a tremendous boon to the nonwhite population of both islands. He opposed the establishment of a U.S. naval base on the Chaguaramas peninsula, and he championed the creation of the West Indies Federation in 1958. His nation was the second to pull out of the federation four years later, however, when consensus proved impossible to achieve. This pullout followed Jamaica's withdrawal, and Williams uttered one of the more famous statements of his public career with the quip, "One from ten leaves nought [zero]," reflecting the idea that the federation was undone without the leadership and financial resources of Jamaica.

Became Prime Minister

In August of 1962, three months after withdrawing from the federation, Trinidad and Tobago achieved independence from Britain, and Williams became the first prime minister of the newly sovereign state of Trinidad and Tobago. He remained in office until his death in 1981 and usually held a cabinet position or two besides his duties as prime minister and party leader. He was the country's minister of external affairs in the early 1960s and again from 1973 to 1974, then served as minister of finance, planning, and development from 1967 to 1971, as well as minister of national security during that same period. From 1975 until his death, he was minister for finance. He held power through a period of great change and economic growth in the country, which has a relatively high standard of living thanks to its oil exports. Bouts of labor and political unrest periodically flared, but Williams dealt with these firmly. One such incident was a 1970 uprising that included strikes, marches, and the mutiny of a regiment that had become politicized as part of the Black Power movement sweeping through several Caribbean countries. Williams declared a state of emergency and pushed through a law that outlawed all strikes. An oil boom after 1973, prompted by a worldwide oil crisis, helped him remain in power.

One significant threat to the PNM's rule was a growing dissension among East Indians in Trinidad and Tobago and their desire to play a larger political role in the country. Their United Labour Front group had support from Cuba, and the group became a significant chal-

to devote himself full time to improving the lot of Trinidadians and Tobagans. "I have dealt too much in the past years with the historical background of problems and with the statistics," the *Times* of London quoted him as saying. "What I intend to do now is to see the living humanity behind the statistics."

In 1956 Williams founded a political party, the People's National Movement (PNM), which won a majority of seats in the Legislative Council in the general elections that year. The PNM was somewhat of a rarity in West Indian politics in that it was not allied with any trade union. As its leader, he "called for an end to lenge to Williams and the PNM in the late 1970s. As prime minister, Williams pleaded for an end to ethnic unrest with another famous quip: "Forget mother Africa; forget mother India," he was fond of saying, according to *Americas* writer James Patrick Kiernan. "Think of mother Trinidad. She does not discriminate among her children."

In 1976 Williams declared Trinidad and Tobago a republic, and under the new system a president would serve as head of state, while the prime minister would be the head of government. Following the elections that year, however, he retreated from the public eye, urging the PNM to designate a successor to him as party leader, and he refused to attend regional conferences. He had been the most famous person in the dual-island nation for a generation, known for the ever-present dark glasses he favored and a hearing aid that resembled a Secret-Service earpiece. He died of a heart attack on March 29, 1981, in St. Anne, a suburb of Port of Spain.

Throughout his years as prime minister, Williams continued to publish tomes on history and the economic development of the Caribbean. These included a *History of the People of Trinidad and Tobago* from 1962 and *From Columbus to Castro: The History of the Caribbean, 1492–1969, Inward Hunger: The Education of a Prime Minister, British Capitalism and Caribbean Slavery: The Legacy of Eric Williams.* This collection of essays discusses the impact of his doctoral dissertation, which was published in book form in 1944 as *Capitalism and Slavery.* "Despite almost a half-century of revisionism," remarked Ralph A. Austen in *Business History Review,*

Selected writings

Nonfiction

The Negro in the Caribbean, Associates in Negro Folk Education, 1942.
Capitalism and Slavery, University of North Carolina Press, 1944.
Education in the British West Indies, Guardian Commercial Printery, 1950.
History of the People of Trinidad and Tobago, People's National Movement Publishing, 1962.
Documents of West Indian History, People's National Movement Publishing, 1963.
British Historians and the West Indies, People's National Movement Publishing, 1964.
Britain and the West Indies, Longmans, 1969.
Inward Hunger: The Education of a Prime Minister, Deutsch, 1969.
From Columbus to Castro: The History of the Caribbean, 1492–1969, Deutsch, 1970.
Forged from the Love of Liberty: Selected Speeches of Dr. Eric Williams, compiled by Paul K. Sutton, Longman Caribbean, 1981.

Sources

Periodicals

Americas, July 1999.
Business History Review, Winter 1988.
Miami Herald, June 15, 2007.
New Statesman, February 13, 1998.
New York Times, March 31, 1981.
Times (London, England), March 31, 1981.

—Carol Brennan

Cumulative Nationality Index

Volume numbers appear in **bold**

American

Aaliyah **30**
Aaron, Hank **5**
Abbott, Robert Sengstacke **27**
Abdul-Jabbar, Kareem **8**
Abdur-Rahim, Shareef **28**
Abele, Julian **55**
Abernathy, Ralph David **1**
Abu-Jamal, Mumia **15**
Ace, Johnny **36**
Adams Earley, Charity **13, 34**
Adams, Eula L. **39**
Adams, Floyd, Jr. **12**
Adams, Jenoyne **60**
Adams, Johnny **39**
Adams, Leslie **39**
Adams, Oleta **18**
Adams, Osceola Macarthy **31**
Adams, Sheila J. **25**
Adams, Yolanda **17**
Adams-Campbell, Lucille L. **60**
Adams-Ender, Clara **40**
Adderley, Julian "Cannonball" **30**
Adderley, Nat **29**
Adkins, Rod **41**
Adkins, Rutherford H. **21**
Agyeman, Jaramogi Abebe **10, 63**
Ailey, Alvin **8**
Akil, Mara Brock **60**
Al-Amin, Jamil Abdullah **6**
Albright, Gerald **23**
Alcorn, George Edward, Jr. **59**
Alert, Kool DJ Red **33**
Alexander, Archie Alphonso **14**
Alexander, Clifford **26**
Alexander, Joyce London **18**
Alexander, Khandi **43**
Alexander, Margaret Walker **22**
Alexander, Sadie Tanner Mossell **22**
Alexander, Shaun **58**
Ali, Hana Yasmeen **52**
Ali, Laila **27, 63**
Ali, Muhammad **2, 16, 52**
Allain, Stephanie **49**
Allen, Byron **3, 24**
Allen, Debbie **13, 42**
Allen, Ethel D. **13**
Allen, Marcus **20**
Allen, Robert L. **38**
Allen, Samuel W. **38**
Allen, Tina **22**
Allen-Buillard, Melba **55**
Alston, Charles **33**

Amaker, Norman **63**
Amaker, Tommy **62**
Amerie **52**
Ames, Wilmer **27**
Amos, Emma **63**
Amos, John **8, 62**
Amos, Wally **9**
Anderson, Anthony **51**
Anderson, Carl **48**
Anderson, Charles Edward **37**
Anderson, Eddie "Rochester" **30**
Anderson, Elmer **25**
Anderson, Jamal **22**
Anderson, Marian **2, 33**
Anderson, Michael P. **40**
Anderson, Mike **63**
Anderson, Norman B. **45**
Anderson, William G(ilchrist), D.O. **57**
Andrews, Benny **22, 59**
Andrews, Bert **13**
Andrews, Raymond **4**
Angelou, Maya **1, 15**
Ansa, Tina McElroy **14**
Anthony, Carmelo **46**
Anthony, Wendell **25**
Archer, Dennis **7, 36**
Archie-Hudson, Marguerite **44**
Ardoin, Alphonse **65**
Arkadie, Kevin **17**
Armstrong, Louis **2**
Armstrong, Robb **15**
Armstrong, Vanessa Bell **24**
Arnez J **53**
Arnold, Tichina **63**
Arnwine, Barbara **28**
Arrington, Richard **24**
Arroyo, Martina **30**
Artest, Ron **52**
Asante, Molefi Kete **3**
Ashanti **37**
Ashe, Arthur **1, 18**
Ashford, Emmett **22**
Ashford, Evelyn **63**
Ashford, Nickolas **21**
Ashley-Ward, Amelia **23**
Atkins, Cholly **40**
Atkins, Erica **34**
Atkins, Juan **50**
Atkins, Russell **45**
Atkins, Tina **34**
Aubert, Alvin **41**
Auguste, Donna **29**
Austin, Gloria **63**

Austin, Jim **63**
Austin, Junius C. **44**
Austin, Lovie **40**
Austin, Patti **24**
Avant, Clarence **19**
Ayers, Roy **16**
Babatunde, Obba **35**
Bacon-Bercey, June **38**
Badu, Erykah **22**
Bahati, Wambui **60**
Bailey, Buster **38**
Bailey, Clyde **45**
Bailey, DeFord **33**
Bailey, Philip **63**
Bailey, Radcliffe **19**
Bailey, Xenobia **11**
Baines, Harold **32**
Baiocchi, Regina Harris **41**
Baisden, Michael **25**
Baker, Anita **21, 48**
Baker, Augusta **38**
Baker, Dusty **8, 43**
Baker, Ella **5**
Baker, Gwendolyn Calvert **9**
Baker, Houston A., Jr. **6**
Baker, Josephine **3**
Baker, LaVern **26**
Baker, Maxine B. **28**
Baker, Thurbert **22**
Baker, Vernon Joseph **65**
Baldwin, James **1**
Ballance, Frank W. **41**
Ballard, Allen Butler, Jr. **40**
Ballard, Hank **41**
Bambaataa, Afrika **34**
Bambara, Toni Cade **10**
Bandele, Asha **36**
Banks, Ernie **33**
Banks, Jeffrey **17**
Banks, Michelle **59**
Banks, Tyra **11, 50**
Banks, William **11**
Banner, David **55**
Baquet, Dean **63**
Baraka, Amiri **1, 38**
Barber, Ronde **41**
Barber, Tiki **57**
Barboza, Anthony **10**
Barclay, Paris **37**
Barden, Don H. **9, 20**
Barker, Danny **32**
Barkley, Charles **5**
Barlow, Roosevelt **49**
Barnes, Roosevelt "Booba" **33**

Barnes, Steven **54**
Barnett, Amy Du Bois **46**
Barnett, Etta Moten **56**
Barnett, Marguerite **46**
Barney, Lem **26**
Barnhill, David **30**
Barrax, Gerald William **45**
Barrett, Andrew C. **12**
Barrett, Jacquelyn **28**
Barrino, Fantasia **53**
Barry, Marion S(hepilov, Jr.) **7, 44**
Barthe, Richmond **15**
Basie, Count **23**
Basquiat, Jean-Michel **5**
Bass, Charlotta Spears **40**
Bassett, Angela **6, 23, 62**
Bates, Daisy **13**
Bates, Karen Grigsby **40**
Bates, Peg Leg **14**
Bath, Patricia E. **37**
Baugh, David **23**
Baylor, Don **6**
Baylor, Helen **36**
Beach, Michael **26**
Beal, Bernard B. **46**
Beals, Jennifer **12**
Beals, Melba Patillo **15**
Bearden, Romare **2, 50**
Beasley, Jamar **29**
Beasley, Phoebe **34**
Beatty, Talley **35**
Bechet, Sidney **18**
Beckford, Tyson **11**
Beckham, Barry **41**
Belafonte, Harry **4, 65**
Bell, Derrick **6**
Bell, James "Cool Papa" **36**
Bell, James A. **50**
Bell, James Madison **40**
Bell, Michael **40**
Bell, Robert Mack **22**
Bellamy, Bill **12**
Bellamy, Terry **58**
Belle, Albert **10**
Belle, Regina **1, 51**
Belton, Sharon Sayles **9, 16**
Benberry, Cuesta **65**
Benét, Eric **28**
Ben-Israel, Ben Ami **11**
Benjamin, Andre **45**
Benjamin, Regina **20**
Benjamin, Tritobia Hayes **53**
Bennett, George Harold "Hal" **45**
Bennett, Gwendolyn B. **59**

Cumulative Occupation Index

Volume numbers appear in **bold**

Cumulative Subject Index

Volume numbers appear in **bold**

Active Ministers Engaged in Nurturance (AMEN)

Actors Equity Association

Actuarial science

ACT UP

Acustar, Inc.

ADC

Addiction Research and Treatment Corporation

Adoption and foster care

Adventures in Movement (AIM)

Advertising

Advocates Scene

Aetna

Cumulative Name Index

Volume numbers appear in **bold**